MEASURING Sustainability

MEASURING Sustainability
LEARNING by DOING

Simon Bell and Stephen Morse

London • Sterling, VA

First published in the UK and USA in 2003 by Earthscan
Reprinted 2006

Copyright © Simon Bell and Stephen Morse, 2003

ISBN-10: 1 85383 843 8
ISBN-13: 978 1 85383 843 9

Typeset by JS Typesetting Ltd, Wellingborough, Northants
Printed and bound by Creative Print and Design (Wales), Ebbw Vale
Cover design by Danny Gillespie

For a full list of publications please contact:

Earthscan
8–12 Camden High Street
London, NW1 0JH, UK
Tel: +44 (0)20 7387 3558
Fax: +44 (0)20 7387 8998
Email: earthinfo@earthscan.co.uk
www.earthscan.co.uk

22883 Quicksilver Drive, Sterling, VA 20166–2012, USA

A catalogue record for this book is available from the British Library

Library of Congress Cataloging-in-Publication Data
Bell, Simon.
    Measuring sustainability : learning by doing / Simon Bell.
        p. cm.
    Includes bibliographical references and index.
    ISBN 1-85383-839-8 (alk. paper) – ISBN 1-85383-843-8 (pbk. : alk. paper)
        1. Sustainable development. 2. Economic development–Environmental aspects.
        3. Environmental indicators. I. Title.

HC79.E5 B435 2002
338.9'27–dc21

2002153087

Earthscan is an imprint of James and James (Science Publishers) Ltd and publishes in association
with the International Institute for Environment and Development

This book is printed on elemental chlorine-free paper

Contents

List of Figures, Tables and Boxes

FIGURES

TABLES

BOXES

Preface

In all modesty, maybe in some trepidation, we need to say at the outset that this book has some considerable range to it.

At one level it is a review of the chaotic and contrasting landscape of literature in the field of sustainable development and sustainability indicators (SD and SIs). This should be enough for a single book but . . .

It is also a discussion of the project nature of the world at the beginning of the 21st century. This is an immensely contentious area needing at least 400 pages to discuss but . . .

It is also a review of the adapted methodology – Systemic Sustainability Analysis (SSA) – and a conversation as to how this evolved from the pages of a book to its first 'use-form' in practice as Systemic and Prospective Sustainability Analysis (SPSA) – a tortuous business needing many pages to describe but . . .

It is also a description of the roll-out of SPSA in the context of the Mediterranean island of Malta. A rich, two-year process of learning is described, but then there is more . . .

It is also a leap forward, away from the forest of hype in which the SD/SI world can be experienced, into a full-on exploration of how we learn, why so much of our experience of the projectified world is the way it is and how it might be different.

At this point we ran out of steam – and rather worried for the sheer content of the book.

Dante sums up how we felt at the beginning of this process:

> *Half way along the road we have to go,*
> *I found myself obscured in a great forest,*
> *Bewildered, and knew I had lost my way.*
> *It is hard to say just what the forest was like,*
> *How wild and rough it was, how overpowering;*
> *Even to remember it makes me afraid.*

(Dante's *Divine Comedy*, Canto 1)

However, by the end of the process, although we remain unsure of the exact direction for our further engagement, using rear-view vision we are sure of the places we will not venture into again. Keeping with Dante's forest, Sam Walter Fosse sums up our experience of the SD/SI process:

The Calf Path

One day, through the primeval wood,
A calf walked home – as good calves should,
But made a trail all bent askew
A crooked trail, as all calves do.

That trail was taken up next day
By a dog that passed that way.
And then a wise bellwether sheep
Pursued the trail o'er vale and steep,
And drew the flock behind him, too
As good bellwethers always do.

And from that day, o'er hill and glade,
Through those old woods a path was made,
And many men wound in and out,
And dodged, and turned, and bent about,
And uttered words of righteous wrath,
Because 'twas such a crooked path.
But still they followed (do not laugh)
The first migrations of the calf.

Each day a hundred thousand rout
Trailed that zigzag calf about.
And o'er his crooked journey went
The traffic of a continent.
A hundred thousand men were led
By one calf near two centuries dead.

A moral lesson this might teach,
Were I ordained and called to preach;
For men are prone to go it blind
Along the calf paths of the mind.
They work away from sun to sun
To do what other men have done.
They follow in the beaten track
And out and in and forth and back.
And still their devious course pursue
To keep the path that others do,

But how the wise old wood gods laugh
Who saw that first primeval calf.
Ah! Many things this tale might teach –
but I am not ordained to preach.

(Sam Walter Fosse, 1858–1911)

The book will begin with two chapters that set out the state of play in SD and SIs at the turn of the 21st century. This is certainly not exhaustive, and a reader may be frustrated that his/her favourite example, paper, book etc has not been mentioned. We apologize, but hope that any omission will not detract from the main thrust of what we are saying – most notably that SD, and by definition any SIs to gauge it, are highly contested. These chapters cover a lot of ground in only a few pages, but are intended to provide a taste of the diversity of approach and opinion in SD rather than seek a 'best way' forward. At times the diversity can be bewildering, and it certainly takes a great deal of effort to digest and keep up with, but it cannot be ignored.

Chapters 3 and 4 will describe our experience of applying SPSA in Malta. Chapter 3 provides the context to the project – why it existed and what it set out to do – and Chapter 4 gives the outline of the SPSA methodology. Chapter 4 makes extensive use of diagrams to illustrate the steps in the narrative, and the reader is urged to digest these in order to fully appreciate the SPSA process. In addition, we have linked elements of Chapters 3 and 4 back to Chapters 1 and 2 so the reader, having read what we actually did, can then go back and check the diversity of approaches that are taken by others in similar circumstances. The reader may agree or disagree with our own particular choice at that point of the process, but at least he/she can see something of the range of options that were open to us. After all, we did not do what we did in isolation, but drew on the work of others as well as our own ideas. Yet at the same time the overall plan of what we did was of course largely our decision – albeit with important inputs from stakeholders, not least the donor agency. Chapters 5 and 6 will draw out the main lessons we gained out of Malta and suggest ways forward.

Acknowledgements

Whilst taking full responsibility for the majority of the ideas contained in this book, we should like to acknowledge the patience and resilience of all those who assisted us, separately and together, over the last two years.

First, it has to be said that this book has arisen from the combined thoughts and experiences of literally hundreds of academics, practitioners and lay people working in and around the field of sustainable development (SD). The ultimate aim of SD is to make our lives and the lives of our children better, and the efforts of this army of workers in many places and over many years is testament to the human spirit.

A special note of thanks goes to Blue Plan and particularly the director, Mr Guillaume Benoit, who provided us with the opportunity to test out and develop our methodology in Malta.

Many, many thanks are due to Mrs Elisabeth Coudert, the Blue Plan Programme Officer (and our friend) in charge of the roll-out of SPSA in Malta. Elisabeth read our first book, and on the basis of a meeting in Sophia Antipolis had the courage to engage us in the Maltese CAMP. She has been tireless in her attention to the detail of this work and has attended all workshops as both a presenter of the Blue Plan message and a participant. Finally, she has been wonderfully acute in reading and commenting on drafts of this book.

This book would not exist today without the assistance of all our friends in Malta. A major vote of thanks is due to the Maltese SPSA team leader/coordinator, Mr Ray Cachia Zammit, and to Mr Louis Vella, the national project coordinator who had responsibility for the CAMP as a whole.

Our work was made light by the active and passionate attention of Mr Tony Ellul, who undertook much of the SPSA groundwork in Malta, combining his existing workload in the Planning Department with SPSA and a passion for amateur dramatics. Regrettably, we never had the chance to experience him in this latter capacity.

Thanks are due to so many people, but we would particularly like to mention: Carol Agius, Joslyn Magro, Christine Tanti, Michelle Borg, Prassede Grech, Avertano Role, Anthony Borg, Paul Micallef, Lucianne Licari, Marguerite Camilleri, Ernest Azzopardi, Hadrian Bonello, Claire Albani Wilson and Andrew Vella.

Many, many others have worked with the authors over the last two years, and we apologize that space does not permit us to mention them all here.

Finally, we would like to thank all those who took the time to provide us with feedback after reading our first book on sustainability indicators. This current book builds on that effort, and while Malta gave us an opportunity to try our ideas in practice, the comments and advice provided by readers of the first book provided us with encouragement and much food for thought. We would like to urge readers of this book to do the same.

Simon Bell (s.g.bell@open.ac.uk)
Stephen Morse (s.morse@reading.ac.uk)

List of Acronyms and Abbreviations

BP RAC	Blue Plan Regional Activity Centre
CAMP	coastal area management programme
CATWOE	client, actors, transformation, worldview, owner and environmental
CBA	cost–benefit analysis
CSDI	community sustainable development indicators
DEFRA	Department for Environment, Food and Rural Affairs (UK)
DFID	Department for International Development (UK)
DSR	driving force–state–response
EDS	ecosystem distress syndrome
EF	ecological footprint
EPD	Environment Protection Department
ES	environmental sustainability
ESI	environmental sustainability index
FAO	Food and Agriculture Organization (UN)
FLAG	Florida Local Assessment Guide
GDP	gross domestic product
GIS	geographical information system
IA	integrated assessment
ISD	indicator of sustainable development
LGMB	Local Government Management Board (UK)
lm	Maltese pounds
LQI	land quality indicators
MAFF	Ministry of Agriculture, Fisheries and Food (UK)
MAP	Mediterranean Action Plan
MCSD	Mediterranean Commission on Sustainable Development
mg/l	milligrams per litre
MIPS	material intensity per unit of service
MIS	management information system

MOV	means of verification
NGO	non-governmental organization
NRM	natural resource management
OVI	objectively verifiable indicator
PA	planning authority
PAP RAC	Priority Actions Programme Regional Activity Centre (Split, Croatia)
PAR	participatory action research
PHC	poly-hydrocarbon
PLA	participatory learning and action
PM&A	power relations, mindset and assumptions
PMPA	performance measurement and progress assessment
PRA	participatory rural appraisal
PSIR	pressure–state–impact–response
PSR	pressure–state–response
QLI*	qualitative and implicit indicators
QLII	qualitative, implicit and internal
QNE*	quantitative and explicit indicators
QNEE	quantitative, explicit and external
QNEI	quantitative, explicit and internal
QoL	quality of life
SD	sustainable development
SGI	sustainability gap index
SI	sustainability indicator
SLM	sustainable land management
SLSA	systemic learning for sustainability analysis
SNIP	Sustainable Northern Ireland Project
SPSA	systemic and prospective sustainability analysis
SSA	systemic sustainability analysis
SSM	soft systems methodology
SWOC	strengths, weaknesses, opportunities and constraints
USAID	United States Agency for International Development
VBA	Visual Basic for Applications
WBCSD	World Business Council for Sustainable Development
WCED	World Commission on Environment and Development
WGP	weighted goal programming

Chapter 1

The Brave New Frontier of Sustainability: Where are We?

INTRODUCTION

It is often said that 'development' as envisioned today is largely a post-Second World War phenomenon that has moved, not necessarily progressed, through various forms and fashions. The 1950s and 1960s were the days of grand development theories all applied at the macro-scale (country, region). The Green Revolution in Asia is such an example based on modernization theory. The grand theories became less fashionable in the 1970s, and the 1980s and 1990s were the age of the 'micro-intervention' in development. The boundaries of state intervention and control were rolled back and efforts were instead focused on allowing individuals to help themselves. Terms such as 'stakeholder', 'farmer first' and 'participation' rapidly gained ground. Yet the 1980s saw the rapid expansion of one development theory that successfully managed to combine both macro- and micro-perspectives: sustainable development (SD). It is perhaps hard to appreciate it now, some 20 years or so later, but this may really be said to be different. In SD the individual is seen as central, but one could scale up from that to quite literally the globe. All were involved, no matter where on the globe one lived or what one did for a living. No one is exempt and no one can pass on the responsibility to others; not even to the next generation. Add to this a multi-disciplinary focus encompassing economics, culture, social structures, resource use, etc, and it's not difficult to see how the all-encompassing nature of SD – multi-scale, multi-disciplinary, multi-perspective, multi-definition – has ensured that it is perhaps the ultimate culmination to development theories. Indeed it is much more than the adding together of 'development' and 'sustainability' (Garcia and Staples, 2000) and at the turn of the century SD has become the dominant paradigm within development. After all, as Bossel (1999) puts it:

There is only one alternative to sustainability: unsustainability.

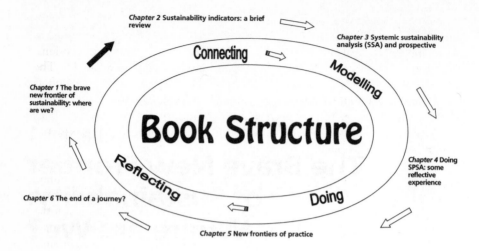

Put in those stark terms, who wants unsustainable development? SD made the world a place where individuals had a stake, and was not just a matter for the economists and politicians (the traditional view). As a result SD has helped spawn the wide range of 'direct action' groups such as those that now protest at meetings of the most industrialized countries.

In this chapter we will explore some of the issues in SD at the turn of the century. The chapter will begin by addressing the contested nature of SD, and the reason why that should occur. It will then proceed to discuss some of the methods used to track progress towards SD, with particular focus on the use of indicators as a device. A commonly expressed central element in all of this is the need for public participation; experts should not solely drive SD. Addressing a wider audience does inevitably mean that one has to work with multiple perspectives on SD. Facilitating such participation and handling multiple perspectives within it require specialized methodologies and skills. Some of these, particularly the adaptation of soft systems methodology (SSM), will be outlined. But participation does not automatically mean painless or easy transition to SD. Indeed, the practice of public participation brings problems, and some of these will be discussed at the end of the chapter.

WHAT IS SUSTAINABLE DEVELOPMENT?

Sustainable development has many definitions,[1] but perhaps the most commonly quoted within the extensive literature on the subject is:

> *Development that meets the needs of current generations without com-*
> *promising the ability of future generations to meet their needs and*
> *aspirations.* (WCED, 1987)

This definition arose out of the United Nations-sponsored World Commission on Environment and Development (WCED), chaired by the former Prime Minister of

Norway, Gro Harlem Brundtland. Its report, *Our Common Future,* (WCED, 1987) contains the above definition, and this has been repeated verbatim, or modified to suit specific institutional or individual needs, ever since. It comprises two dimensions: the notion of development (to make better) and sustainability (to maintain). The word 'sustainable' is often attached to other human-centred activities such as agriculture, natural resource management, health care provision, urban centres, etc. These are all elements of SD, and are based on the same underlying principle of not compromising the future, and in a sense we can refer to a 'sustainability movement'. Indeed, the term 'sustainability' is often used synonymously with SD.

Like other development approaches, SD is all about an improvement in the human condition, yet unlike many of the others it does not emphasize economic growth or production. The difference from other macro theories of development rests not so much on its focus on people, because they all have that, but more on the underlying philosophy that what is done now to improve the quality of life of people should not degrade the environment (in its widest bio-physical and socio-economic sense) and resources such that future generations are put at a disadvantage. In other words, we (the present) should not cheat the future; improving our lives now should not be at the price of degrading the quality of life of future generations. At the same time, the 'sustainable' element to SD does not imply stasis. Human societies cannot remain static, and the aspirations and expectations that comprise a part of 'needs' constantly shift (Garcia and Staples, 2000). How all of this has been set out in definitions is a fascinating discussion in itself, with almost every organization involved in SD putting its own spin on the wording and phraseology that reflects its own mission and vision. While this may be exasperating, we agree with Meter (1999) that 'one of the joys of the sustainability movement is to learn how many different definitions people use of the term sustainability'.

SD is classically portrayed as the interface between environmental, economic and social sustainability (Goodland and Daly, 1996), and the ideas inherent in SD are often presented in visual terms. Indeed, a study of the visual devices used in the literature (SD art) and the ideas behind them could be a fascinating topic for analysis in itself. Figures 1.1 and 1.2 are two forms in which this relationship has been visually presented. In Figure 1.1, perhaps the most common type of presentation of SD, there are three interlocking circles, with SD representing the point where all three overlap. This diagram has had much appeal in the literature, perhaps because of its stress on circularity and non-linear inter-linkage. By way of contrast, in Figure 1.2 the components and relationships are presented in a more mechanistic form, as boxes and arrows respectively. Here we see an emphasis on linear, almost mechanical, linkages.

However, although a desire for 'improvement' of the human condition and a concern for future generations (or 'futurity') rest as twin pillars at the heart of SD, the detail of what all this implies in practice has been open to much debate. As with all development approaches, one is always left with the basic question as to which people we are talking about. Just who is supposed to be developing sustainably? Where are they in terms of 'space' (meaning more than just physical location, but also including socio-cultural dimensions)? Part of this is the ever-present question as to what exactly 'development' and 'improvement' means to them. Extending this further raises questions as to the timescale involved. How many generations ahead should we consider?

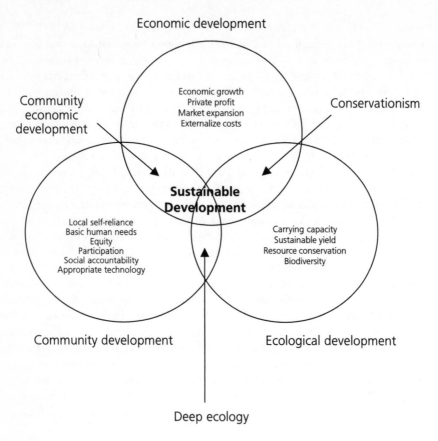

Economic development

Community
economic
development

Conservationism

Economic growth
Private profit
Market expansion
Externalize costs

**Sustainable
Development**

Local self-reliance
Basic human needs
Equity
Participation
Social accountability
Appropriate technology

Carrying capacity
Sustainable yield
Resource conservation
Biodiversity

Community development

Ecological development

Deep ecology

Figure 1.1 *The interactions between ecological, economic and social (community)
development*

As one may guess, answers to all these questions can depend a great deal upon who
is asked for an opinion (Meppem and Gill, 1998). Perspective is critical, and as soon
as more than one person in included then, by definition, this becomes multiple.
Globalization may have helped induce some uniformity in perception and aspiration,
but the extent of this is surely debatable, and in any case the likely outcome is a
'ratcheting up' of expectation rather than a levelling down (Deb, 1998). Yet SD is all
about equity (Templet, 1995), not just in inter-generational terms ('don't cheat our
kids'), but also within the same generation.

Indeed, the very soul of SD is that it is participatory. It is not something that can
be imposed by a small minority of technocrats or policy-makers from above. Instead,
SD should involve people from the very beginning. This is embodied within Principle
10 of the Rio Declaration on Environment and Development:

> *Environmental issues are best handled with the participation of all con-
> cerned citizens. Each individual should have . . . [information], and the
> opportunity to participate in decision-making processes.* (UNCED, 1992;
> cited in Curwell and Cooper, 1998)

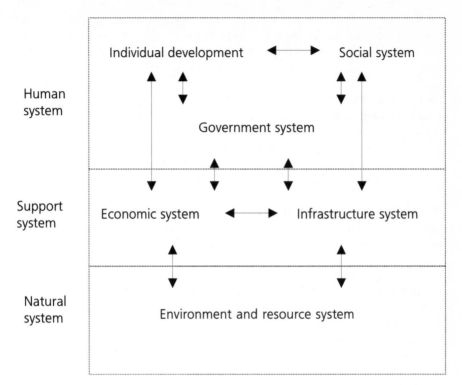

Source: after Bossel, 1999

Figure 1.2 *The six key sub-systems of human society and development*

Some even see SD as impossible without a parallel emphasis on good governance. Yet while this is laudable, it can be difficult in practice. With the best of intentions, can we really include everyone's views? Do we not inevitably hear those with the most power or those with the loudest voice? The result may be feelings of disenfranchisement, and perhaps the emergence of the direct action groups mentioned earlier.

The lack of a common understanding of SD, beyond very broad mission statements such as that of the WCED, seems to have been a source of frustration for some (de Kruijf and van Vuuren, 1998). At one level, if SD is founded upon a requirement to address the local perspective then it would seem to be unlikely that a global consensus will ever emerge. But can we determine a community's SD without correlations to larger scale, including global, processes (Allenby et al, 1998)? If nothing else, SD is a shared responsibility, and some express a desire to apply some common understanding across similar systems (de Kruijf and van Vuuren, 1998). Whilst appreciating that a system is the outcome of an individual's understanding, multiple perspectives can trip us up if we are not careful. A system is quite literally defined by the person experiencing it, and it will be different to different stakeholders. Solow (1993) has also decried what he sees as the 'expression of emotions and attitudes' that have dogged discussions of SD, with 'very little analysis of sustainable paths for a modern industrial society'.

It is interesting to note that attempts to derive such a 'common understanding' have often focused directly on the underlying basic science of SD (Stirling, 1999), and the turn of the century has seen the emergence of what some term 'sustainability science' (Kates et al, 2000). A focus on 'science' here is perhaps not unsurprising, given that SD has strong roots in scientific perspectives of natural resource management and the environment (Bell and Morse, 1999; Kates et al, 2000), even if this involvement has waned in more recent times:

> *Over the last 15 years, however, with few exceptions, science and technology have not been active partners in the societal and political process of sustainable development.* (Kates et al, 2000)

Nevertheless, it can be comforting when looking for underlying principles of SD to return to the ideas and language that helped spawn it. For example, the following broad principles, or variations of them, are commonly espoused:[2]

- Rates of utilization of renewable resources must not be greater than rates of regeneration.
- Waste emissions must not be greater than the assimilation capacities of the environment.
- Rates of use of non-renewables must not be greater than the rate of creation of renewable substitutes.

These ideas, encapsulated in the general notion of 'environmental sustainability', albeit bereft of appropriate spatial and time scales over which these rates apply, can be found in many forms. Goodland and Daly (1996), for example, suggest we must:

- learn how to manage renewable resources for the long term;
- reduce waste and pollution;
- learn how to use energy and materials more efficiently (including more use of solar energy); and
- invest in repairing the damage done to the Earth.

These ideas are also encapsulated in the ethos of the Natural Step organization, and its four 'system conditions' for the maintenance of system 'quality' (Hardi et al, 1997; Curwell and Cooper, 1998). The Natural Step was founded in Sweden in 1989 by Karl-Henrick Robert, and its principles arose out of a consensus among that country's top scientists as to what conditions are required for a sustainable society:

- Materials from the Earth's crust must not be systematically increased in the ecosphere.
- Materials produced by society must not be systematically increased in the ecosphere.
- The physical basis for the productivity and diversity of nature must not be systematically diminished.
- There must be fair and efficient use of resources with respect to meeting human needs.

The first three of these tell us what we must not do (ie despoil), while the third brings out the importance of equity – today and tomorrow. There is also an undercurrent of emphasis on 'production' and 'consumption'. Indeed, given this language it is perhaps not surprising that the Natural Step is said to be particularly pertinent to business, with the intention being to break out of a linear production process (resources lead to raw materials, lead to manufacturing, lead to utilization, lead to waste) and into a more cyclical one that makes better use of the four Rs: re-use, repair, recycling and reconditioning (Curwell and Cooper, 1998).

While the four Natural Step conditions have an understandable appeal, particularly as they provide a firm basis for action by business, they can perhaps be seen as too mechanistic in emphasis. For example, we could translate these steps into the sort of issues list presented in Table 1.1 (Tyteca, 1996; Ditz and Ranganathan, 1998). Note that all of the impacts listed in Table 1.1 are measurable in quantitative terms. A similar input–output approach can be taken for any industry, including farming (Lefroy and Hobbs, 1992).

Table 1.1 *Sample list of environmental impacts of industrial activities*

Issue	Impacts (to measure)
Resources	raw materials uptake
	energy consumption
Waste emissions (water)	biochemical oxygen demand (BOD)
	total suspended solids
	acidity/alkalinity (pH)
	concentration of phosphates, nitrates, heavy metals, etc
Waste emissions (air)	carbon dioxide, nitrous/nitric oxides, sulphur dioxide
Waste emissions (other)	solid wastes
	toxic wastes
	noise
Further impacts	impacts on landscape
	impacts on biodiversity
	contribution to the greenhouse effect
	contribution to ozone layer depletion
	contribution to acid rain deposition

Source: after Tyteca, 1996

However, something seems to be missing from this rather mechanical analysis. Where are the people? To state the obvious, SD is something rationalized and implemented by people for people, by definition and not by accident. SD is not an entity that sits outside of our heads and independent from human thought and action: just the opposite. No people, then no SD. One consequence of this is that SD can mean very different things to different people. What is one person's SD is another's despoliation, degradation and exploitation (Dahl, 1997). After all, SD is something that everyone, not just scientists and technicians, can relate to and form an opinion on:

> *This is not rocket science. Sustainability is something that everyone can understand.* (Hart Environmental Data, 1998)

Understand, yes – but on whose terms? Here is the crux of the matter. Everyone really does have a view if asked what SD should be and how to get it. But how much agreement is there? Some have even tried to categorize SD as 'belief systems' (Table 1.2), and there may well be religious undertones to such diverse perspectives on SD (Dahl, 1997). Interestingly, van Asselt and Rotmans (1996) and van Asselt et al (1996) use a similar categorization of perspective – hierarchist, egalitarian and individualist – to describe a spectrum of biases in the way that people deal with uncertainty. This may even be used to create 'perspective-based' models of future projections in issues central to SD such as population, health, gross domestic product (GDP), energy and emissions (Rotmans and van Asselt, 1999).

Table 1.2 *Four simplified belief systems and sustainable development*

Belief system (simplified)	Group	Some characteristics
Liberty	Libertarians	• free markets necessary and sufficient for SD • fairness and equity are irrelevant
Efficiency	Corporatists	• sustainability marginally relevant and not inconsistent with maximizing output over time
Equality	Egalitarians	• all humans have natural rights which require social, economic and political equality
Community	Communitarians	• global perspective • inter-generational and inter-specific equity are important • economic growth undesirable

Source: after Allenby et al, 1998

The groups portrayed in Table 1.2 do not necessarily sit in benign indulgence of each other's existence. Indeed, the 'community' belief system of SD may be seen by libertarians as a threat to individual freedom. Communitarians may also see libertarians as a threat to their emphasis on equity. Indeed, even if a vision of SD that includes an emphasis on 'equity' could be agreed to by all in Table 1.2, the likelihood is that it would be interpreted by the various groups in quite different ways: equity in distribution of resources (Templet, 1995) vis-à-vis equity in opportunity. These inevitable stresses and strains are important in SD:

> *Until these stakeholder differences are accepted, and normative statements regarding the necessity to move toward sustainability are avoided, it is unlikely that all groups will be equally represented; they may even avoid participation in debates on the environment–economy interface.* (Allenby et al, 1998)

Yet, despite this truism, determining what SD means to stakeholders is 'an obvious but often neglected step' (Gardner et al, 1995). Seeing the sustainability dimension in SD as 'science' may not be an entirely helpful step; after all:

> *it is clear that incomplete knowledge, and limitations in our ability to utilize it, will permanently challenge sustainability science as it tries to link research to action and to reconcile scientific excellence with social relevance.* (Kates et al, 2000)

Science is also a grand narrative/worldview that comes with its own baggage, and given the stereotypical groups presented in Table 1.2, the words 'utilize' and 'relevance' are open to many interpretations, making this statement quite literally boundless. Recognizing that a wide range of perspectives exist is one thing; engaging with them in a meaningful way based on genuine participation and equity of perspective is something entirely different. Compare the above quotation, and a vision of sustainability as a 'science', with the following:

> *Conversely, scientists and managers must understand and consider the values and needs of people, rather than concluding what is good or bad for society from their own, often technical, perspectives.* (Kessler et al, 1992)

> *When providing society with advice about the sustainability of natural resource use, we keep in mind the explosion of the space shuttle Challenger. If rocket scientists can make such a big mistake, we ecologists, working in a much harder field, need to be aware of the limitations of our understanding.* (Hilborn and Ludwig, 1993)

Both these quotes come from papers with a specific focus on sustainable natural resource management rather than SD, but many others throughout the sustainability movement echo the essence of what they say. Hence there is something of a conundrum. Attempts to derive broad principles for SD tend to lean heavily on 'technical' perspectives (sustainability science, Natural Steps, etc), yet most agree that SD means nothing without people – all people, not just the technically adept few. Science has limitations in what it can contribute in such an emotionally charged and value-judgement-centred arena (Gatto, 1995):

> *To operationalize sustainable development requires moving from literary or scientific definitions towards a process that recognizes diversity of perspective.* (Meppem and Gill, 1998)

Stirling (1999) is critical of what he sees as attempts to engage with SD as if it were 'an objectively determinate quantity', and attempts to convert 'the fuzzy and controversial socio-political problems of sustainability into precisely defined and relatively tractable analytical puzzles'. He refers to this as an 'analytical fix', and suggests its appeal may at least in part:

> *be due to the strong convergence of interest between those seeking to promote particular academic disciplines and those seeking convenient ways to justify difficult or potentially unpopular decisions.*

Strong words indeed! Nonetheless, the interface between the technical ('analytical fix') perspective and the role of other stakeholders, including the public, has been a matter of some debate and even double-think. Just how much of SD should be a 'top-down' process ('omniscient modelling' – Rubenstein, 1993) driven primarily by technical specialists, and how much should be 'bottom-up', driven by a dynamic of public participation ('stakeholder trading' – Rubenstein, 1993)? If there is a compromise between these two extremes, just where it should be has been the subject of much debate.[3] What determines the location of this compromise? Cost, place, ability, data, ethics? Who should be involved, who decides this, what are the means for engaging in the conversation (and who says so), and what is the valid format for the conversation to take place? Indeed, is it possible for us to use this compromise to outline a path for SD and to follow it (Gatto, 1995)? Reconciliation of top-down and bottom-up visions of SD may be problematic, but nonetheless it is necessary, and much can depend upon the level of trust between these various groups (Crilly et al, 1999). Unfortunately there is evidence to suggest that trust between the public and scientists, let alone politicians, is at a low ebb in much of the developed world at least (Pinfield, 1996; MacNaughton et al, 1995).

But such flexibility in perspective can also be an advantage. After all, the detail of what comprises SD will be very context-specific, and it would be illogical to expect the same conditions to apply everywhere. That is why there is no detailed global blueprint, only a broad statement of philosophy. Yet the flexibility afforded by such a broad philosophy also allows for multiple interpretations, and these can operate at various levels. We can illustrate this with a four point 'sustainability checklist' (Table 1.3). In our view, Table 1.3 is one way we can explore an individual's engagement with SD, even if it all boils down to the maintenance of quality of life (QoL), as some suggest. For the most part, the QoL relates to an individual's immediate environment, hence the emphasis on Local Agenda 21 initiatives, but people also engage at a wider scale (caring for distant people and environments). Therefore, the answers to the questions in Table 1.3 will depend upon our own 'space': the complex cultural, socio-economic and political context that we occupy (de Kruijf and van Vuuren, 1998). In practice, an individual will have many such concerns that could interact in all sorts of complex ways. These concerns may also be ranked – an individual may see traffic as more important than litter – and this ranking could change over short, medium and long terms. The list is also likely to be quite different for other people.

Historically, most of the focus has been on the first two questions of the sustainability checklist. There has been less formal emphasis on the final questions: 'what do I do (or expect someone else to do) about it?' We find this surprising given that SD has always been intended as a practical approach rather than just an academic exercise. SD, by its very nature, is a move towards the 'peoplization' of development; taking it out of the hands of the technocrats and making it a matter of key interest to all. Indeed, here we have another conundrum. Perhaps for the majority of people, SD is seen in terms of others (rather than themselves) not doing the right thing: 'The government is not trying to improve public transport as much as it should, therefore it is not behaving sustainably'; 'Farmers are using fertilizers and pesticides, therefore they are not farming sustainably'.

Indeed, although it has been exaggerated here, studies do suggest that what people say they want and what they actually do can often be at variance. People, for example,

Table 1.3 *A sustainability checklist*

Question number	Checklist question	Explanation
1	What is important to me in sustainable development?	What are the key considerations I regard as important to the maintenance of my quality of life? This can include the response 'I don't care!'
		For most people this will be a complex combination of environmental, social and economic concerns that may change with time and space (where the individual lives), and also depend upon whom one is interacting with.
2	How do I engage with or relate to the key considerations identified in 1?	How do I engage with, interact with or relate to the things I identify as important?
		For most people it may simply be via everyday experience and the media (newspapers, TV, radio).
3	What do I do about it? (internalized response)	Once I know what is important and how I engage with it, what do I then do about the information I receive, especially if it suggests that things are 'wrong'?
		This can vary from 'doing something' to talking. The response may be 'internalized', eg worry.
4	What do I expect others to do about it? (externalized response)	As with 3, only 'What do I expect others to do about it?' and 'How do I interact with them in order to achieve this?'

may want fewer cars on the road, and chastise the government and others for not doing more to achieve this, as long as it is not their own cars that can't be used. Consumers complain about the use of fertilizer and pesticides by farmers, yet seem reluctant to pay a premium for organic produce in the supermarket. In essence the problem is that SD speaks volumes at the level of an individual, but loses much when brought to the more charged atmosphere of politics and policy. Perhaps that most inclusive of development approaches is visualized by most in external (rather than internal) terms! Wouldn't this be ironic? As Curwell and Cooper (1998) put it:

> *Thus the essential paradox of a sustainable society is the conflicting requirements of providing the flows of production and consumption needed to maintain a good quality of life for all humankind, while simultaneously sustaining the local and global environment and bio-diversity.*

This paradox could be compounded by trends such as the increasing urbanization of humankind.

The spatial and temporal scales upon which SD is considered are continuous from the individual to the global (Dahl, 1997). For example, at the global scale are the problems associated with human-mediated global warming thought to be linked to greenhouse gas emissions. Although these issues are often discussed in terms of national and international politics, there are also roles for industries, companies, communities and even the individual. After all, these may be the very groups that pay the price, directly or indirectly, for any reduction. It would appear that historically, and perhaps even at present, the temptation is often to degrade now and let future generations pay the price, or at least let them take the risk if there is any uncertainty:

> *We can think of inter-generational discounting as a concession to human weakness or as a technical assumption of convenience (which it is)*. (Solow, 1993)

For example, whether human-mediated global warming is 'real' has been the subject of much debate and uncertainty, particularly in the US, and part of the comfort zone that allows such a debate to take place is the reassurance that if CO_2-mediated global warming is a proven (beyond all doubt) cause–effect then we will not have to pay the price – our children will.

Issues of scale (both space and time) are often presented within SD in a largely technical sense. For example, spatial scale is deemed to be important in terms of deriving physical system components and flows between them.[4] Factors outside of this are said to be 'externalities'. But there is far more to this than just technical issues. After all, people perceive and interact with scale to varying degrees of tolerance and concern. We might be highly concerned about a site-specific effect arising out of global warming that results in damage to our house or farm, but perhaps be less concerned if that damage is to someone else's property thousands of miles away. Similarly, we may be more likely to show such concern if the damage occurred tomorrow as distinct from a hundred years time. As a result, some have visualized various horizons (influence, attention and responsibility) that link time and space in SD (Figure 1.3). There is much scope here for trade-offs and negotiation between different groups. Not surprisingly, many of the definitions of SD reflect these points and in a sense encapsulate the multiple perspectives, interaction with scale and negotiations that have occurred between those formulating any one definition.

Nevertheless, although the precise meaning of SD in any one context may be open to negotiation, once arrived at we are presumably concerned with the practicalities of achieving it. Even if the starting point is a definition that corresponds more to a vague mission statement of intent than precisely defined goals, the requirement for implementation forces through an analysis of what needs to be done, by whom, where, for how long and when. Naturally we will also need to know whether all of this is successful in terms of achieving the desired change. In other words, there is a need to be able to check progress towards a goal. After all, as Solow (1993) puts it, 'talk without measurement is cheap', and for Hardi et al (1997) 'management requires measurement'. Of course the assessment of what constitutes 'good' or 'effective' measurement is very much the value judgement of the stakeholder involved, a point we will continually return to in the next three chapters. It is here, in the assessment of SD as a necessity for action, that in our opinion the current frontiers of SD rest (Mitchell, 1996).

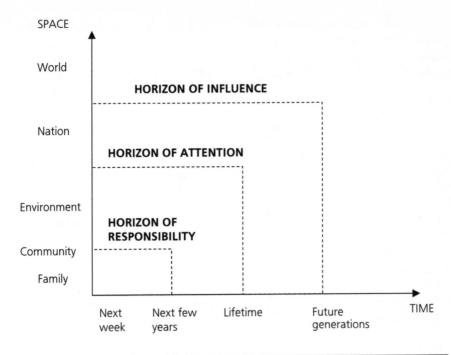

Horizon of	Comprising
Influence	Systems in time and space that are significantly affected by an actor's influence
Attention	Systems whose behaviour, development and/or fate is of some interest to an actor
Responsibility	Systems where an actor would be willing to carry some responsibility in order to see them survive or improve

Note: For sustainable development the horizon of attention must not be smaller than the horizon of responsibility
Source: after Bossel, 1999

Figure 1.3 *Horizons of influence, attention and responsibility in sustainable development*

GAUGING PROGRESS

There are a number of tools and methodologies designed to help gauge progress towards SD, but given the disparity of views already described it shouldn't be surprising that 'there is no textbook which gives a methodology that is generally accepted and applicable across regions and sectors' (Hardi et al, 1997). Nevertheless, there are some broad approaches that we commonly come across in the extensive SD literature. One of these is the popular concept of an ecological footprint (EF), based on the notion of carrying capacity. Carrying capacity has had a substantial influence in the origins of SD and is the subject of much debate to this day.[5] There are various definitions. For example:

> *Carrying capacity is the maximum load (population × per capita impact)*
> *that can safely and persistently be imposed on the environment by people.*
> (Catton, 1980)

A spatial unit (eg urban area, country) can thus be described in relation to its impact in terms of the land area required to support it: the ecological footprint. This is quite distinct from the physical footprint, the physical land area occupied by the spatial unit (Curwell and Cooper, 1998). Hence the EF is usually expressed quantitatively as a plot of land area required to maintain the unit, and the larger the EF then, by implication, the greater the resources required to sustain the unit's existence (Allenby et al, 1998). Examples of the EF calculated on a per-country basis are presented in Figure 1.4. The EF can be a simple yet visually striking device, and has provided a powerful metaphor for gauging sustainability (Haberl et al, 2001).[6] It utilizes a human frailty that almost all of us are sensitive to: avarice; and has deep issues of equity embedded within it. The immediate implication is that a large EF is 'bad' and smacks of greed.

Unfortunately, it is also possible to interpret EFs in terms of competitive ability; those with larger footprints could be seen as more competitive and hence 'successful' (Newman, 1998). Up to a point it does appear as if at least one measure of output, GDP/capita, increases as the EF (taken as a measure of input) increases (Figure 1.4). However, the rate of increase of GDP/capita slows and levels out completely once the EF reaches 5ha/capita. Beyond that point there is no evidence to suggest that higher EFs are linked to higher GDP/capita. Much also depends upon assumptions of productivity (Haberl et al, 2001). If productivity is low then more land area will be required to sustain a city or country. The EF also says little about qualitative issues, and there is no 'output' component to balance against input. For example, although we could argue that the EF should be as small as possible, does size really matter that much? After all, provided that the land area required to support the unit does not suffer from resource degradation, pollution or negative socio-economic impact, then cannot the unit be regarded as sustainable? What matters is where the system boundary is drawn, and all the EF does is ensure that the system boundary is widened beyond the physical limits of a spatial unit. In other words, the EF device allows a discussion to take place in terms of spatial units that people can readily engage with. In itself it may not say much about what could or should be done to improve matters.

At the more limited spatial level of a productive unit such as a firm, one could gauge similar measures to the EF, but modified to include output. One could, for example, measure the material intensity per unit of service (MIPS). This is the mass of material input per total units of service delivered by the good over its entire lifespan (Hinterberger and Schmidt-Bleek, 1999). Inputs would include manufacturing, transport, packaging, operating, re-use, recycling, re-manufacturing and even waste disposal. The aim, of course, is to get as much service for as little material as possible. It's a sort of EF, but with output included:

> *Products are environmentally sound when either the amount of material*
> *input per amount of services is decreased, or the number of services provided*
> *by the product is increased.* (Hinterberger and Schmidt-Bleek, 1999)

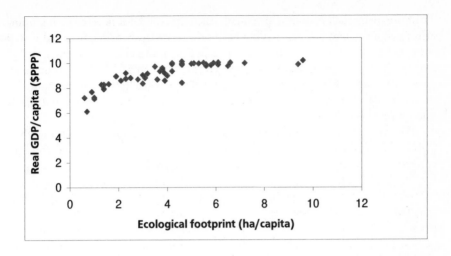

Country	Ecological footprint (ha/capita)	Country	Ecological footprint (ha/capita)
United States	9.6	Portugal	3.8
Australia	9.4	Spain	3.8
Canada	7.2	Korean Republic	3.7
Singapore	6.6	Brazil	3.6
New Zealand	6.5	Israel	3.5
Hong Kong	6.1	Malaysia	3.2
Sweden	6.1	Hungary	3.1
Denmark	5.9	Argentina	3.0
Finland	5.8	South Africa	3.0
Ireland	5.6	Costa Rica	2.8
Netherlands	5.6	Mexico	2.5
Norway	5.5	Chile	2.3
France	5.3	Colombia	2.3
Belgium	5.1	Turkey	2.1
Iceland	5.0	Thailand	1.9
Austria	4.6	Jordan	1.6
Germany	4.6	China	1.4
Russian Federation	4.6	Egypt	1.4
Switzerland	4.6	Peru	1.4
United Kingdom	4.6	Philippines	1.4
Greece	4.2	Indonesia	1.3
Italy	4.2	India	1.0
Japan	4.2	Nigeria	1.0
Venezuela	4.0	Pakistan	0.9
Czech Republic	3.9	Ethiopia	0.7
Poland	3.9	Bangladesh	0.6

Source: GDP/capita taken from the United Nations Human Development Report, 1998. EF calculated on a country basis for 1995 taken from Chambers et al, 2000.

Figure 1.4 *Ecological footprint (EF) for some selected countries, and the relationship between EF (ha/capita) and real GDP/capita ($ purchasing power parity)*

There are many such measures of eco-efficiency that can be applied to such output-orientated units, and business has not been slow to see the benefits, financial as well as in public relations, of such devices. The inclusion of two elements, input as well as output, allows for greater flexibility on the part of firms compared with an input-only device like the EF. There is also the possibility of externalizing some of the inputs (ie, don't consider them as such, but assume that someone else has), and much depends upon where boundaries are drawn (Foxon et al, 1999; Stirling, 1999).

Placing such input–output components and flows into common units has received a great deal of attention. One approach has been to use the concept of 'emergy'; converting inputs/flows into a common energy equivalent (usually solar energy – Odum, 1988). The emergy involved in a process, including industrial, is thus a measure of the 'work done by the environment, including everything it supplies free' (Bastianoni et al, 1998). Another popular approach has centred upon the use of cost–benefit analysis (CBA) to compare the financial values of the costs of achieving sustainability with the benefits. Costing the environment in this way is what some refer to as 'weak sustainability'. It implies that manufactured capital of equal value can take the place of natural capital, and hence the environment can be 'valued' in such terms, and notions of depreciation and resource substitution applied in economics can be used here as well (van der Hamsvoort and Latacz-Lohmann, 1998). Distilling sustainability down to money certainly has an appeal that must be hard to resist for those charged with paying for it. CBA also presents sustainability in terms that are quantitative and seemingly objective and precise. This can be dangerous, however:

> *At worst the veneer of false confidence implied in an analysis may well be part of the problem, not the solution.* (Meppem and Gill, 1998)

Pearce and Atkinson (1993) also point out the need for a complementary appreciation of 'strong sustainability' elements to the natural resource base and environment. With strong sustainability, the existing stock of natural capital must be maintained and cannot be replaced by manufactured capital. Put simply, it is exceedingly difficult to 'value' in purely economic terms dimensions such as 'clean air, scenic views and wildlife' (Mitchell, 1996). In weak sustainability, what Meppem and Gill (1998) refer to as 'intangibles' tend to be left out of the analysis. Humans have very diverse values that they apply to 'nature', and CBA will be insensitive to such value pluralism, and may even distort it to fit into a simple model. The other extreme, strong sustainability, has also had its critics, mainly on grounds of practicality (van der Hamsvoort and Latacz-Lohmann, 1998).

However, perhaps the most popular approach to gauging SD has been the employment of indicators and indices, an index being an amalgam of more than one indicator (Liverman et al, 1988; Quarrie, 1992). Gardner et al (1995) describe them as 'sign and signals which should be monitored in order to predict a good future'. Terminology is rather fluid, with labels such as sustainability indicators (SIs) and indicators of sustainable development (ISDs) being employed in various contexts. There are many definitions of an 'indicator' (Gallopin, 1997): the current consensus is 'an operational representation of an attribute (quality, characteristic, property) of a system' (Gallopin, 1997), while data are actual measurements or observations of the values of indicators.

There are many examples of indicators and indices designed to measure attainment of SD or its elements, and no one set has emerged with universal appeal (Mitchell, 1996). There is also much overlap between indicators and the approaches mentioned above. The EF, for example, may be utilized as an indicator within SD (Chambers et al, 2000). However, given that SD is typically envisaged as having environmental, social and economic dimensions then the usual approach is to develop a framework of indicators that cover all of these, perhaps in conjunction with a single index that tries to bring them all together into a numerical value (Mitchell, 1996). The EF may be a part of such a framework, but would need to be combined with social and economic indicators. Although this may sound simple, there is clearly much complexity at play.

Indicators can be translated into visual forms for presentation to an audience. This can take many forms, but one approach increasingly being applied is to present the value of indicators in a map format, perhaps with a geographical information system (GIS – Langaas, 1997; Winograd and Eade, 1997). GIS is a technology whereby values of indicators can be overlaid on a map and related to a range of other variables. This may be allied with the use of computer-based models to generate the predicted value of indicators in various policy scenarios. An example of the latter is the QUEST model of SD produced by the University of British Columbia and Envision Sustainability Tools (EST, 2000), and its use within a 'sustainability atlas' in the UK (Lindley, 2001). As with the EF, such 'visualization of sustainability' is seen as a critical development in making the data 'accessible, manageable and comprehensible' (Lindley, 2001). It also provides a way in which options for the future can be explored. 'Futurity' is, by definition, a universal concern in SD, and although there may be difficulties in deriving consensus over what a sustainable future would look like, tools that help to predict options and present results in an easily digested form exert a powerful fascination. Understandably, given the 'futurity' within SD, such scenario-building has itself become an important dimension in attempts to influence policy (Braat, 1991; Rotmans, 1998; Bauler and Hecq, 2000).

While indicators are a logical device to use in SD, especially given their long record of use in fields such as economics, social accountability and environmental science (Bell and Morse, 1999), there are a number of key questions related to their development and application. These include:

- What indicators should one select?
- Who selects them?
- Why are they selected?
- What are they meant to help achieve?
- What about the balance between the various dimensions of SD?
- How are the indicators to be measured?
- How are the indicators to be interpreted, and by whom?
- How are the results to be communicated, to whom and for what purpose?
- How are the indicators to be used?

Some of these questions also apply to tools such as the EF, and clearly, given the level of 'value judgement' in SD, there is much scope for variation here (de Kruijf and van Vuuren, 1998). Indeed, there are almost as many answers to the above questions as there are indicator projects. For example, we can immediately distinguish between the sustainability of what one is trying to achieve (ie development) and the institutions and mechanisms in place to achieve it (institutional sustainability). These can be mutually exclusive rather than compatible or reinforcing. Indeed, some indicator sets are perhaps far more in tune with the notion of institutional performance, accountability and survival than with SD per se. It is with these questions, and perhaps with some more than with others, that the crux of the complexity in engaging with SD rests. At the heart of the matter is the inevitable and unbreakable connection between SD and people.

MULTIPLE PERSPECTIVES

For the most part we have seen a great deal of effort in terms of defining SD and the identification of tools, such as indicators, as devices for helping to gauge progress towards attainment. Yet the link between all of this and actually 'doing' something about it has not been so strong beyond a sometimes vague notion of 'let's tell everyone about our indicators'. Local and national Agenda 21 websites abound, and some publish their indicators in newspapers and other 'hard' media, but that is just about it. With the notable exception of indicators that are normally gathered and acted upon by governments (eg unemployment, crime rate), linking SD indicators through to policy and change is still very much in its infancy.

Part of the emphasis in 'doing' SD has been to include stakeholders in the determination of what needs to be done and how (Guy and Kibert, 1998). What do stakeholders want to include in SD and what are the indicators and methods they want to use? There are a number of rationales behind this inclusion, including an ethical stance surrounding democracy through to a more utilitarian assumption that such participation will make the implementation of necessary change easier and/or more effective. However, it is highly likely, if not inevitable, that there will be multiple perspectives even on the same issue. Studies addressing the same issue in SD will get quite different results depending on who is asked, when and how (Stirling, 1999). Not unsurprisingly, public participation has become a cornerstone of community development projects in many countries, and the US is particularly rich in examples (Besleme and Mullin, 1997). Guy and Kibert (1998), for example, referring to the Florida Local Assessment Guide (FLAG) in the US, suggest that such community participation can help in SD programmes because:

- it can help ensure that local government focuses on areas of concern where money will be wisely spent;
- it can result in a reduced risk of public opposition when hard choices are made based on limited resources;
- it is cheaper than employing professionals!
- citizens feel a sense of worth that makes them more willing to make contributions;
- it personalizes the process, resulting in greater feelings of public ownership and greater degrees of care than more objective outside 'experts'; and
- it builds community empowerment and self-accountability, especially relevant at a time of 'downsizing government'.

As part of FLAG, citizens will be asked to help identify a future 'vision' as to how their system should appear at a future date, combined with measurable goals to be achieved in fixed timeframes. While the rhetoric sounds good, the history of social indicators in policy decision-making in the US has been rather mixed. Attempts during the 1960s and 1970s at such 'social accounting' met with failure (Besleme and Mullin, 1997), and even some of the flagship community indicator projects, such as Sustainable Seattle, that have been founded upon public participation have had their critics (Brugmann, 1997a, b). The reasons for this will be discussed in later sections.

There are many ways to engage stakeholders, and the SD literature is full of examples and case studies. Everyone, it would seem, has his or her own favourite approach and set of methods, and we are no different. Interestingly, there is perhaps much experience that can be drawn from the developing world, where participatory tools have long been in vogue. The rise of what is called the 'participatory movement' within development can be traced back to the 1970s. The objective of what was initially termed participatory rural appraisal (PRA), and in more recent times participatory learning and action (PLA) or participatory action research (PAR), was to catalyse community awareness and action. In other words, the techniques could be employed to let communities learn about themselves and instigate change as a result: a facilitation of empowerment. PRA was built on three assumptions that resonate well with developed-world literature on community participation in SD:

1   the unpredictability of social phenomena;
2   the subjective nature of data; and
3   the endemic nature of problems.

The first of these is a reiteration of the complexity of human beings and the social, cultural and economic systems they create and live in. In order to deal with such complexity, the guiding principle of 'optimal ignorance' was coined. This means knowing only what is 'useful' and being appropriately imprecise – ie drawing a line in terms of what you need (not necessarily want) to know.

The second assumption is wrapped up with notions of multiple perspective:

> *All views of activity or purpose are heavy with interpretation, bias and prejudice, and this implies that there are multiple possible descriptions of any real-world activity.* (Pretty, 1998)

The third stresses the close inter-relationships of problems with many other issues, and the need to avoid a reductionist separation. This can be dangerous, as a focus on one problem in isolation could at best achieve nothing and at worse create more intractable problems elsewhere.

While the desirability of including the public in any setting of an SD agenda, including its meaning, has been broadly accepted, there are debates over the degree of top-down and bottom-up involvement. The issue is perhaps no longer about the desirability of such public involvement, but its practicality. How can the public be best involved? Clearly there are potential issues of unequal power. One interesting direction for the practical implementation of public participation in an SD context is the use of integrated assessment (IA).[7] These are frameworks for combining

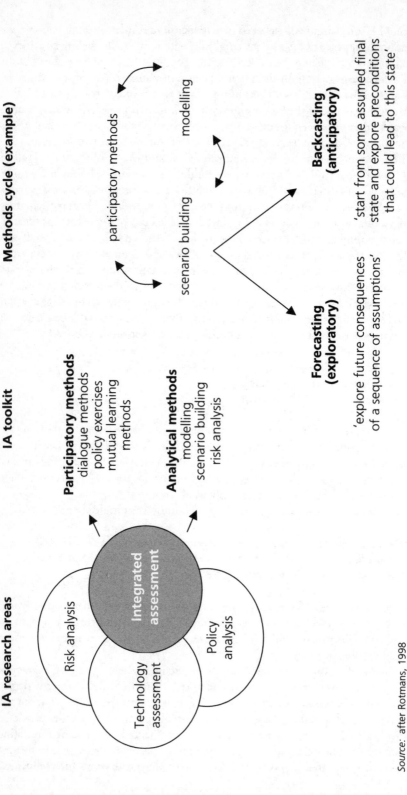

Figure 1.5 *Areas covered by integrated assessment (IA)*

Source: after Rotmans, 1998

knowledge from a wide variety of disciplines (Figure 1.5), and have three goals (Kasemir et al, 1999):

1   the coordinated exploration of possible future trajectories of human and environmental systems;
2   the development of insights into key questions of policy formation; and
3   the prioritization of research needs.

Given that SD is a contested concept, IA seeks to bring the various actors together and provide them with a forum for fruitful dispute. However, there is no universal and best way of doing this (Rotmans, 1998), and there are various tools and approaches that could be used. In practice, participation within SD often takes the form of focus groups, citizen juries, study circles, community conventions, consensus conferences and planning cells to name but a few (sometimes these are given the generic name 'deliberative institutions'). In a developing-country context, there is a host of devices commonly employed within PLA, many of them based on visual devices.[8] All of these approaches have their strengths and weaknesses and, of course, outcomes will be dependent upon who is included in the process, when and how. Each of them has to deal with all sorts of motives, desires and expectations, and are often negotiated through competition as well as cooperation (Ballard, 2000). There is much debate in the literature over the various merits and demerits of these approaches, and frankly much appears to depend upon local context and personal opinion. There is clearly more scope for research here (Kasemir et al, 1999).

One example (systemic sustainability analysis, or SSA), based on the soft systems methodology (SSM) of Peter Checkland and others (Checkland, 1981, 1990), has been developed by us (Bell and Morse, 1999) and tested in Malta in 2000 and 2001. While SSM has epistemological commonalities with other approaches in SD, for example in its reliance upon tools such as the focus group, it also has its disadvantages. It should be noted that there was never any intention to suggest that SSM was the only or indeed the best method that could be employed to facilitate participation in SD. For example, SSM only works well with relatively small numbers of people, and is time-consuming. Nevertheless, SSM is attractive as an approach in SD precisely because it is designed to deal with 'messy' situations. It is based on an assumption that in many cases a well-defined problem is a rare luxury, and people involved often cannot agree on what is wrong or what should be done. As we explain in our earlier book, this struck us as relevant considering the highly contentious and messy nature of SD. SSM is designed to allow multiple viewpoints on a problem and/or solutions to be considered, and 'practitioners with very different viewpoints can step out of role to test assumptions' (Ballard, 2000).

A simplified illustration of SSM is shown in Figure 1.6. One of the steps involves the use of a visual device termed the 'rich picture'. This is a holistic and qualitative device intended to help a group of actors present, understand and negotiate what they perceive as the relevant actors and processes involved in the 'mess'. It is a no-holds-barred approach, and may include such qualitative aspects as character and characteristics, points of view, prejudices, spirit and human nature. The idea is to develop relevant 'problem themes' that those involved agree need to be addressed. Following on from this, the group can move on to make a statement as to what needs to be done

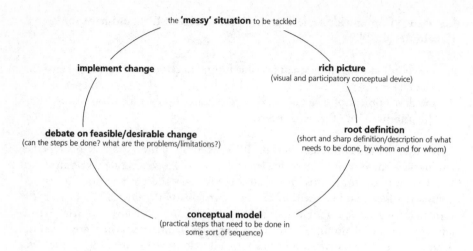

the **'messy' situation** to be tackled

implement change

rich picture
(visual and participatory conceptual device)

debate on feasible/desirable change
(can the steps be done? what are the problems/limitations?)

root definition
(short and sharp definition/description of what
needs to be done, by whom and for whom)

conceptual model
(practical steps that need to be done in
some sort of sequence)

Figure 1.6 *Simplified stages in the soft systems methodology*

(a root definition) and create a conceptual model for implementing change. What does the root definition imply should be done? Are these activities sequential and does one depend upon another? If so, how are they linked? Finally, one looks at the desirability/feasibility of what is proposed. The process is a circular one with continued scrutiny and analysis following any implementation.

One other feature of SSM that we found attractive in SD was that the methodology could easily be passed to stakeholders and not remain the intellectual property of the researcher. We saw this as important given the historical tendency of SD to be driven by top-down and technocentric agendas. Also, SSM may be liberating in itself (lots of new insights and ideas) rather than necessarily generating a defined end product. In that sense it acts as a form of 'collaborative inquiry' (Ballard, 2000), and can allow participants to deal with issues of SD in a learning environment. It is the learning and awareness that the method facilitates that could be of great value, even if there is no defined deliverable.

PUBLIC PARTICIPATION: TALK AND ACTION

Participation brings problems. A major problem with the practical inclusion of the public in setting indicators of SD is with resources. While inclusion helps to ensure social relevance, can public interest be sustained? To maintain any momentum may require substantial investments of personnel, time and money, the three resources that are most limiting in any project. The result may be that project personnel have to press on with minimal public involvement, if any, while hoping that this can be brought in more solidly at a later time. While the public may be interested in SD, at least when it affects them, and more than willing to voice an opinion, a stronger commitment may not be forthcoming. After all, people have busy lives. Voicing a quick opinion in a survey may be one thing; devoting hours of valuable time to SD projects may be something else. The result may be an apparent indifference, as the public does not devote the attention that the topic seemingly requires (MacNaughten et al, 1995; Owens, 1994).

The way forward is often presented in terms of indicators. The chain of reasoning is a simple one: the public is interested in SD and desires information on progress in an easily digested form, and indicators are ideally suited to this. Ideally one would want the public to participate in helping to set the indicators. However, just because the public has been informed, does this mean that they will act by bringing about change in their own lives or putting pressure on those in a position to influence policy? Can we even expect that SD indicators will be a consideration in election campaigns? Being hungry for information does not in itself result in action (MacGillivray, 1994), and there may be various reasons for this (Camilleri, M, 1996):

- Many people are locked into lifestyles with little opportunity for change (Grove-White, 1993), especially when they are concerned with day-to-day economic problems, eg commuting to work.
- The individual can feel a powerlessness to challenge key institutions (MacNaughten et al, 1995), eg the fuel protests in the UK during 2000.
- There may be mistrust of institutions, especially those of the government (MacNaughten et al, 1995), eg consumer distrust of the Ministry of Agriculture, Fisheries and Food (MAFF) (now known as the Department for Environment, Food and Rural Affairs, or DEFRA) in the UK following the food scares of the 1980s and 1990s (BSE, genetically modified food, salmonella in eggs, etc).
- People may be alienated by the rather technical discourse on environment, which has tended to become dominated by interest groups and scientism (ie science knows best) (Grove-White, 1993).

All of this results in tension between what the public wants and what it does, and urging change may not be easy (MacGillivray and Zadek, 1995).

There may also be some difference of opinion as to what 'participation' actually means in any particular context, as it is not an 'all or nothing' concept. The spectrum illustrated in Table 1.4 shows how 'participation' can mean quite different things; from a pretence (eg powerless representative on a committee) through to self-mobilization. There are many intermediate positions between these extremes. This plasticity of meaning can be an advantage. It may allow a project to proclaim its participatory credentials and appear eminently virtuous, while in practice this 'participation' may amount to nothing more than a carefully selected 'street' representative who sits on a 'people's committee' with six external experts. As one may expect, an underlying issue throughout is the meaning of the word 'people'. In some cases, where numbers are small, it could refer to all of the stakeholders, but this is rare. Normally, participation is intended to occur with a representative sample of stakeholders; 'representative' in terms of gender, socio-economic status, culture, occupation, etc. Techniques and methodologies exist for trying to ensure such representation, but inevitably this could mean that those not involved may not feel any ownership of what is discussed in their name, even if they are broadly in agreement. This can instill feelings of disenfranchisement, and perhaps even lead towards the sort of direct action that we see at meetings of world leaders.

Table 1.4 *Different types of public participation in sustainable development*

Type of participation	Characteristic
Passive	People told about a decision related to SD or what has already happened, with no ability to change it.
Functional	Public participation seen by external agents as a means to achieve SD goals (eg to reduce costs) usually after major decisions have already been made.
Consultative	People answer questions related to the planning of SD, but who to ask, the form of the questions and analysis of results is done by external agents.
Manipulative	A pretence (no real power), eg the presence of one or a few 'people's' representatives on a board or committee charged with planning SD. They may be outnumbered, and hence outvoted, by external experts.
Interactive	People involved in analysis of condition, development of action plans, etc as part of SD. Here, public participation is seen as a right and not just as a mechanical function.
Self-mobilization	People mobilize themselves and initiate actions without the involvement of any external agency, although the latter can help with an enabling framework.

Source: Pretty, 1995

There is also the issue of negotiation. Unless 'people' are uniform, it is highly likely that there will be multiple and often quite divergent views as to what needs to be done, by whom, for whom and how. Minorities could easily become alienated in such a situation, and one could be left with SD at the expense of a minority. This may be acceptable and even desirable in a broader scheme, but could immediately sow the seeds of discord. The opposite danger is that the vision of SD and the ways in which it is gauged become dominated by relatively few stakeholders, perhaps those with the most power (Kasemir et al, 1999) or perhaps become over-focused on dominant local issues at the expense of other concerns important in SD (Mitchell, 1996; Crabtree and Bayfield, 1998). What one is left with may be indicators that equate much more to agency (eg local government) performance than SD.

Allied to all of this are considerations of cost. It can be expensive and time consuming to consult. It is much easier, cheaper and quicker to 'tell':

> *The history of sustainable development policy-making to date is still one characterized by top-down decision-making. To an extent this approach characterizes the development of indicators, with much activity taking place in United Nations institutions, the OECD, the European Union and many national governments. Such an approach is certainly the classic way that international policies are developed.* (Pinfield, 1996)

But even with all of these issues, perhaps the biggest problem with participation is expectation. Even if the mechanics are imperfect, engaging stakeholders in the process does raise expectations that someone will act upon the outcomes. In some cases it may be that the stakeholders themselves are able to act with the indicators they help develop, but many of the points that will be raised will inevitably be ones that can only be acted upon by various branches and agencies of government. It all comes down to power and an expectation that those with the power to do something will act. Unfortunately there has been something of a tendency for governments to stress local action by the public while giving vocal support (and little else) to the bigger issues. Quite frankly, attempts to heighten people's awareness of constraints may achieve little of value if opportunities to overcome them are also very limited. This has been starkly portrayed in a developing-country context where people, in addition to being poor, may even lack basic democratic rights. Poverty reduction programmes are increasingly being built on the need for participation by those who are poor, but 'there is little recognition of the fact that poor people are diversely embedded in unequal meso, macro and global economic and social power structures' (Bevan, 2000). If people have little, if any, ability to change a situation, and unfortunately this is often the norm rather than the exception, then highlighting the problems they face is not in itself going to improve their circumstances (Pinfield, 1996). Also, as Bevan (2000) states, 'participatory approaches do not sit well with hierarchically structured organizations, and institutional cultures are embedded in wider cultures that are not so easily transformed'. After all, much of what is done in development is done through professions, institutions and agencies that have strong tendencies towards erecting barriers to maintain their self-sustainability. By contrast, SD requires, almost by definition, that such barriers be broken down, yet change can be slow and painful. Similarly, the almost inevitable requirements of development revolve around defined limits on time and resources and strong mechanisms of accountability and performance required by the funder. This can reinforce linearity in SD by stressing the need for defined outcomes at a defined cost and in a defined time. However, one could argue that with 'real' SD there should be no end to this process, and there should be a conscious and continuous reflection as to what it all means followed by a return to the starting point. In other words, SD should be circular rather than linear.

This circularity in SD certainly has a great logical appeal: 'sustainability does not represent the end point of a process; rather, it represents the process itself' (Cornelissen et al, 2001). After all, as we live we continuously engage with new ideas and concepts. Life is a learning process and our beliefs, values and attitudes are not static but may change so as to alter what we perceive as quality of life. In addition, we balance and negotiate our perceptions with those of others, and the interpretive ranges that we are willing to entertain may change as a result. Perhaps the issue of traffic no longer becomes important as we shift our lifestyle, for example from commuter to tele-worker, or perhaps we become more willing to entertain other evidence that suggests that traffic is not getting any worse, despite the evidence of our eyes to the contrary. Our vocabulary may grow, allowing us to verbalize and debate change with others in ways that could again alter our perception. This extends to our views as to what should be done. Just as our informal vision of SD is subject to change, then more formal views should also be open to the same sort of continuous learning and flexibility.

Hodge et al (1999) describe this desired circularity in SD in terms of a perform-ance measurement and progress assessment (PMPA) cycle. A 'story' about SD (an amalgam of peoples visions, perspectives, wishes, etc) is enacted through 'measures'

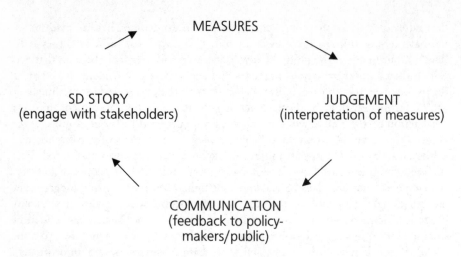

Note: the process is circular – there is no final 'end product' where the process stops.
Source: Hodge et al, 1999

Figure 1.7 *The performance measurement and progress assessment cycle*

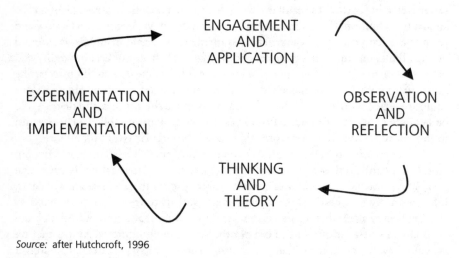

Source: after Hutchcroft, 1996

Figure 1.8 *The learning cycle*

that are interpreted ('good' or 'bad' for SD) and communicated back to stakeholders. Like SSM, the process doesn't have a final end product as such (Figure 1.7). Others have drawn parallels with the 'learning cycle' (Hutchcroft, 1996), a point that will be explored in more depth in Chapter 5 (Figure 1.8). Similarly, policy development is often portrayed as a circular process (Figure 1.9). However, circularity and participation imply an extension of the issues we have described over time.

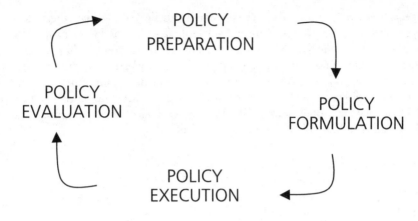

POLICY
PREPARATION

POLICY
EVALUATION

POLICY
FORMULATION

POLICY
EXECUTION

Source: after Jimenez-Beltran, 2001

Figure 1.9 *The policy cycle*

SUMMARY

By the turn of the 20th century, SD had become the battle cry of almost everyone concerned with improving the human condition. The unanimity of this popularity suggests that SD does resonate with the human spirit, and of course is to be welcomed, but there are problems. The inherent and necessary flexibility in the meaning of SD and how to achieve it does allow for a host of responses and perspectives. While scientists have continuously sought to create an underlying essence of SD expressed in more objective ecological terms – a sustainability science – this tends to avoid rather than address the value judgments that are at the very heart of SD. Whether we like it or not, SD is of ALL people, by ALL people and for ALL people.

While the frustrations of those not familiar with dealing in the inevitable diversity of opinion and subjectivity is understandable, and while ecological principles obviously have much to contribute, SD cannot become the sole preserve of a few. To put it bluntly, keeping SD 'alive' in learned journal papers is like accepting the inevitability of keeping beautiful yet endangered species alive in books while refusing to address their potential demise in nature. SD has to be practised to be alive, and this is not possible unless ALL of us are involved.

Yet if one does acknowledge the centrality of people in SD, then one does have to engage with difficult issues of multiple perspective and public participation. These are not optional extras to be tagged onto a science-based analysis; they are central. This does, inevitably, insert SD into politics, economics, policy formulation and culture. Sustainability scientists might decry this 'dilution' and 'distraction', as they see it, but there is simply no choice. We would suggest that the decision is not so much whether participation has to happen, but how best to achieve it.

Of the methodologies developed by SD practitioners to help gauge progress, indicators have perhaps had the greatest popularity. Condensing complex information so as to allow digestion and interpretation by non-specialists is clearly desirable, especially when the indicators can be presented visually. Yet these have their disadvantages, not least of which is the truism that having an indicator does not automatically mean that the public have been engaged in any real sense. Neither does it mean that supplying information in such a condensed form will automatically ensure that managers and policy-makers will act on it. Without these, indicators will not help bring about SD. They will remain technically elegant images in journals and reports of what a few individuals want as SD. In the next chapter, the development and use of indicators in SD will be discussed in more depth.

Chapter 2

Sustainability Indicators: A Brief Review

INTRODUCTION

Although the use of indicators as a device for 'doing' sustainable development (SD) is logical given the context set out in Chapter 1, it does present some immediate difficulties. We can summarize these as:

- What indicators do we use to measure sustainability?
- How do we measure them?
- How do we use them?

The irony is that these appear to be very simple questions. After all, with a blank sheet of paper we can rapidly list the main elements important in SD. It is also possible to ask small groups of people to negotiate a list of indicators amongst themselves, and within 30 minutes or so a basic list usually emerges. Both of us have carried out this exercise with undergraduate and postgraduate students as well as professional planners, and can readily assure the reader that it is not difficult. Topics such as pollution, density of cars, noise, the environment, litter, the countryside, quality of food, etc will rapidly emerge. Indicators bubble up out of this cauldron with ease, and with feeling. Even a methodology can be discerned. For example, car density can be 'measured' by the time it takes to get to work in the morning.

Given that indicators have perhaps been the most commonly applied tool to help gauge progress towards attaining SD, in this chapter the theory and practice behind their use will be discussed. We feel it is vital to cover the literature of the creation and use of indicators in SD in order to demonstrate the complexity and variety of approaches to this subject. However, it has to be said that in reading this chapter the reader may in places be perplexed by the detail of the description. While this may be bewildering, the description is important as it provides a summary of the background to the choices facing us in developing systemic sustainability analysis (SSA) within the Malta project.

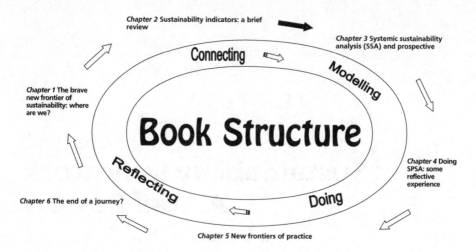

We have set out to provide the reader with a taste of the diversity and complexity of the sustainability indicator (SI) literature, but not necessarily to analyse the underlying patterns (points of agreement or disagreement). The two of us did discuss this, but we wanted to present our Malta example against a backdrop of the complex and highly contested terrain of SIs without worrying too much at the moment about mapping out the terrain in depth. We felt it was more important to highlight the main steps in the SI process so as to allow a comparison with the steps in Malta described in Chapters 3 and 4.

The chapter will begin with a discussion of the theory behind the use of indicators in SD and criteria commonly applied in their selection. This will be followed by a summary of the debate surrounding the ways in which indicators of SD should be presented. Of central import here is the decision to aggregate indicators into a single index or keep them separate. There are many options between these extremes, and all manner of indicator diagrams have been suggested as ways of presenting the information to users. The third section of the chapter will explore the setting of reference conditions in SD. Just what value of the indicator would suggest that sustainability has been obtained? Indeed, is it even possible to do this, or should a user be content with knowing the direction in which the indicator is moving over time? Who makes these decisions? The final section of the chapter will discuss the various uses of indicators in SD, and in particular what have been the problems with these.

INDICATORS OF SUSTAINABLE DEVELOPMENT

The first point to make is that people use indicators all of the time without actually realizing it.

> *Indicators are used by people on a day-to-day basis for making decisions. A blue sky in the morning indicates that we should wear a T-shirt because the weather will be good. All around us there are indicators that tell us something about the state of the world. The media and television are littered with indicators.* (Acton, 2000)

Indicators really are a vital part of people's lives, yet at the same time the term 'indicator' has a technical and cold feel to it. It conjures up assumptions of numbers and statistics that mean nothing to the lay person and can only be used by specialist technocrats. It is certainly true that for SD there has been an emphasis on selecting indicators deemed to be 'relevant', largely by applying a set of indicator rules, by technicians. Such checklists are common in the SD literature. For example, one could stress that an indicator should be:

- specific (must clearly relate to outcomes);
- measurable (implies that it must be a quantitative indicator);
- usable (practical);
- sensitive (must readily change as circumstances change);
- available (it must be relatively straightforward to collect the necessary data for the indicator); and
- cost-effective (it should not be a very expensive task to access the necessary data).

There are other lists of criteria besides this, and another example is presented in Table 2.1 (Guy and Kibert, 1998). Mitchell (1996) echoes these concerns and summarizes them into a five-point set of criteria that those attempting to obtain indicators of SD should follow. These include the need for a clear definition of the objective that the indicators are meant to achieve, who is going to use the indicators and how. Although the criteria of Guy and Kibert (1998) or Mitchell (1996) do not rule out the possibility of qualitative indicators, a general assumption has been that indicators of SD should be quantitative.

Table 2.1 *Guy and Kibert's suggestion for criteria to help select indicators for sustainable development*

Criteria	Questions
community involvement	were they developed and acceptable by the stakeholders?
linkage	do they link social, economic and environmental issues?
valid	do they measure something that is relevant?
available and timely	are the data available on a regular basis?
stable and reliable	are they compiled using a systematic method?
understandable	are they simple enough to be understood by lay persons?
responsive	do they respond quickly and measurably to change?
policy relevance	are they relevant to policy?
representative	do they cover the important dimensions of the area?
flexible	will data be available in the future?
proactive	do they act as a warning rather than measure an existing state?

Source: Guy and Kibert, 1998

Yet the irony, as Acton (2000) says in the earlier quotation, is that we use indicators all of the time, but these are qualitative in nature (eg a blue sky) and seemingly far removed from the 'hard' indicators of Guy and Kibert (1998) and Mitchell (1996). Some do suggest conditions under which qualitative indicators would be preferable to quantitative (Gallopin, 1997), including considerations of cost and ease of data collection. Yet in terms of SD there is much contradiction in this balance. After all, if one examines the theoretical assumptions that lie behind more qualitative approaches to research then there is much that resonates with the very essence of SD summarized in Chapter 1 (Paulesich and Reiger, 1997). For example, reality in qualitative research is understood to be a social construct. Hence much depends upon perspective, and this will be multiple as in SD. An understanding (analytical) approach (as distinct from descriptive) is indispensable in such research, and case studies are central. Similarly, much of the reported SD work is very site- and time-specific. Also, the researcher is not separate from the researched (ie an objective and neutral observer) but has an integral relationship with the system being analysed. This is sometimes not appreciated in SD, and some even talk of a sustainability science (Kates et al, 2000) that can imply an empirical objectivity that may be an illusion at best. The resonance between the nature of qualitative research and SD as set out in Chapter 1 is indeed marked.

Nevertheless, whatever the individual rights and wrongs behind such indicator criteria, they do provide some limits to the indicators that may be 'allowed' in any one context. Even so, different authors tend to stress different characteristics. Crabtree and Bayfield (1998), for example, suggest that operational feasibility, an issue that encompasses much of the above discussion, is important. This consideration may be at the expense of technical soundness, a thought echoed by de Kruijf and van Vuuren (1998), who quote an Indonesian minister as saying, 'If a theoretically sound indicator is not possible, then find me one that is rather less theoretically sound.' As a result Crabtree and Bayfield (1998) suggest that a more cost-effective strategy would be to influence bodies that already collect indicator data rather than put new bodies in place. Yet at the same time there may be a clear concern that data availability should not be a constraint in selecting relevant indicators (Meter, 1999). If it is, then the result could be a maintenance of the status quo with people using what is available rather than taking a more imaginative stance (Crilly et al, 1999; Meter, 1999).

Some workers also suggest a structure that can be applied to selecting SD indicators. At a basic level this could comprise the standard pressure–state–response (PSR) indicator framework.[1] Various forms of the basic PSR model have been suggested. Two examples, linear and cyclical, are presented in Figure 2.1. Some suggest the inclusion of a further category of impact indicators in this model: the pressure–state–impact–response model (PSIR; Figure 2.2). The United Nations applies this framework in the selection of its indicators of SD, although it uses the term 'driving force' instead of pressure (driving force–state–response; DSR). Others see the inclusion of 'driving force' in the PSR model as adding a new dimension rather than as a synonym; ie driving forces generate pressure (Figure 2.2). Driving forces would be factors such as demand for food, water, revenue, etc. In turn these generate specific pressures within the system. Whatever the terminology and detail, this family of approaches usually seeks to categorize indicators in terms of cause and effect. The result is typically (but not always – see, for example, Mortensen, 1997) a framework with the categories of indicators in columns and an assumption of horizontal links between columns.

(a) Linear PSR model

Example: pesticide application to a river watershed and its relationship to pesticide pollution of the river

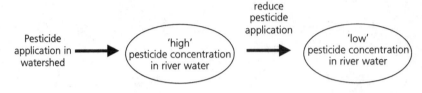

For example, by:
- increasing price of pesticide
- legislation
- voluntary limits on pesticide use
- discouraging crop cultivation

In this case, indicators could measure:
- application rate of pesticide (active ingredient applied per area of watershed)
- concentration of pesticide in river water
- price of pesticide, taxes
- number of laws/measures to limit pesticide use
- number (eg meetings, media messages) and success rate (eg attendance at meetings, surveys of awareness) of campaigns designed to heighten farmer awareness of the issue and discourage pesticide use

(b) Cyclical PSR model

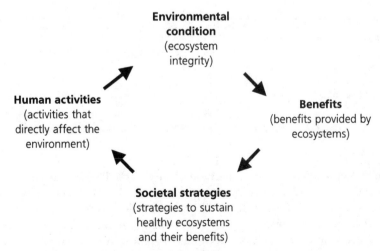

Figure 2.1 *Some pressure–state–response (PSR) models*

Example: pesticide pollution of a river

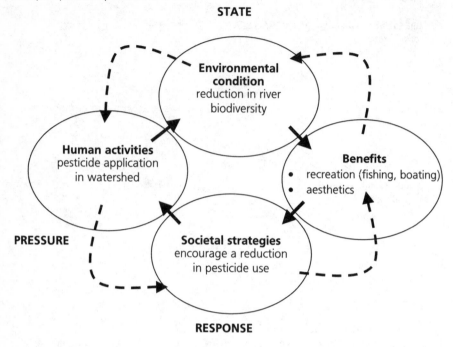

The traditional 'linear' PSR model assumes a target (the desired state) which one reaches by altering management.

The cyclical PSR model includes a notion of 'benefit' (aesthetic or otherwise) which in turn could drive strategy and activity so as to arrive at the condition one requires (solid arrows in figure). It is also possible to see the relationship in the reverse (dashed arrows). A desired benefit will allow a prediction as to the environmental condition required and change in activities necessary to arrive at this.

With the cyclical version of the PSR model, it is implied that change will always be present in a society. For example, the advent of new technologies and strategies will open up new threats and possibilities, and desirable benefits may alter as societal values and structure change.

Source: Meter, 1999

Figure 2.1 *Some pressure–state–response (PSR) models (continued)*

While conceptually convenient, and indeed popular, the PSR family of models does have some serious problems. Spangenberg and Bonniot (1998) describe some of these, including a tendency for the 'R' of PSR to encourage short-term curative policies rather than the 'development of cause-orientated approaches'. They suggest that the PSR models reflect a sort of 'political end-of-the-pipe thinking' that militates against more proactive responses. An additional problem is that PSR models may not capture

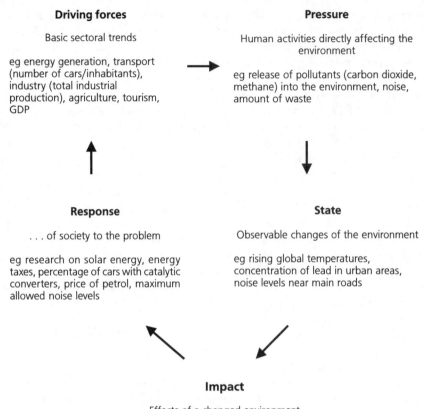

Driving forces

Basic sectoral trends

eg energy generation, transport
(number of cars/inhabitants),
industry (total industrial
production), agriculture, tourism,
GDP

Pressure

Human activities directly affecting the
environment

eg release of pollutants (carbon dioxide,
methane) into the environment, noise,
amount of waste

Response

. . . of society to the problem

eg research on solar energy, energy
taxes, percentage of cars with catalytic
converters, price of petrol, maximum
allowed noise levels

State

Observable changes of the environment

eg rising global temperatures,
concentration of lead in urban areas,
noise levels near main roads

Impact

Effects of a changed environment

eg decrease in agricultural production, hurricanes, floods

Source: Jesinghaus, 1999

Figure 2.2 *Pressure–state–impact–response (PSIR) model for indicators of
sustainable development*

the richness of multiple causality and interaction, which inevitably exists between
most indicators of SD (Gallopin, 1997; Hardi et al, 1997). The danger is that those
developing indicators with this model in mind may shoe-horn them into categories
and think one-dimensionally about which pressure indicator influences which state
indicator, and what we can do about it. In practice, a single indicator may be
categorized either as pressure or state, and a single state indicator could be influenced
by a number of pressure indicators (Hardi et al, 1997). One can impose further
conditions on indicator selection to avoid this, but the danger is that the essentially
organic nature of SD will be reduced to a highly simplistic and mechanical model
(Gallopin, 1997) that encourages quick-fix solutions. As a result, some have rejected
the PSR model in favour of more context-relevant approaches. For example, Meter
(1999) refers to the use of 'linkage analysis' in the community development of indicators, where the major concern was whether the indicators were linked to issues that
are important to a community rather than worry about cause–effect relationships.

In other situations, SD indicators could be created within a broad analytical framework. An example is the use of the 'multiple capital' framework (Howlett et al, 2000; Woodhouse et al, 2000) where sustainability is seen in terms of available capital (natural, human, social, physical and financial) and the vulnerability context (trends, shocks and stresses) in which these assets exist. There are numerous examples of sustainability indicators within each of these asset bases, and one could, of course, combine the PSR approach with multiple capital by identifying a suite of indicators within the asset bases. For example, in the natural capital base, Syers et al (1995), Dumanski and Pieri (2000) and Lefroy et al (2000) have developed land quality indicators (LQI) to be applied in sustainable land management (SLM; Herrick, 2000). Lefroy et al (2000) suggest using a decision support system to help generate a suitable set of such indicators, although they also stress that validation is not easy. Part of this is a familiar, to those who work in SD, lack of a consensus over what is important within SLM (Syers et al, 1995). Indeed, arising out of this has been a suggestion by some (eg Jodha, 1991) that sustainability is best assessed through unsustainability, as the latter is often more apparent (Fuentes, 1993) and easier to gauge by using indicators (Newman, 1998). Mageau et al (1995), for example, have described an ecosystem distress syndrome (EDS), and the sort of characteristics that could be looked for in order to detect it, including a reduction in biodiversity and primary productivity.

'Capital' is a widely employed notion in SD, particularly in terms of describing and analysing the sort of trade-offs that can occur between these different assets (Goodland and Daly, 1996). Substitution of capital is the basis of the 'weak' verses 'strong' sustainability debate summarized in Bell and Morse (1999). However, some do see land as quite distinct from what economists usually put forward as the meaning of the term 'capital' with 'an implicit assumption that it [land] can be substituted by other forms of capital, that it is reproducible and that it is there to be managed in much the same way as manufactured capital' (Victor, 1991).

Another approach to formulating indicators, claimed to rest on a basic analysis of what is deemed necessary for SD, is described by Bossel (1997, 1999). Here, indicators are selected on the basis of their ability to address a set of questions concerning 'basic oriental satisfaction'. This is meant to contrast with other indicator sets that Bossel regards as being 'developed by various ad hoc methods'. In his approach, indicators of 'system sustainability' are determined in response to a 'very specific set of questions covering all essential aspects of viability and sustainable development'. The result is a set of basic orientors that can be applied to systems as a means of representing 'basic system interests'. Bossel (1999) lists these as in Table 2.2. They can act as a sort of checklist for what is 'important in and for systems, ie the basic system needs'.

In all of the above examples, one is applying a set of criteria to generate indicators deemed important within the development context. For the most part, and as the reader may have gleaned from the above, such lists have been derived in a largely top-down and technical mode, with technical excellence (what people would like to know) rather than practical use (what people need to know) as the prime concern (Rigby et al, 2000). They may be in line with a social-economic environment, PSR or asset base perspective, but it is clear that one indicator to cover all these will not be adequate. Instead, a common approach is to present the indicators within tables

Table 2.2 *The basic orientors of system sustainability as described by Bossel*

Basic orientor	Key questions	Worldwatch examples
Existence	Is the system compatible with and able to exist in its particular environment? Is the speed of escape from an existing danger greater than the speed of its approach?	Grain surplus factor Debt as share of GDP in developing countries World fish catch
Effectiveness	Is it effective and efficient? Is the rate of increase in resource use efficiency greater than the rate of erosion of resource availability?	Unemployment in the EU Gross world product per person Grain yield efficiency
Freedom of action	Does it have the necessary freedom to respond and react as needed? Is the rate of increase in the spectrum of possible responses greater than the rate of appearance of new challenges?	Share of population age 60 and over Energy productivity in industrial nations Water use as share of total runoff
Security	Is it secure, safe and stable? Does the rate of installation of protective measures keep up with the rate of increase of threats?	Share of population in cities World grain carryover stock Economic losses from weather disasters
Adaptability	Can it adapt to new challenges? Does the rate of structural change in the system keep up with the rate of irreversible changes in the environment?	Persons per television set Capital flow (public funds) to developing countries Carbon emissions
Coexistence	Is it compatible with interacting sub-systems? Can the rate of change in interaction and communication keep up with the rate of appearance of new actors?	Income share of richest 20% of population Number of armed conflicts Recycled content of US steel
Psychological needs	Is it compatible with psychological needs and culture? Does the rate of appearance of psychological stresses and strains remain below the rate at which they can be absorbed?	Refugees per 1000 people Immunization of infants Chesapeake oyster catch

Source: Bossel, 1999

(indicator frameworks). Numerous examples of such indicator frameworks exist,[2] and while there may be many differences there may also be commonalities. For example, a Local Government Management Board report (LGMB, 1995) identified a set of commonly suggested indicators of SD within UK local initiatives, and the following common denominators can be extracted:

- Resources and waste
- Pollution
- Biodiversity
- Local needs
- Basic needs

- Satisfying work
- Health
- Access
- Living without fear
- Empowerment
- Culture and aesthetics

Much of this is not surprising, and indeed as mentioned at the start of the chapter, when prompted to do so these are the sort of issues that emerge out of discussions with students and professionals. Naturally there is substantial diversity in terms of the precise indicators for these categories and how they are to be measured (LGMB, 1995).

The number of indicators to be included within a framework also provides some constraint on choice. Suggested numbers of indicators vary a great deal. Guy and Kibert (1998), describing the Florida Local Assessment Guide (FLAG) in the US, suggest that an initial list of 100 indicators will need to be 'distilled down to more manageable sets of 15–20', although manageable to whom is not described. Indeed, although there is variation, the figure of 20 indicators as a compromise between manageability and depth of information appears a great deal in the literature, although with little if any rationale as to why this ballpark figure in particular should be so magical. Crilly et al (1999), for example, suggest the use of 21 indicators of SD in order to resonate with Local Agenda 21, and the Local Government Management Board (LGMB) in the UK, having reviewed a number of pilot indicator projects, noted that the average number selected was 23 (range from 13 to 27; LGMB, 1995). A comment from Bossel (1999) probably best sums up the prevailing feelings of SD practitioners: 'the number of indicators should be as small as possible, but not smaller than necessary'. This leaves plenty of room for manouevre, but still doesn't explain the magic of 20.

Although much effort and thought has gone into the creation of numerous indicator frameworks, there is something of a conundrum here. As discussed in Chapter 1, everyone has their own opinion as to what is good or bad in SD, and the fact that there are so many SD indicator frameworks and projects is testament to this. This is the very essence of what makes SD so popular and yet so difficult to do in practice. The devil really is in the detail! On the one hand, given the site-specific (case study) nature of what SD entails, this would seem to be inevitable, and some even call for more of the same as a way of making progress (Syers et al, 1995; Gardner et al, 1995). Indeed, there may be few, if any, key indicators that could be applied across even quite similar systems (Gardner et al, 1995). However, the result of such a rapid and diverse process of SD indicator creation, often starting anew each time, can be a bewildering choice of approaches, matrices, classifications and types (Mitchell, 1996). Nevertheless, there have been attempts to create guidelines that could be applied to similar systems worldwide. The UN list of indicators arising out of the Rio conference is an example of this, as are the United Nations Food and Agriculture Organization (FAO) guidelines for fisheries (Garcia et al, 2000). Even here, though, there is still great emphasis on local flexibility and an avoidance of being too prescriptive.

INTEGRATION OF SUSTAINABLE DEVELOPMENT INDICATORS

Indicator integration is basically a means by which individual and quite different indicators in a framework can somehow be viewed together to provide an holistic view of SD. It attempts to get around two problems often attributed to indicator frameworks (OECD, 1998):

1   Complexity. Many indicators may be sensible from a technical perspective, but one can lose sight of the bigger picture and become enmeshed in detail.
2   Compromise. An indicator framework may not allow an immediately apparent analysis of trade-offs between some indicators and others.

Aggregating them into a single index can help address both points. It is particularly seen as important in terms of presenting the information to the public and decision-makers who, it is assumed, do not need to be aware of the detail but only the broad message as to what is happening.

There are two main approaches here. One could keep the indicators entirely separate, but listed or presented together within a single table or diagram (visual integration), or one could combine the indicators to yield a single index of SD (numerical integration). Many examples exist for both, involving all sorts of mathematics from the simple to the complex. Mitchell (1996) summarizes some of the approaches taken to integrate (or aggregate) indicators into a single index of sustainability, many of them founded on monetary valuation of resources – money can be a powerful medium for aggregation! Tyteca (1996) provides a review of examples for the narrower field of environmental performance of industry.

One non-monetary example of integration is described by Manyong and Degand (1997). They describe an approach to measuring the sustainability of agriculture using a technique called weighted goal programming (WGP). The technique is based on a measurement of deviation of the actual value of a set of indicators from some nominal target or goal. The aggregate deviation from the target, after weighting the relative importance of the individual indicators in the wider scheme, is given the symbol 'Z'. Clearly, if the target is deemed to be the sustainable condition then the nearer Z is to zero (ie the lower the deviation), the more sustainable the system. In Manyong and Degand's example, Z is an attempt to integrate human nutrition, soil fertility and income, although most of the indicators are for human nutrition and all indicators have the same weight. However, this issue of weighting during integration is highly contentious and driven in the most part by value judgement (Dahl, 1997).

A further approach described by Cornelissen et al (2001) is based on the use of fuzzy set theory. For example, assuming that there are three indicators of SD, these can be measured and checked against an 'acceptable' level (Table 2.3). What is deemed to be acceptable is, of course, a matter of some value judgement. The pattern of response to all three indicators can then be aggregated to provide an overall condition for SD (a numerical value symbolized by μ_{SD} rather than Z). Therefore, although the attitude towards SD is highly subjective, the use of fuzzy set theory can allow a link between human expectation and the numerical nature of indicators. It could be one way of combining quantitative and qualitative information in SD (Rotmans, 1998).

Table 2.3 *The use of fuzzy logic in determining an overall assessment of sustainable development*

Rule	SI_1 acceptable		SI_2 acceptable		SI_3 acceptable	RESULT sustainable development
1	yes	**AND**	yes	**AND**	yes	very good
ELSE						
2	yes	**AND**	yes	**AND**	no	good
ELSE						
3	yes	**AND**	no	**AND**	no	poor
ELSE						
4	no	**AND**	no	**AND**	no	very poor

Note:
* At the end of each rule there is an 'ELSE' that forces the reader to consider the next line in the table.
* Answers to the lines can be either completely 'true' or not, or 'true' to varying degrees.
* The result is a numerical assessment of SD (called μ_{SD})

Source: Cornelissen et al, 2001

A more economic example of such integration is sustainability calculated on the basis of national savings, national income and depreciation to man-made capital, natural resources and the environment (Pearce and Atkinson, 1993; Rennings and Wiggering, 1997). The idea is that an economy should be able to save more than the combined depreciation of all forms of capital. The result is a single value, again symbolized by Z, which represents the sustainability of the economy (sustainability in its 'weak' sense; Bell and Morse, 1999). This is an example of what some term 'green accounting', and can include entries in the standard systems of national accounting.[3] As long as the depreciation of natural resources is made up for by replacement with other assets of equal value, then Z will indicate sustainability: 'the cardinal sin is not mining; it is consuming the rents from mining' (Solow, 1993). The calculation of a single value for sustainability on a country basis opens up the possibility of league tables; a sort of 'name and shame' policy.

The use of money as a common unit to integrate indicators of SD certainly has a logic that appeals to those charged with raising (eg as taxes) and spending it. Some would even go so far as to claim that monetization is the only practical solution to combining different types of indicator.[4] Bio-physical indicators are far more difficult to integrate because of their different units of measurement (Bartelmus, 1999). Despite the advantages, the problem with the use of money as a common denominator is that it implies that all assets and processes involved in SD can be valued. While this has been attempted, it may not be easy or even possible (Dahl, 1997).

All three above examples are examples of numerical integration – the generation of a single value for sustainability. Other integrative approaches are based on the use of diagrams. The AMOEBA (or RADAR), where indicators are arrayed as arms, is one example.[5] As originally designed, it essentially comprises a bar graph of indicator values turned into a circular presentation. Figure 2.3 is an example of a RADAR diagram for 'company sustainability' (in this case, eco-efficiency indicators for the pharmaceutical industry; adapted from Joly, 2001). The arms of the RADAR represent actual performance by the industry in terms of eco-efficiency. Other variants on the AMOEBA/RADAR theme are 'star' and 'kite' diagrams (Garcia and Staples, 2000) and sustainability polygons and webs (Woodhouse et al, 2000). For example, Bossel (1999) presents his six 'basic orientors' for system sustainability as an 'orientor star' (Figure 2.4). The underlying mechanic of the orientors is based on the ratio of the rate of response to the rate of threat, with the former having to be greater than the latter in order to ensure sustainability. The circle in the centre of the diagram represents the minimum value for SD (ie, a ratio of 1; rate of response to threat = rate of threat), with each arm having to at least match this for SD.

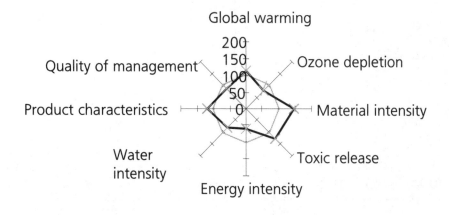

Indicator	Value
Global warming	113
Ozone depletion	78
Material intensity	145
Toxic release	128
Energy intensity	61
Water intensity	80
Product characteristics	118
Quality of management	85

Note: This particular example comprises eight eco-efficiency indicators for the pharmaceutical industry (adapted from Joly, 2001).

Figure 2.3 *Example of a RADAR diagram for company sustainability*

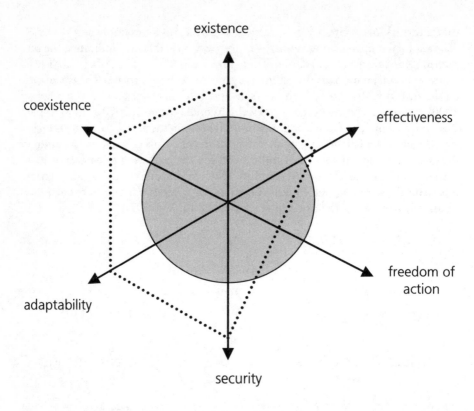

The circle in the centre of the diagram (the unit circle) represents the zone of non-viability (unsustainability). If any of the six 'orientor satisfactions' (ratio of the rate of response to the rate of threat) is less than one (eg freedom of action in the above diagram) it will fall inside the circle and indicate unsustainability.

The six orientor satisfactions are:

	Orientor	Numerator	Denominator
1	Existence	Speed of escape from a danger	Speed of approach of danger
2	Effectiveness	Rate of increase in resource efficiency	Rate of erosion of resource availability
3	Freedom of action	Rate of increase in spectrum of possible responses	Rate of appearance of new challenges
4	Security	Rate of installation of protective measures	Rate of increase of threats
5	Adaptability	Rate of structural change	Rate of irreversible changes
6	Coexistence	Rate of change of interaction and communication	Rate of appearance of new actors

Source: Bossel, 1999

Figure 2.4 *The orientor star of sustainable development*

Although in such AMOEBA-type diagrams the visual 'whole' provides some basis for integration, the individual indicators are still presented separately. This can be an advantage, as it allows the reader to disaggregate the whole. The appeal of such a compromise was one reason behind our selection of the AMOEBA as a presentation device in the systemic sustainability analysis (SSA) described in Bell and Morse (1999). There are alternatives, and the 'sustainability dashboard' (Hardi, 2001) is gaining in popularity. Here the approach is to draw an analogy between a vehicle dashboard, and all its dials and lights, and SD. Separate dials and warning lights are included for various dimensions of SD, so there is some disaggregation. By way of contrast, a diagrammatic approach that doesn't allow any disaggregation is the 'sustainability barometer' (Prescott-Allen, 1997; Figure 2.5). This involves mapping the particular state of a system on to a two-dimensional structure of human and ecosystem wellbeing. Sustainability equates to a defined area of the structure (top right of Figure 2.5). The reader, from the diagram itself, cannot discern why a system happens to occupy the location it does in the barometer.

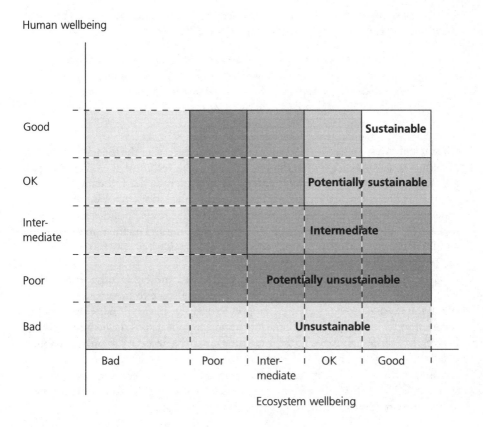

Source: adapted from Prescott-Allen, 1997

Figure 2.5 *The IUCN barometer of sustainability*

Numerous writers and practitioners have discussed the desirability of integrating a suite of indicators into a single index for SD.[6] Experts are divided into those who see this is a good thing, and those who stress the dangers. The following quotation sets out the basic difficulty:

> *[I]t would be counterproductive if new indicators were to become weighted and averaged together – leading to more fetishing of one single index, which tries to add up all the apples and oranges into a single number coefficient. This can turn out to lead to the same kind of nonsense as the GNP indicators. It is better on scientific grounds, as well as those of public education and efficient, democratic government to have a group of indicators covering different dimensions. [O]nly transparent and tangible indicators that people can readily understand and visualize and relate to their own lives will provide the desired political constituency for needed governmental policy. This has been an endemic problem with economics, and its arcane formulae which have left people mystified, alienated and demotivated.* (Henderson, 1991, p176)

The lack of transparency afforded by highly aggregated indicators is a serious problem (Moffatt, 1994; Allenby et al, 1998; Jesinghaus, 2000). Yet:

> *The challenge for the scientific community is that highly aggregated indices of sustainable development are being pushed by political demand, despite the hesitancy of experts and scholars to tackle questions that involve human values and political processes as much as, or more than, scientific method-ologies.* (Dahl, 1997)

This lack of transparency is at the 'communication' level (ie in the form it is generally presented to an audience) rather than necessarily at the 'technical' level. For example, the documentation associated with an index may include the full data set so that anyone can disaggregate the index and monitor the calculations involved. While such transparency may be applauded, it is unlikely that the groups (politicians, decision-makers, etc) intended to use the index will have the time and inclination to go to the lengths of disaggregating its components. After all, that is precisely why the index was created in the first place!

Clearly, there is a demand for highly aggregated indices (Hodge et al, 1999; Persson, 2001), even if 'their purpose may indeed be more to provoke by shocking sum totals than to provide statistical support to decision-making' (Bartelmus, 1999). A compromise may be in order. Some integration to appease politicians and decision-makers may be desirable, but at the same time it may be necessary to provide enough detail to allow transparency at the level of communication. There have been various attempts to do this, many of them revolving around the use of compromise diagrams such as the AMOEBA, although these have also had their critics, and some see them as biased more towards addressing a need for aggregation.

> *From a methodological point of view, it [the AMOEBA] can be criticized for the aggregation process, simple addition of indicators and the reference to historical situations; it is a very crude, preliminary solution for measuring sustainability.* (Rennings and Wiggering, 1997)

However, while this fear does resonate with many,[7] a workshop held at the OECD in 1998 made the point that:

> *Many participants had found that it was easier to gain attention for an issue with a simple graphical presentation or a limited numerical index than with a more complex concept. This comes back to the essential problem of whether the priority is to guide policy in the 'right' direction as opposed to getting the indicators strictly comprehensive and correct.* (OECD, 1998)

Sustainability diagrams, and indeed indices, have received a high level of prominence in the literature. The basis upon which these devices are founded – clarity for users – is bound up with the uses to which they will be put. As Wefering et al (2000) suggest, there are very different views about clarity with regard to SD. Scientists and technicians are interested primarily in data presented as tables, graphs, etc, and possibly even raw uncondensed data, while decision-makers and managers typically require some condensation of the data, particularly in terms of how it relates to goals and targets. With this group, visual devices such as those described above may be useful, but should also be capable of being unwrapped to reveal underlying data. On the other hand, individual users (the public) prefer highly aggregated data (perhaps as an index) and visual devices.

A pragmatic approach, given the contested views of the SD indicator technicians and those wanting to use them, points towards a hybrid approach with layers of aggregation for different groups. OECD (1998) referred to a 'pyramid of indicators sets' (Figure 2.6). At the top level would be a few (or even one) highly aggregated indicators for the public and decision-makers, and as one moves towards the bottom of the pyramid the indicators would become increasingly disaggregated (Braat, 1991).

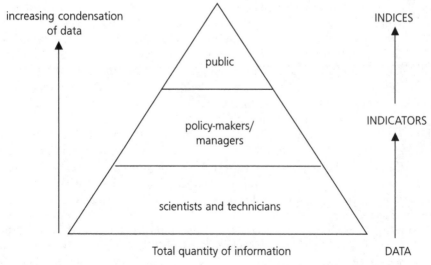

Source: Braat, 1991

Figure 2.6 *Relationships between indicators, data and information: the OECD 'pyramid of indicator sets'*

THE REFERENCE CONDITION

Assuming that we are able to develop a set of indicators, or perhaps just one index, that can be used to gauge progress towards the goal of SD, we are still left with the question: What is the goal? Just what are we aiming for? There are two broad approaches:

1   A defined target for an indicator/index. The aim is to get some/all of the indicators to this target.
2   A defined direction for an indicator/index. The aim is to get some/all of the indicators to move in the desired direction.

The notion of a defined target or threshold, equating to a sort of best practice for indicators of SD, is perhaps the most common approach.[8] It allows decision-makers to judge the gap or distance between what is and what should be (Gilbert, 1996; Crabtree and Bayfield, 1998). It is also a familiar approach in a number of fields where indicators have been applied. In environmental management, for example, there are legal targets for levels of pollutant emission ('critical loads') and 'critical concentrations' in air and water (Kellogg and Goss, 1997; Rennings and Wiggering, 1997). This is what some call a 'target frontier', with the 'ideal frontier' being zero (Tyteca, 1996). The difference here may well be based on a recognition that the 'ideal frontier' may be difficult to achieve in practice (Tyteca, 1996). In SLM, 'the threshold value may be regarded as the level of that indicator beyond which the particular system is no longer sustainable' (Syers et al, 1995). Naturally, each indicator would have its own threshold, but knowing what these are is not by any means an exact science. Even with the more bio-physically based environmental indicators (Syers et al, 1995), there is much subjectivity.[9]

The reference condition could be a single value for an indicator or index, although perhaps backed up by legislation, or it could be a desirable range (a band) as used in the Malta project, to be discussed later. As one may imagine, the setting of a reference condition for indicators of SD might not be an easy process. Crabtree and Bayfield (1998), for example, put such difficulties down to a lack of experience of individual indicators and their interpretation, a nationally agreed set of standards for most indicators and consensus mechanisms for setting SD standards.

Some have used an historical state for the system as a reference condition (an 'historical reference system'). For example, Ten Brink et al (1991), in their AMOEBA methodology for indicators of sustainability, suggested a reference condition for the North Sea system that pertained to the year 1930. This year was selected because data were available and it corresponds with a time when exploitation of the North Sea was not seen as excessive and hence could loosely be regarded as sustainable. In a variation on this theme, Rotmans and van Asselt (1999), in their AMOEBA of future projections arising from multiple perspectives, use 1990 as the baseline, and the arms of the AMOEBA represent future trends up to the end of the 21st century. The year 1990 was not selected because it represents sustainability (unlike 1930 in the Ten Brink et al example), but was simply a convenient baseline against which to plot the future. An alternative to the use of a reference year is to compare the system to one currently in existence and assumed to be sustainable, or at least to have better 'system health' (a 'geographical reference system'; de Soyza et al, 1997; Wefering et al, 2000). We could also try and reconstruct what the reference condition should be from first principles rather from anything we have seen (a 'theoretical reference condition').

Historical, geographical and theoretical reference systems are attempts to base decisions on some notion of a quasi-objective condition rationalized to represent sustainability. We can take a different approach and ask the stakeholders what they think the reference condition should be (ie the 'worst' and 'best' cases for each indicator, providing a 'stakeholder reference system'). Woodhouse et al (2000) provide an example of such an approach, and – as we will discuss in Chapters 3 and 4 – this was essentially the basis of our work in Malta. Naturally, there may be much inherent subjectivity and value judgment in such stakeholder reference systems, and opinions may be diverse. Also, it should be borne in mind that nothing prevents us from combining all of these approaches, using different ones for each indicator in the framework.

Once a reference condition has been established, it is a simple matter to calculate the deviations of indicators from the reference condition, taking into account the 'polarity' of SD in each case. The value of an indicator may be well outside the reference condition, but that may not be a problem for SD provided they are the right side. In essence this is over-achievement! An example here is the incidence of pollution. One may set a maximum target level for a pollutant in a river, and one could back this up with legislation, but values lower than this would be highly desirable. With a number of indicators one could sum 'bad' deviations from the reference condition (a sort of sustainability gap index; SGI). An example of an index of this sort is the Ecological Dow Jones Index, calculated as the sum of the deviations of indicators from the reference condition (Ten Brink et al, 1991; Wefering et al, 2000). With 32 indicators, this would vary from zero (32 × 0 per cent difference) to 3200 (32 × 100 per cent difference), with 0 representing sustainability and 3200 representing unsustainability. A further example is provided by Ekins and Simon (2001), who describe the gap in terms of time taken to address the standard required for SD.

What level of deviation from the reference point is acceptable could vary from zero to all sorts of compromises arising out of an essentially political process (Wefering et al, 2000). We could, of course, build such concerns into the setting of the reference condition in the first place, as with the stakeholder reference system, for example. After all, if decision-makers help set the targets then they also have some responsibility to ensure attainment; they are as much stakeholders as anyone else. To some extent this may be included even when the indicators are of an apparently technical derivation. For example, the AMOEBA of Ten Brink et al (1991) has indicators based to some extent on the level of acceptability to decision-makers rather than just scientists.

One danger with such a focus on SD 'gaps' is that only indicators on the 'bad' side of the target may be prioritized for consideration. This may result in some complacency with regard to indicators on the 'right' side of the reference condition at the time the measurement was taken. It could also cause some shifting of resources away from indicators deemed to be OK to those with 'bad' gaps. Much also depends upon which indicators have been included. In practice, the aim is typically to limit the number of indicators for logistical and/or presentational purposes, and decisions have to be made as to which indicators to include and how they are to be measured. As already discussed, this is a highly subjective and value-ridden process, but it will influence the magnitude of any deviation from the reference condition. A danger here, of course, is what Crabtree and Bayfield (1998) refer to as 'institutional capture'. Powerful individuals or groups may set the agenda in terms of what indicators of SD to include and, in essence, what gaps to address.

It is possible to do away with a reference condition per se, and instead present the value of indicators (eg across countries) in the form of league tables. In this case, the aim is to present status in relative terms rather than use an absolute standard. Hence the motivation for change is not to do better relative to a standard, but to do better relative to other countries. Great care needs to be taken with such an approach, given that developed countries tend to take the lead in developing such tables, and 'institutional capture' can occur. The debate surrounding the calculation of the Environmental Sustainability Index (ESI) is but one example of what can happen.[10] The importance of including Southern voices in the process has been reiterated by many (eg de Kruijf and van Vuuren, 1998).

There are other examples that are much less overtly reference condition or league table orientated, and instead look to present indicator trends over time. A good example here is the list of indicators provided by *Vital Signs*, a publication of the Worldwatch Institute. First published in 1992, the series attempts, in the words of Worldwatch, to 'broaden the base of information available to decision-makers around the world by assembling a unique and eclectic set of global indicators'. In the mode of all indicator sets, the Worldwatch publication attempts to address a common problem: 'there is a widening sea of data but, in comparison, a desert of information' (Mitchell, 1996). As an example, the 2000–2001 offering (Brown et al, 2000) lists 32 key indicators, ranging from the usual environmental suspects (carbon emissions, global temperature, use of fertilizer) through to the not so usual (bicycle production, internet use) to the unexpected (cigarette death toll, peacekeeping expenditure). Although some indicators do have graphs that break trends down into regions and/ or countries, for the most part this is avoided. The commentaries do bring out regional and/or country comparisons, but one does not detect a strong 'name and shame' style. The result is perhaps more of a feeling that we are all in this together. Bossel (1999) uses examples of the Worldwatch indicators to illustrate his basic orientors of system sustainability (Table 2.2).

USING INDICATORS OF SUSTAINABLE DEVELOPMENT

Once a set of indicators has been established, measured and compared with a reference system, the results have to be communicated to those intended to use them. After all, indicators of SD are means to an end, and are not ends in themselves (Stirling, 1999).

There seems little point in developing an approach to monitoring the things that are meaningful to local people if they never find out about it. (Acton, 2000)

Of course, this quotation could equally apply to all those who are meant to 'do' something with the indicators, and not just the public! Although this may sound blindingly obvious, the danger with indicators is that people sometimes lose sight of the ultimate goal ('what we want to be') and instead become wrapped up with 'what we want to measure and how'.

The form in which this communication occurs has significant consequences in terms of how the indicators are to be applied (Corvalán et al, 1997). Communication to end-users may take a number of forms: internet (Garcia et al, 2000), printed mass media, television/radio, leaflets, technical reports (for example, see Global Reporting Initiative, 2000), and conferences and workshops. Just who should be told will have an influence on both the form of indicator presentation and the means of communication (Crilly et al, 1999). It may be that indicators have to be translated into other forms (such as financial cost–benefit analysis), or aggregated, before they are communicated. Given the centrality of communication in all of this, it is perhaps surprising that this has received remarkably little attention (Acton, 2000), a point that will be returned to in Chapter 4 when we discuss the Malta project.

Two key questions at this stage are who will use the indicators; and how (Mitchell, 1996)? It certainly appears as if some SD indicator projects have been, to say the least, a little 'fuzzy' over the answers to these (Acton, 2000). However, one answer has been summarized by Moldan et al (1997):

> *The potential uses of ISDs (indicators of sustainable development) include alerting decision-makers to priority issues, guiding policy formulation, simplifying and improving communication and fostering a common understanding of key trends with a view to initiating necessary national action.*

This is a commonly stated position, if perhaps rather unmet in practice, and unsurprisingly is no different to the use of indicators in a wide variety of fields (Tyteca, 1996). De Kruijf and van Vuuren (1998) suggest that SD indicators have two related purposes, as:

1   tools in the policy planning process; and
2   communication tools.

But the second use should not be a passive process of technocrats telling others, such as the public and decision-makers, what they have found, ie seeing the public as nothing more than passive consumers of someone else's indicators (MacGillivray and Zadek, 1995). Indicator exercises should be founded on a participatory process that helps provide new goals for politicians and decision-makers (Pinfield, 1996; Meter, 1999). However, there have been mixed experiences with all of this. For example, in the more specific context of SLM, the land quality indicators (LQIs) summarized by Dumanski and Pieri (2000) are intended to act as foci for research policy. These have generally been developed by experts with the aim of providing indicators upon which decision-makers can act. Yet Herrick (2000) fears that adoption of LQIs, particularly those centred on soil quality, has not been good. Rigby et al (2000), also working in the broad sphere of natural resource management (NRM) and livelihood, make the candid claim that:

> *Much of the measurement of indicators has, at the end of the day, largely resulted just in the measurement of indicators. The actual operational-ization of indicators to influence or change, for instance, policy is still in its infancy.*

And this after more than 20 years of effort into the development of indicators within a field (NRM) where much experience of the process exists, and indeed helped to generate the broader vision of SD seen today! But it gets worse: in the broader field of SD there also seem to be problems with this assumption of an indicator–policy change link, with some suggesting that 'there is little evidence of indicators leading directly to the formulation of policies for sustainable development' (Pinfield, 1996). Is this suggestive of a problem with the indicator approach or is there something bigger involved? Reid (1995), for example, is critical of progress towards the attainment of SD and suggests a number of reasons for this, including:

- lack of awareness of the issues;
- political unacceptability of most action;
- opposition from entrenched interests; and
- inadequacy of institutional mechanisms for bringing together development and environment

These are substantial issues, particularly the second and third points, but the use of indicators as a tool was supposed to help with some of them. Are there other issues involved? For example, we could question factors such as a lack of involvement from decision-makers in the setting of indicators in the first place. This may be due, at least in part, to unwillingness from more technical-orientated SD researchers to fully engage with the socio-political environment (including laws and regulations) within which decision-makers operate (Moran, 1994). It may also be that decision-makers are not so familiar with many of the basic concepts in SD, for example the notion of carrying capacity (Pinfield, 1996).

> *To date, there are severe difficulties in translating the outputs of environ-mental science into appropriate inputs for policy formulation. This does not come as a surprise, as the two worlds, of scientific inquiry and political decision-making, are dissimilar in both their cognitive and social aspects.*
> (Kasemir et al, 1999)

Yet as Reid (1995) points out, politicians may well place conflicting demands upon the institutional structures meant to help facilitate SD, including the setting and use of indicators. For example, in the UK the national government has established a set of headline indicators of SD that it expects local governments to adopt and amend as they see fit. The result has not only been some confusion over the importance of 'local' issues, with perhaps an emphasis on the 'environmental' flavour of SD, but conflict with the national government's stated priority of encouraging economic growth.[11] Yet some are adamant that SD is certainly not sustained growth and neither is it related to an 'environmental movement' (Hart Environmental Data, 1998).

Perhaps understandably given the above morass, it seems at times as if the emphasis in setting indicators has been technical excellence rather than helping managers to manage (Rigby et al, 2000; Pannell and Glenn, 2000). Indeed, while the literature has much to say about methods of selecting indicators and participation, the advantages of specific suites of indicators, methods of presentation, etc, there is little on the practical use of these tools, for example to explore policy and investment options (Stirling, 1999; Pannell and Glenn, 2000). If included, the latter is often dealt with as a once-off application rather than as a sustained activity. Some suggest that this could even be deliberate so as to delay action (Pinfield, 1996). At the very least, given that SD indicators have been around for some 20 years, and much time and effort has gone into indicator-based research, this lack of use may be surprising.

For those involved in SD there may be some uncomfortable truths in all of this. It's not that people don't want indicators. We use qualitative indicators all of the time, and even some quantitative and technical indicators are widely used and familiar to much of the public (eg gross domestic product (GDP), unemployment rates). Yet with indicators of SD there has perhaps been a failure to convince decision-makers and politicians about the costs, financial or otherwise, of not implementing SD (O'Neill et al, 1996). Wiggering and Rennings (1997) suggest that the financial (bottom-line) costs of environmental damage be made far more explicit. After all, there is evidence to suggest that publicly reporting indicators of company environmental performance is enough to drive firms to improve this performance (Ditz and Ranganathan, 1998). There may be various mechanisms at play, including ethical investment, but there does seem to be a correlation between transparency and performance (Tyteca, 1996). The World Business Council for Sustainable Development (WBCSD) is a group that monitors such environmental performance indicators, and its philosophy with such indicators is that it is better to be 'approximately right rather than precisely wrong' (Allenby et al, 1998).

Yet to be useful in a 'management' sense, indicators have to be set and measured on a regular basis. Monitoring, unfortunately, may be regarded by some as an inferior grade of inquiry relegated to managers rather than scientists, and perhaps even worse, could become so routine that it becomes an end in itself with little application in management (Kessler et al, 1992). Hence, from the point of view of researchers, there may well be a greater incentive to keep generating new sets of indicators, or indeed other tools and methods to gauge SD, rather than getting involved in or even considering too deeply the less glamorous side of the business. This would include issues such as how will these tools feed into what could be the fairly routine and repetitive yet critical decision-making required in part for SD? The danger must be that the routine measurement of indicators ends up being relegated to a data collection branch of an agency that generates tables of numbers that no one ends up either looking at or using. The key here may well be convincing those who are intended to use the indicators that the process of routine monitoring is cost-effective, ie that it is worth doing (Pannell and Glenn, 2000). There have been surprisingly few cost–benefit analyses of the use of indicators in SD. The theory has been clearly set out by Pannell and Glenn (2000) with reference to indicators of agricultural sustainability:

> *The fundamental criterion for choosing to monitor an indicator is that the benefits from doing so must exceed the costs. A decision-maker (either*

*farmer or policy-maker) should choose to monitor the set of indicators for
which the total benefits exceed the total costs by the greatest absolute
amount.*

However, while the costs of monitoring are relatively easily determined, as always with
SD the crux comes down to how the benefits are assessed. If one takes a financially
pragmatic view of 'benefits' in the sense of saving expenditure on agricultural inputs,
unemployment benefit, health care etc, then this may be possible, as illustrated by
Pannell and Glenn (2000). But what about the 'value' of biodiversity, a good view,
clean air, less noise, etc? Having a close relationship between the use of an indicator
and a pay-off will no doubt make the 'use' of that indicator more likely, but what are
the pay-offs, and who receives them?

By way of contrast, others are sceptical about the use of indicators as tools for
stakeholders to influence policy:

> *In more than 20 years of grassroots organizing experience I have neither
> personally used nor come across a grassroots group that has used indicators
> as a primary tool to encourage a party or government to change its political
> objectives.* (Brugmann, 1997b)

> *A 'The Tail Wags the Dog' strategy, ie 'let's produce an index that tells people
> what should be really important for them', is bound to fail – there is no
> shortage of attempts to tell people what they have to do, and it becomes
> boring after a while.* (Jesinghaus, 2000)

However, there is another direction that employs indicators more as devices to help
people understand themselves and what they want in SD. The focus here is not so
much at the level of influencing macro-policy, but at the level of inspiring a community to take control of change. Kline (2000) suggests that 'indicators can be an effective
mechanism for understanding people's values, needs, concerns and expectations', a
point echoed by Besleme and Mullin (1997) in their summary of community
indicator projects, including those focused on SD, in the US. While early (1960s–
1970s) attempts at using indicators in social accounting within the US died out due
to funding cuts and a 'perception that indicators had no direct and useful application',
a rebirth in the 1980s has seen a host of examples of community indicator projects
in the US (Besleme and Mullin, 1997), including the famous 'Sustainable Seattle' project. In a more bullish statement of the advantages of indicators as part of community
development that stands in some contrast to the point made by Brugmann (1997b)
above, there is the following quotation:

> *Indicators are an excellent tool for communities working toward a
> common goal. When properly designed, they can forewarn a community
> about a potential problem or negative trend before its effects become
> irreversible. They can demonstrate the linkages among large social,
> economic and environmental systems and help to identify the causes of
> complex problems. They can measure the effectiveness of policies and
> projects. Most of all, they can simplify, yet comprehensively track a
> community's progress towards its goals.* (Besleme and Mullin, 1997)

As a result some distinguish another type of indicator, community sustainable development indicators (CSDIs, or neighbourhood sustainability indicators), quite distinct from the sort of SD indicator discussed so far (Acton, 2000; Table 2.4). The difference between these two is largely in terms of who has set them and what for. CSDIs may have a more indirect effect on policy, while the traditional SD indicators may be intended to directly influence policy rather than facilitate change at local level (the 'attempts to replace GDP' of Jesinghaus, 2000). Some have subdivided the CSDI category. The result may be a set of 'nested indicators' (Meter, 1999; Table 2.5) that operate at different spatial and time scales, and may have varying relevance to external groups (researchers, decision-makers etc).

Table 2.4 *Two different types of sustainable development indicators*

Characteristic	Sustainable development indicators (SDIs)	Community sustainable development indicators (CSDIs)
Public participation	Limited	Extensive
Who collects data/statistics?	Experts	Community
Communication of indicators	Extensive within the policy-maker/manager group More limited with other groups	Via media and other means
Use	Directly to drive policy	Encourage individuals to make changes in their day-to-day lives Affects policy indirectly
Resonance	Policy-makers/managers	Public

While indicators are often seen in terms of their use as tools to help understand linkages and processes in complex systems, some do put limits on the depth of this understanding:

> To me, indicators are a very poor tool for deepening our understanding of the system(s). They should be primarily used to track whether or not we are imposing our newly redefined, ie sustainable development, values on the system . . . [W]e want to use indicators to establish that essential link of accountability to the sustainable development agenda. (Brugmann, 1997b)

The problem may simply be that decision-makers and managers have other agenda, and indicators of SD frankly have little influence. They may even be a useful (to some) device for diverting attention into avenues that make for pleasant rhetoric but don't mean much in practice. As Brugmann (1997b) puts it, 'in one aspect of such planning

Table 2.5 *Four types of community sustainable development indicators (CSDIs)*

Type of CSDI	Purpose	Linkages	Main use	Potential limitations
Data poetry (community)	Highly linked indicators that are most useful for stakeholders (internal groups) Designed to help transform the discussion of the community towards a more long-term view	high	internal	do not allow for comparisons across neighbourhoods focus more on action steps than complete picture of local sustainability concerns
Core (community and experts)	Linked indicators useful for local residents as well as external groups (researchers, funders, policy-makers) Designed to allow comparisons among diverse communities	high	internal and external	difficult to define one set of indicators that apply to diverse neighbourhoods
Background (experts)	Offer interesting background information that helps define the context in which SD takes place Useful for both internal and external groups	few	external	less integrating than data poetry and core indicators
Deep sustainability (community and experts)	Help local stakeholders to define a long-term vision for their community Highly linked and look far into the future Evoke long-term visioning	high	internal and external	may be impractical to implement in the short term

Notes: 'Linkages' refer to relationship with local concerns and goals. 'Main use' (internal and external) refers to the groups that would primarily use the indicators. 'Internal' refers to the neighbourhood community while 'external' refers to those outside of the neighbourhood (such as researchers).

Source: Meter, 1999

[for sustainable development] – the use of "sustainability indicators" – we have failed to be methodical and articulate'. This author goes on to illustrate why he believes indicators have failed to have an impact in planning. One reason is their tendency to be applied to meet a variety of needs (planning, public education, accountability), and he suggests that a better approach may be to focus instead on a defined set of performance indicators to which decision-makers and managers can be held responsible (see also Jimenez-Beltran, 2001).

This potential confusion between indicators of sustainability and indicators of 'quality provision' (including access and demand) has arisen within various contexts besides the local government context described by Brugmann (1997a and b). The United States Agency for International Development (USAID), for example, has tried to separate these out within a context of health and family planning provision in Africa. The results can be subtle and somewhat confusing. For example, USAID distinguishes between indicators of the 'sustainability of demand' and indicators of 'demand', yet at the same time acknowledges 'there is a great deal of potential overlap between indicators of access, quality and demand and indicators of sustainability' (USAID, undated)!

Given the ambiguities that can arise, it is perhaps not unsurprising that the ability of local stakeholders ('dedicated generalists') to both set and apply indicators to meet the complex issues surrounding sustainability are, to use Brugmann's word, problematic. Even if it were possible to set indicators of SD, Brugmann argues that their usefulness in influencing behaviour would be limited given the other more pressing influences, including legal requirements, that managers and decision-makers face on a regular basis. The result can be inconsistency between SD indicators and other performance indicators, with the former losing out in the struggle (Table 2.6).

Table 2.6 *A comparison of sustainability indicators for Seattle with some of the city's performance indicators*

Parameter used in both 'sustainability' and 'performance'	Consistent in terms of:	
	vision	indicator measurement
Air quality	✓	✓
Water consumption	✓	
'Open space'	✓	
Volunteering	✓	
Neighbourhood perception (eg safety)	✓	
Unemployment	✓	
Crime	✓	✓
Recycling	✓	
Household income	✓	
Biodiversity		
Equity and justice		

Note: ✓ indicates that the indicator is compatible in its use to gauge both 'sustainability' and 'performance'.

Source: after Brugmann, 1997a

Instead, Brugmann (1997a) suggests that it would better if 'stakeholders would ideally focus on preparing the goals and targets of a strategic plan that has legal standing' rather than taking part in an exercise to get indicators that 'measure sustainability – which in the face of effecting real change takes on a more academic or pedagogical appeal'.

Of course, one could go on to think of indicators in more organic terms than the 'end product' (a 'deliverable' in project parlance) of a public consultation exercise to be applied by managers. We could see the whole process of participation, consensus building and debate as a desirable process in itself, resulting in 'reflective insight and the genuine sharing of ideas', without necessarily arriving at an end point of 'positive and normative definition' (Meppem and Gill, 1998). The role of decision-makers here is to 'facilitate learning and seek leverage points with which to direct progress towards integrated economic, ecological and socio-cultural approaches for all humanity' (Meppem and Gill, 1998).

Indicators of SD could certainly play a role here as useful tools to play out such debates and learning (Acton, 2000), although they cannot by themselves empower people (LGMB, 1995).

> *In the process of their development, indicators do serve to stimulate community visioning and unite different interests, but they cannot single-handedly bring about change.* (Besleme and Mullin, 1997)

> *Even if we never use a single indicator the process [of their development] has given us so much.* (Meter, 1999)

This is quite distinct from the use of indicators, such as newspaper readership, to passively measure public participation, for example in the political process or in social programmes (MacGillivray, 1997; Kline, 2000) or indeed participation as a means of getting the indicators. Instead the indicators are in part a product of a vision of SD but at the same time help to define as well as implement it! This logic implies a constant circularity with a starting vision of SD and indicators that in turn generate greater participation and interest in SD, which in turn leads to a new definition of SD and a new set of indicators, etc ad infinitum. Indicators are no longer a neutral end product to aid implementation of a positive and normative definition of SD but exist explicitly as a catalyst for further change. As Kline (2000) puts it, 'they can be a critical element in helping people gain more control over their lives and in ensuring a healthier future for the next generations'.

Seeing sustainability within a learning context rather than a defined target has much to commend it, and it is one emergent feature of our work in Malta that will be expanded upon in Chapters 4 and 5. Crilly et al (1999), for example, describe how the Sustainable Northern Ireland Project (SNIP) acted as a catalyst to encourage local government officers to think beyond their statutory remit as well as allowing community and pressure groups to expand upon their understanding of SD. The problem is that such increased awareness can lead to frustration if the individuals or groups concerned are unable to do anything about it. It can become learning for learning's sake rather than resulting in desired change. While this has a logic, we have to be careful not to get carried away with despair. Heightening awareness of problems and perspective can be liberating at the level of an individual's life, and may increase the questioning as to how larger-scale change can be brought about.

SUMMARY

This chapter has covered a number of key issues that arise out of the creation and use of indicators as tools to help achieve SD. Criteria for their selection, the number to be selected, the degree (if any) of aggregation, presentation and use are all important and indeed central considerations. However, the last point, use, is perhaps the one that has received the least attention. Projects geared to generating SD indicators tend to become myopically focused on technical issues (what indicators, how many, how to aggregate, etc) rather than really consider usage to bring about change. The result is a substantial literature that deals with methodological issues, but with little to say on how, or even if, the indicators were applied to help improve the quality of people's lives. The assumption is that they do, but where is the proof? Various negative comments to the contrary (eg Brugmann, 1997a and b; Kasemir et al, 1999; Jesinghaus, 2000; Rigby et al, 2000) must engender some cynicism about the whole process of generating indicators in order to bring about SD. Their use in a community learning sense may have an appeal (Meppem and Gill, 1998), but could ultimately result in frustration if these groups cannot actually bring about change at larger scales; nothing prevents them making changes to their own lives. Having said that, making someone aware of their problems may be a good first step to initiating change. It's not a bad place to begin!

In the following two chapters, the development and use of indicators of SD will be explored in the context of a project that both authors have worked on over a period of two years. The project was based in Malta and drew, in part, upon much of the foregoing discussion. The reader will be able to see numerous points in the Malta project where we took a particular direction when alternatives were available. We have explained our rationale behind such choices, but as we hope the reader would have seen from Chapters 1 and 2, there is no universally defined set of rules and methods in SD; much is left to personal opinion, and that is framed by a host of factors including culture, experience and livelihood.

Chapter 3
Systemic Sustainability Analysis and Prospective

INTRODUCTION

In the previous two chapters, we explored some of the recent developments in terms of putting sustainable development (SD) into practice. Some of the issues that arose out of this were discussed, particularly those that surrounded the creation and application of indicators as a tool. We also described how in our previous book we developed a method called systemic sustainability analysis (SSA), founded on the soft systems methodology (SSM), which can be used to help develop indicators in a participative mode. In this chapter, the practical application of SSA is set out and explained. It is not assumed that SSA is 'finished' or 'definitive'. Rather, we suggest that it is a developing and changing approach that practitioners can adapt and change to meet the specific needs of the circumstances which confront them. Neither do we wish to suggest that SSA is the best or only such approach. In Chapter 1 we did briefly describe a range of approaches that workers have taken, often under the generic title 'deliberative institutions'. Here, the context in which SSA is applied is primarily Malta. The process of the 12-fold structure is given in some detail and the comments of stakeholders in the context are added.

The purpose of this chapter and Chapter 4 is two-fold. Firstly, the chapters describe the main elements of SSA and set out, step by step, how to undertake it for the development of sustainability indicators. In this sense the chapters constitute a 'how to' guide, including craft tips on the use of methods and tools. Secondly, and leaping into the 'how to' element, the chapters set out a series of observations from stakeholders and participants who have been involved in the development of the SSA. These comments and points provide some external insights into the way in which SSA has been experienced by others and sets out some of the main issues and problems which any such analysis can run into.

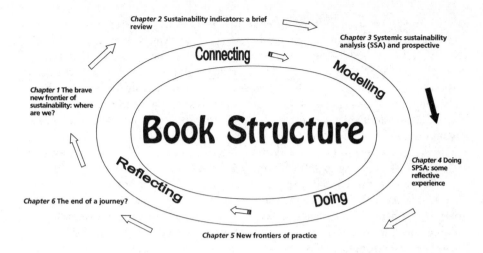

Perhaps there has been a problem in the SD literature in that it tends to be very case-study-orientated. SD does often tend to be quite site- and time-specific. Our focus on Malta is no different in that sense, and a reader may be excused for wondering what Malta has to do with the specific context with which they may be involved. This is something of a common dilemma; generalizations in SD can be dismissed as not taking into account the local context, and site-specific studies can be dismissed as having only limited applicability. We will ask for the reader's indulgence here. Much of the Malta experience is site-specific, but at the same time we will also present issues and learning outcomes that we feel have much wider applicability.

The presentation of these chapters also requires some explanation. Rather than writing an academic treatise in the form of an authoritative 'knows best' and top-down explanation of events, we decided to set out the SSA experience in the manner it was experienced. This contrasts markedly with the style of Chapters 1 and 2, which summarized recent developments in the field. The format for the presentation is somewhere between a diary, a stakeholder review and a toolkit. Our aim is to demarcate external lessons (from the literature) and more internal insights arising out of our sustained contact with the local stakeholders in Malta. This may appear clumsy in places but we feel strongly that only a presentation of this form relates the richness of the experience that we have undergone. To leave out the diary form is to miss the passion and emotion involved in this work, so often ignored in spurious attempts to achieve 'rational' and 'scientific' measures of emotionally supercharged problems like environmental decline, too much tourism and social alienation. To leave out the voices of stakeholders is to miss the other perceptions of the motives of projects and reflection on actions. SSA, as we experienced it, was not a neutral approach derived externally and with no implications for local people. We include their voices and concerns, both about the process of SSA and the implications that learning and using it had for team members. We believe that these voices are representative of many stakeholders outside the context we describe here. Finally, to leave out the toolkit would be to cheat you, the reader, who we assume has picked up this book with a mind to seeing how sustainability indicators may be done differently.

However, we do have three interlaced aspects in the chapter and this might provide the reader with navigation problems, especially if you wish to get to the details of the toolkit in the least time. So, in order to facilitate navigation we have broken the elements of SSA down into 12 distinct stages and presented each of the three aspects of content: diary, stakeholder voices and toolkit in easily identified formats. The toolkit appears as the main narrative of the chapter. Diary aspects are set out in boxes. Stakeholder voices appear in shaded boxes. So, if you only want the toolkit, avoid the boxes.

Insights arising out of the application of SSA will be picked up and explored in Chapter 5. We will flag them in Chapters 3 and 4.

We wish to reiterate that we certainly do not intend to present SSA as the magic answer to sustainability indicators! This was not the intention in the first book and neither is it here, although some colleagues did seem to think that we were championing only one approach and dismissing other equally valid methodologies. As will have been seen from Chapters 1 and 2, there are many ways in which academics and field workers have tried to deal with some central issues in sustainability indicator development/application:

- The need for stakeholder participation in terms of what is meant by SD, as well as the indicators that are intended to gauge it. But given that SD is all about people, their ambitions, desires and dislikes, this inevitably leads to diversity of opinion and issues over 'representation'.
- The forms in which indicators are presented so as to be used.
- The integration of indicators into some overall assessment of sustainability.
- The questions of who wants indicators, and why? In other words, who will use them, and how?

These are all critical points, and SSA as a methodology set out in the first book is but one way of dealing with them. It complements the ideas of Meppem and Gill (1998), and others who see planning for sustainability as a learning concept, and incorporates SSM as a device for facilitating stakeholder participation. In the first book we suggested the AMOEBA as a visual device for indicator presentation, which at the same time could allow for a more qualitative integration rather than go down the road of quantitative integration as set out in Chapter 2. There are, of course, other devices and methods that one could use to facilitate participation, presentation and integration. Indeed, one reviewer of the first book was critical of the potential of soft systems, arguing that there are better approaches. We do not dispute this, but at the same time it should be noted that no approach would be universally ideal: there is no Holy Grail of SD methodology. In Chapter 5 our aim will be to explore the issues that arise out of these rather than the specifics of the methodology and visual device.

PERSONAL BACKGROUND TO THE FIELD WORK

The field work which provides the basis for this chapter arises from the development of SD indicators in Malta from early 2000 to January 2002. In particular, a project for the development of indicators for the northwest of Malta, a part of the island which experiences a relatively high level of coastal tourism on the main sandy beaches and it still has a viable rural economy (relative to the rest of the island). Before providing an overview of the project itself and of the SSA approach as applied here, it is valuable to set out some diary thoughts on experiencing the Maltese context for the first time. This provides the reader with a view of the context as experienced by Simon and some introduction to some of the issues that came up early on arrival.

> One definite indicator which is shared by everybody in this room and probably by the whole country and the people who come to Malta . . . is the indicator that the environment has degenerated. (Stakeholder at a workshop held on 4 October 2000, Luqa, Malta)

Author's diary

I think it is fair to say that inception workshops are not my favourite events. Past experience tells me that they are often political events and opportunities for much 'speechification' around the project aims and objectives. But here I was, making my way on an Air Malta flight, preparing myself for just such an event. On approaching Malta from the air for the first time (in daytime anyway) I was struck by the smallness of this densely populated island set in the wide blue of the Mediterranean sea. Actually, I was mistaken: my first impression was incorrect. The large woman in colourful clothes sitting next to me on the plane exclaimed to her friend 'Look, Gozo is beautiful today'. Gozo is Malta's small relation and partner in this mini archipelago set in the middle of tourist-haunted seas.

The plane lumbered heavily on and Gozo was behind us, but in no time the flight had crossed the diminutive divide between this island and her partner. Malta itself was now in view. There is no doubt about it, the scale is best realized from a few hundred metres. From this height the academic can think objectively about his research, the consultant can assess the nature of problems and solutions and the island itself appears to be deceptively rural and of a relatively encouraging size to the 'fix it' mentality. But this is the north. In no time the ferry terminal to Gozo was behind us and the east-facing coast comes into view. This is an experience. From the beginnings of the urban sprawl that is the wealth and the agony of Malta, which one first notices in Mellieha Bay, past Saint Paul's Bay, down to Pembroke and on to Sliema and Valletta itself, the impression of floating over a white and khaki low-built suburb is inescapable. The extensive, low rise vista goes on and on interrupted only by occasional gold-clad church and warrens of roads. The plane edged inland, passing Mosta, Naxxar, splendid Mdina with the fortress citadel of the Knights of St John and Rabat, as it made its way to the destination of Luqa and final landing. But the first-time visitor is not aware of the districts and villages, the fiercely individual mini-towns and dormitories. All is one in a non-stop collage of residences and Mediterranean sprawl. The memory of the comparatively open spaces of Gozo and the northwest of the island were now long gone, although in reality only minutes had past. I could not help coming to the conclusion that if ever an island needed to consider its sustainable development surely this one did.

Malta has a population of approximately 380,000 on an island no bigger than the metropolitan area of a small city (approximately 246km²) – giving the amazingly high population density of around 1500 people per km². Gozo is tiny by comparison (65km²) and the very junior partner in the trine-coalition, Comino, is almost invisible at 2.5km². Malta is an independent republic and has been so since 1964 although there is a lingering British feel to the place, which is emphasized by the charming English with Maltese dialect of sonorous lilt evident from the chatter of the lady who sits beside me on the plane, red public telephone boxes and the right-hand-drive cars.

Figure 3.1 *Map of Malta, Gozo and Comino*

Descent into Luqa (our pilot was applauded by the Maltese on the flight – my colourful friend was ecstatic) hides the vista of unplanned suburban sprawl from view and leaves the first-time visitor with the immediate worry of immigration (membership of the EU is still a nervous referendum away at the time of writing) followed by the teeming throng of the airport concourse. I was fortunate in not needing to queue for a taxi into Sliema where my hotel was located. I was met by a member of the Sustainability Indicators team and rapidly escorted to a car waiting in the darkening car park.

Driving into the mass of joined-up villages and towns I am again awed by the sheer weight of humanity that is the rich wealth of Malta. Buildings of all types surround the visitor as progress is made on perilous roads through a maze of poorly lit districts. But did I say that the island is small? Well it is, but the journey to Sliema shows how deceptive some quick statistics can be. Fact must wait on perception for confirmation or denial. The journey is beguilingly complex. I like to keep a mental map of where I am in a country which I am visiting for the first time. I guess this springs from a career of working in some quite unruly places and the need to remember how I got in so I could get out again if I had to in a hurry! The darkling drive from Luqa to Sliema defeated my worn senses and soon had me lost in the flurry of turns and curves which made 5km feel like 50. Where was I in this confusion of architectural types and dimly lit roads?

My guide and driver is kindness made manifest. Polite and enquiring conversation goes on as the dark descends and evening gives way to night. I am asked about my preferences for the following day's workshop (room numbers, need for overhead projectors, etc), about the weather in England, about the state of the European Union and of course about the parlous state of English soccer – a topic on which almost all male Maltese have a view, even if the teams of first choice are more likely to be found in the Italian Serie A than the dank turf of the super-rich clubs of the English Premiership. Old loyalties die hard and the immortal indicators of the league positions of Manchester United and Chelsea hold an enduring appeal.

At last, after many a bump and jostle, we arrived at the hotel in Sliema where I was rapidly processed and, following kind wishes for a good repose, I left my hosts and ascended to my globally familiar L-shaped hotel bedroom. A cold beer from the minibar and I was out on the smallest of balconies, staring out over a dark landscape interrupted by lights upon lights terminated only by the brooding black of the sea and the sky. Warm breezes and sounds of laughter from the numerous cafes and restaurants which be-deck the Sliema promenade drifted up to me on my rare (for Malta) vantage point on the sixth floor. One obvious point was that I appeared to be in one of the few multi-storey buildings on this most crowded island (a paradox I needed to wrestle with for some days). Feeling oddly exposed in my lofty eyrie, I retired for the night.

The days which followed that first experience of Malta have led to many a rethink of what Malta is and how it got to its present situation. I can only write about Malta as I experienced it, as I have been allowed to get to know its complexity and diversity. I do not claim privileged knowledge or a superior and scientific worldview. I express my limited understanding in the co-understanding that there are many more equally personal views about Malta which need to be held in mind and kept as a balance to the views I set out here. My work on the island has allowed me to travel with knowing and insightful guides, and for this I am very grateful. This insider knowledge has allowed me to see past some of the presenting outward appearances which Malta provides for the occasional visitor, to some of the struggles and anxieties which seem to lie behind every window in each household.

Let me begin with the north, well actually the west, for the northwest is the subject of this research and nothing is too far from anything else in Malta, even the cardinal points of the compass. On an early spring safari around the island I was taken with Italian and French colleagues from Sliema in the east, across the island via narrow and single-carriage roads. There is almost no dual carriageway for Malta's 220,000 cars and as 10,000 new registrations are made each year, there is a potent challenge for those brave souls seeking parking at office hours. Our journey took us via Birkirkara and its magnificent church of St Helen set amid a chaos of dwellings, and Rabat with the fortress of Mdina glowering over the open land. Our objective was the twee sounding Dingli cliffs, a name which conjures for me images of elves and goblins. I was being taken to the garden of Malta, the natural wonderland which lies outside the crushing urbanity of the east and the subject for the issues of sustainability which are at the core of the project which this note describes. It was early in the year but even so the flourish of spring was everywhere to be seen and smelt on the barren limestone landscape which is the terrain of the island. On approaching Dingli my attention was drawn to stone-wall-enclosed fields containing cages on posts. I asked what they were and was told that they are traps set by the bird-trappers (a lobby nearly as powerful in Malta as their North American cousins, the National Rifle Association of the US). It all seemed so unfair. Bird goes in cage, bird sings, wild bird comes, wild bird is caught, trapped or shot. Surely there is a better sport to play? Dingli itself was now in view. We got out of the car and headed for the precipitous drop of the cliffs. This is one of the highest points of the island. These intimidating cliffs rear up from the Mediterranean and then slope down to the heavyweight townscape of the Valetta conurbation, which seems to weight the eastern side of the island down to certain flood. Standing here, the next conclusion I came to was that even the rural side of Malta appears urban. Limestone scenery can be unforgiving, especially if it is sparsely mantled in green and criss-crossed by ruinous walls. In places an impression like the Burran, in County Clare in western Ireland, is maintained, with small fields and green grass combining to form a likeable if harsh backdrop to sea and sky. But the eye soon wanders from this, and other sadder sights jostle in. The walls are often ruined in aesthetic effect by fill-ins of brick, ugly block or appalling oil tanks and rusty barbed wire. These stone walls have great value now for the cladding of fashionable homes in the upmarket districts around Sliema and Valletta and, as the young of the island turn their backs on the unprofitable labour of agriculture for the golden promises of tourism and gambling, walls are surplus to requirements and can best be cashed in for once-only income. Too often the barren fields remain untilled now, as agriculture looks harsh to the eyes seeking richer and easier pickings elsewhere. Malta, like Ireland, has always been generous in exporting her youth and talent. The jumble of broken, incomplete and ruinous walls form a home for the prickly pear plants which perform a covering job and mitigate some of the scarring, but a lasting impression of thoughtless and artless expediency is fostered. Turning towards the west, the eye scales down the cliff face to the narrow hinterland at the foot between cliff and sea. At first this is more pleasing. Some well-tended fields allow crops to flourish in the micro-climate, and a mix of fields and trees hints at fertility and the yields to come. But again, other forces are at work. Here and there fields have been cleared and left barren. When asked their purpose, I was told that these areas belong to the hunters and they are cleared in this way so as to be a welcome landing site for migrating birds. The purpose of these grisly voids explained, I wished I had not asked the purpose of the numerous hides set in fast-growing eucalyptus trees. The trees make good hides but, dispersing over 70 gallons of water a day in transpiration from this arid, river-less island, they represent a luxury which many think the hunters could do without.

Driving on from west to north, I was aware of some pleasant vistas and views over the small fields and rock walls of the northwest. Past Malta's Great Wall, the Victoria Lines, natural faults built on originally by the Knights and then extended and developed by the British for defence in micro-imitation of its colossal cousin. Past the diminutive resorts of the area at Ghajn Tuffieha and Golden Bay and up to Cirkewwa and the ferry crossing to tiny Gozo and tinier Comino. Passing Marfa Point I took in the illegal development at Armier Bay, where the planners came too late to stop wooden shacks becoming concrete single-storey dwellings, second homes and boathouses to those with the courage to bet on theft going unpunished because of political inertia.

I began to get the point. This is not empty and unspoilt countryside; the northwest is not a rural idyll tremulously positioned on the edge of developer oblivion, but this is space and hope and not urban, and the best which Malta has left to sustain. What is done is done, and there is no clawing back the fields from the rampant block and cement of the east and south (have I mentioned the south?) but, before the island succumbs to 100 per cent coverage, there is a small time for an intake of breath, for some planning and thinking and valuing what is left of the countryside. And this time for thinking can be assisted by information about the scale of the problem and the rate of loss. What does the loss mean to Malta? As I said at the beginning of this entry, if anywhere on Earth deserves a conversation with itself regarding the meaning and doing of sustainable development, then surely Malta does?

At last, the purpose of the visits that I was to make over the coming years and the point of the work which Steve and I were to engage in dawned on me. Here was a vital and urgent need: a need for understanding, communication and desperate dialogue. Colloquy more on a religious footing than an objective appraisal of monetary value is prayed for from the landscape of an island which has sold its soul for other people's holidays. Malta has reaped as it has sown and the cracks in the fields are becoming fissures to match the rill erosion evident in so much of the untilled landscape. With an embryonic planning authority trying to make itself heard over the multitudinous voices of developers (legal and illegal), this is going to be a close-run thing. I no longer had a methodology to be tested and tried in an academically interesting context divorced of any emotion or subjectivity. I had a local difficulty on a national scale to scan, accept, communicate, invite others to consider and hope for. I was already lost as the objective academic looking down the microscope at the victims of my study. I had landed, the context of my study rose up around me like the suburbia of Luqa when I first arrived, and already I cared about the outcome. This was no exercise in a scientific sustainability analysis to form the stuff of learned papers: it was a struggle against time to understand desperate complexity in communion with friends.

Although some of the reflections were revised and changed with subsequent visits, we feel that it shows quite starkly the impact of a context on one of the authors. Such an impact can be ignored or it can be seen as an informing factor for the following work.

THE IMPORTANCE OF THE SUBJECTIVE

A problem for sustainability indicator (SI) activity that we discussed in our first book is the pseudo-scientific nature of much that is presented in the literature (academic and practitioner) and on the internet. Such pseudo-science manifests itself in various ways, for example:

- An inability or unwillingness to have 'facts' denied – especially by unqualified lay persons.
- An inability to see linked factors outside narrow domains or specialisms.
- An unwillingness to share ideas and conclusions.
- A capacity to provide a bewildering set of specialized facts as if they were uncontested truths.
- A spurious attempt to overwhelm argument by reference to authorities beyond those available to local people.

We have tried to avoid some of the more obvious problems that this approach can cultivate. For example, the diary entries used throughout (an example is presented above) set out some of the emotional and personal impacts a context can provoke in those about to engage in sustainability work. To present this field work as if it were an objective analysis without other meanings would cheapen the narrative concerning SSA and fabricate an illusion of authoritative, top-down and remote science. SSA as undertaken here attempts to be both personal and in touch, whilst maintaining clear operational parameters. By presenting a fuller view of the assumptions and subjective concerns of the main actors we are attempting to present a richer and more complex interpretation of what actually happened in the context.

Contexts such as Malta and SD projects such as this are not simple, uncontested or operationally neutral. It is our contention that this type of project impacts on all actors. If the reflections of the authors are informative of the level of complexity experienced, then the reflections of local Maltese are even more meaningful. Issues of contrasting perception which any sustainability project has to deal with are set out in the contradictory statements from two Maltese stakeholders at a workshop in October 2000.

> (Concerning publicizing sustainability issues:) Unless we coopt the public . . . you can't go forward . . . you have to go out and publicize this issue. (But concerning publicizing a specific issue:) You can imagine the boomerang effect – we will create chaos here. I plead with people here with all this necessary information really try and dialogue and convince the government that if this goes public we are ruined.

From this background it is easy to see that sustainability indicators are devices with deeply embedded social, political and moral issues that have implications far beyond the basic logic of any specific methodology or the presentational function of any given statistic.

Background to CAMP Malta

Within the limits of this book, it is not possible or necessary to discuss the full background to the work of the Mediterranean Action Plan (MAP) and the series of coastal area management programmes (CAMPs), which are undertaken by the range of agencies and organizations associated with MAP. Suffice to say for the sake of the coherence of this chapter that there are two main agencies that the authors were in contact or working with under the auspices of CAMP Malta. The first is the Priority Actions Programme Regional Activity Centre (PAP RAC) based in Split in Croatia. PAP has developed a strong expertise in integrated coastal area management and acts as the CAMP implementing centre. The second, and the direct contacting agency for the SSA, is the Mediterranean Blue Plan Regional Activity Centre (BP RAC), which is based in Sophia Antipolis in France. Blue Plan is concerned with systemic and prospective analysis and with developmental/environmental scenarios required by CAMPs. Blue Plan assists in the development, management and roll-out of projects in the Mediterranean, encouraging certain activities and facilitating processes. It is not in a position to dictate to local agencies or to demand adherence to a top-down policy.

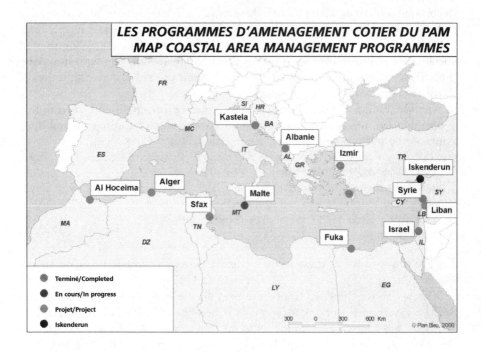

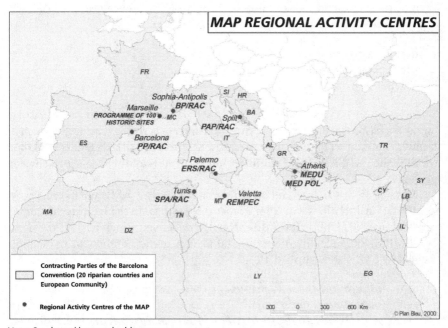

Note: See http://www.planbleu.org

Figure 3.2 *Maps of CAMPs (past, present and future) and the Regional Activity Centres*

At the time of the Malta CAMP there had already been several such projects in different parts of the Mediterranean including Greece, Tunisia and Egypt. Each CAMP has its own focus and central issues of concern but the overriding issue of sustainability has been constant throughout. The main variation with the Malta CAMP project was the inclusion of SSA as the means selected to derive indicators of SD that had local meaning and value.

The Malta CAMP was focused on the northwest of the island. Within this geographic area it was further organized into five thematic sub-projects, and three cross-cutting sub-projects. The five thematic areas were:

1   sustainable coastal management;
2   marine conservation areas;
3   integrated water resource management;
4   erosion/desertification control management; and
5   tourism: impacts on health.

For the arrangement of these teams in the Maltese government organization, see Figure 3.3.

These five were devised from a previous diagnosis process undertaken by the Maltese government working in liaison with members of PAP RAC. To some extent they were pre-selected prior to the indicator activity and so SSA had no impact on the selection process. Also note that the team members were largely drawn from Maltese government ministries and agencies.

The three cross-cutting sub-projects (so named because they were seen as being support projects to the five thematic sub-projects) were:

1   data management;
2   participatory programme; and
3   systemic sustainability analysis.

These were seen as supporting the main CAMP activities by providing a central place for the establishment of all statistics, maps and other data required by the five thematic teams, a common set of participatory techniques for use in all stakeholder workshops throughout the CAMP and common indicator development and presentation methods.

SSA had an overarching and inclusive role within the CAMP and to some extent had operational relations with all the other sub-projects. In the inception document prepared by PAP (UNEP/PAP/MAP, 2000), a document which sets out the nature of CAMP Malta, including timescale and main activities, the actions to be implemented by SSA were identified as:

- *identification of and agreement on the system, stakeholders and main sustainability indicators;*
- *participatory development of the systemic sustainability analysis with description and assessment of the system by main indicators;*
- *provision of inputs to final Project documents and Post-project activities; and*
- *proposal for dissemination of results for scientific and lay communities.* (p7)

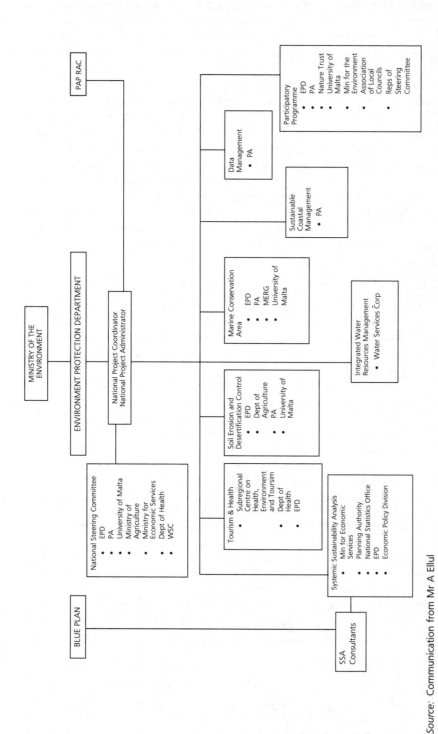

Figure 3.3 *CAMP Malta teams and the Maltese government organization*

Source: Communication from Mr A Ellul

As an aside at this point, the format and language of inception reports is typically as presented above. Documents of this type tend to be prescriptive and 'heavy' in language terms. An issue for an inclusive and learning process such as that suggested for SSA is its ability to work effectively within a project structure which tends to be top-down and focused on outputs before the project is begun. There is a tendency in conventional 'blueprint' (a term used to define projects which follow a blueprint rather than being adaptive to change: see Cusworth and Franks, 1993, pp8–11) project processes to require exact clarity on outputs before projects, prior to inception. The result is typically a set of documents and plans agreed between all contracting partners that specify outcomes, how they are to be achieved and ways in which achievements are to be assessed. In an era of accountability and stress on value for money by governments, this is readily understandable. However, this exactitude can tend to militate against progressive learning processes within projects and the emergence of outcomes as projects progress. It can also militate against local people setting and changing agendas. These issues will be shown to have had consequences throughout the project.

Thus the SSA activity, although focusing on indicator development, was also concerned with 'the system', ie the coastal area of Malta as a whole, although working initially within the northwest region.

The inception report goes on to set out the objectives for the SSA:

- *to contribute to efforts towards a sustainable development of the island, and in particular of its NW area, by preparing a set of sustainability indicators and a systemic sustainability analysis, to be made on the basis of description and assessment of level of sustainability by main indicators;*
- *to introduce and apply systemic sustainability analysis as a specific tool for sustainable management, in this case of coastal and marine areas;*
- *to contribute to preparation of comprehensive integrated final project documents, by presenting a crucial analysis; and*
- *to create inputs of interest for the activities of the Mediterranean Commission for Sustainable Development, for wide use in the Mediterranean region.* (UNEP/PAP/MAP, 2000, p10)

The first and second points are particularly relevant in terms of the analysis set out here. The third and fourth are less relevant, although obviously important for Blue Plan.

The specific focus on sustainable management meant that SSA would be applied as a means to develop awareness of sustainability within Malta and provide it as a means to make further assessments of the Maltese context.

The Maltese project had these activities and objectives and yet these were seen to still leave the SSA team with a free hand to adapt the existing SSA structure and adopt new and insightful methods, tools and techniques widely from a variety of different sources.[1]

At the same time as the inception visit was progressing two parallel activities were taking place. Firstly, the technical specification for the SSA was being developed (UNEP/MAP/BluePlan, 2000) and secondly, the initial Maltese SSA team were being familiarized with the main themes of SSA (Bell and Coudert, 2000). Both of these activities require a little explanation.

TECHNICAL SPECIFICATION FOR SSA

The draft technical specification was a core document which set out the main agreed procedures and content for SSA as drawn down from the previous experience which Blue Plan has had with systemic approaches to sustainability analysis in previous CAMP activity and the original book (Bell and Morse, 1999). These two similar but separately developed approaches were then melded and developed to meet the needs of Blue Plan in Malta. Several core items need to be stressed. Certain rules and meanings of terms were set out in this document. Many terms have contested meanings and it was recognized by Blue Plan that agreed, if not definitive, definitions would be required. Clear definitions are necessary in most projects which are innovative or perceived as complex. This can be for a variety of reasons:

- Legally, terms need to be of fixed meaning.
- Linguistically, terms need to be defined between contesting concepts of meaning.
- Ideologically, terms may be seen to have inappropriate meanings.
- Contemporary and jargon terms need tying down to specific meanings.

Four terms were of major significance: systems analysis, sustainable development, sustainability indicator and systemic sustainability analysis. The following are the definitions finally agreed for use over the runtime of the project and used in this book.

> *The Blue Plan's definition of a system is the following: a system is 'an intellectual construction, for a certain purpose, constituted by chosen elements in dynamic interaction' in order to describe and represent a complex reality or phenomenon ... The purpose of developing a systemic approach to problem solving is generally to gain an in-depth perception resulting in knowledge of a complex reality or phenomenon represented by the system. The systems approach makes intelligible and understandable the complexity and allows analyst and stakeholders to concentrate attention on mutually agreed elements and above all on the relationships between these elements. The approach is global in its scope and considers the system as a whole capable to change under the interactions of different elements within the internal and external context.* (UNEP/MAP/Blue Plan, 2000, pp3–4)

It is important to stress here that the Blue Plan definition of 'system' is an intellectual construction and not an item in-the-world as such. Hence, systems are defined differently according to the different perspectives of different people. For example, a farming system may be defined in different ways by different stakeholders. A farmer might define it as 'a means to develop family income and sustain the current family standard of living by means of the surplus profit generated from agricultural practices'. A grocer might define it as 'a system to provide me with cheap and seasonal produce at a price which enables me to sell on the produce for a reasonable mark-up, thus maintaining the economic viability of my outlets'. A green activist might describe it as 'a system designed to pollute the countryside and impoverish local biodiversity in order to provide short-term profit at a cost of long-term ecological concerns'. A consumer might describe it as 'a system to provide me with cheap, convenient and tasty produce that my family and I can eat wherever and whenever we want'.

All these definitions of a farming system are strongly held and all have some truth to them. The definition chosen by politicians and then adopted as 'the' definition thereafter may well decide the way in which whole populations and generations develop. For example, in the UK we have seen a changing emphasis amongst politicians from the definition of the farmer to that of the consumer.

'System' is a term applied by actors to a context and its meaning will vary with the actor and with the actor's perception. This raises the important issue that sustainability is a concept that encourages multiple perceptions of meaning. In this work we were determined not to simplify or reduce this complexity of meaning.

What do we mean by sustainable development? Sustainable development is defined by Blue Plan as follows (a mix of Brundtland's definition and the FAO's):

> *A development which is respectful of the environment, technically appropriate, economically viable and socially acceptable to meet the needs of present generations without compromising the ability of future generations to meet their own needs.* (UNEP/MAP/Blue Plan, 2000, p4)

Note the addition of 'economically viable' and 'socially acceptable' to the usual emphasis on futurity.

Part of the work of the project was to test the understanding of this idea in the Maltese context and explore its implications as a cost and an issue to local people. Having said this, one should note that local Maltese participants were not invited to come up with their own definition. At an early meeting one Maltese stakeholder questioned if Malta needed or wanted to be sustainable, but the term was not defined at this time so it is unclear what was actually meant. Questioning at this fundamental level and so early on indicated that the teams would face a major task in establishing the legitimacy of the project processes.

What are sustainability indicators? This has been covered in depth in Chapters 1 and 2, but from the perspective of Blue Plan:

> *Sustainability indicators (SIs) have been variously designed to measure impacts of practice and policy. There is a vast literature on this subject and little agreement on matters of detail but it can be argued that indicators have as their primary aim the need to give useful information about:*
>
> * *The **State** of the environment as well as social, economic and ecological components of development and changes observed.*
> * ***Pressures** which act to the detriment of an already degraded status by breaking the highly fragile balance between development and the environment. These pressures can also be essential **Driving Forces** for economic and social development whose impact on the condition of the environment is not directly perceivable or quantifiable.*
> * *Economic, political and institutional **Responses** which aim to reduce these pressures and improve the situation.*

> *Sustainability indicators are intended to give the level of sustainability in the past, for the current situation and in the future according to certain assumptions about change and evolution. The definition of the level of sustainability for any given indicator is a difficult task which assumes an acute knowledge of both the indicator and of its milieu. Developing and evaluating indicators is further complicated because this process as applied in the current context is being undertaken in a subjective and participatory manner.* (UNEP/MAP/Blue Plan, 2000, p5)

Note the focus on the classic (Chapter 2) pressure–state–response (PSR) framework in this definition. This framework commonly appears throughout the literature, but does have its problems (Chapter 2). Also note the clear emphasis on the use of indicators within an 'impacts of practice and policy' context, rather than in terms of community learning. This had repercussions that we will come back to later.

Another theme evident in the definition of sustainability indicators is the focus on participation. From the perspective of the authors, and indeed Blue Plan, such indicators are not to be developed in a remote and top-down manner. Whenever possible the objective is to include views and multiple perceptions and feed back these views to the stakeholders in the project. Hence indicators should not be presented by powerful stakeholders as a fait accompli. Rather, they should be derived from shared understandings concerning matters of mutual concern. And what is meant by SSA?

> *SSA combines the main themes of systemic analysis and core elements from sustainability indicators, ie it allows a team engaged in analysis to explore, describe and assess the level of sustainability of an agreed system by the use of indicators, in the past, present and future . . . By definition, SSA provides a global approach and has a dynamic characteristic because it takes into account the relations between the indicators which describe the elements of the system and their interactions. The system is represented by indicators chosen by the team of participatory stakeholders engaged in the SSA. The external context is considered in terms of beneficial or harmful influence. The level of sustainability is assessed by the team according to a deep understanding of the relevance and interpretation of the combined messages of the selected sustainability indicators. A view of the sustainability of the system can be built by the use of systems diagrams. The sustainability of the system can be monitored over time. Periodical re-examination is necessary in order to take into consideration changes occurring over time.* (UNEP/MAP/Blue Plan, 2000, p5)

The SSA idea is challenging and demanding. It requires local teams to become familiar with tools and techniques and become proficient at managing the approach as a whole. A major requirement is for the approach to be handed over to local stakeholders. In many areas of consultancy and research there remains a divide between 'expert' and team members. Experts can be quite reluctant about their approaches being 'given away'. To some extent this is a justifiable concern. Without restricted access to ideas experts begin to run short of justification, and perhaps even livelihood! However, there is no room for this type of intellectual conceit in SSA. If the approach is to work it has to work for local practitioners. Without this the approach remains rarefied and the preserve of an elite. Such an approach is more likely to generate indicators for the elite and not for the population as a whole, and this is one of the elements of most conventional indicator development methods that the authors are trying to avoid. Many indicator programmes are linear (even if they do espouse a circularity):

participation → sustainability indicators → collection of data → policy

On the other hand, we saw participation as central throughout this process, and instead of a linear process we saw it as truly cyclical. Whether this was achieved in practice will be returned to later, but in practice one couldn't have this unless the tools and techniques are 'owned' by the stakeholders. But even this ownership doesn't guarantee use. I suppose we are looking at a sort of de-professionalization and de-institutionalization of indicators while at the same time trying to help give birth to something that will in itself be self-sustaining.

FAMILIARIZING THE MALTESE SSA TEAM

The second major work being undertaken at this time was the familiarization of the Maltese SSA team with the detail of the approach. It was essential for the Blue Plan team to agree on core terms, but when these were provided as working definitions it was possible to go on to explain the detail of the SSA itself. From the outset it was agreed with Blue Plan and the Maltese government that the SSA would be undertaken in a manner that was commensurate with the need for the local project to learn from its own activity and to develop an approach which was internally reflective. This is important to emphasize and also to note that such an approach can be contradictory to the nature of much contemporary project thinking as highlighted above. To this end, the two years of activities that were set out in the traditional Blue Plan phases of understand, explore and suggest correlated to the form of an action learning cycle (variously described but see Kolb, 1984; Bell, 1996; Paton, 2001). This cycle, used extensively throughout this book, originating in the work of Kolb, sets out a four-fold process of reflecting on the current situation, connecting with other forms of knowledge, experimenting with the new understanding, and acting. All such cycles are expected to be continuous, with each process of action being followed by subsequent reflection and learning. The cycle underpins the SSA itself, but in the technical document it is used as a means to organize the activities of the SSA. In brief, the SSA activity was organized in the following four phases:

Phase 1: Definition and knowledge of the system: Reflecting

In a first step, we will consider the system as a whole, recognizing that it is (for the purpose of this project) represented by the five thematic activities which are sub-systems.

A training or 'kick off' workshop will be held at the beginning of the activity. This workshop will permit a wide range of stakeholders to discuss the system in terms of

relevance and consistency, to change or add elements if necessary, to have presentations and participatory training concerning SSA (systemic analysis, sustainability, sustainability indicators, etc) which will be vital for the implementation of the activity. After this workshop, the project will require a series of follow-up activities:

- *To delimit the boundaries of the sub-systems and their elements as well as the indicators which represent them and the actors who control them.*
- *To define the number of indicators, which should be between 15 and 20 for each sub-system. The MCSD list[2] as well as Planning Authority's report will be a basis for this choice, however this is not exhaustive as it will be opened to other indicators resulting from conversations with stakeholders.*
- *To calculate each indicator over a long period (possibly many years). Relationships and actors have to be understood and valued.*
- *To identify the external context in term of various influences.*

This work will be led and accomplished by the SSA team in close relations with the five thematic activities. The SSA team will be guided and assisted by Blue Plan SSA team leader.

As these activities begin to generate information, a meeting will be held to discuss the results, to examine the relevance of the whole and if necessary to change or add indicators. After that, key indicators (15 to 20) will be identified, among the 75 to 100 already studied, as well as relationships and main actors.

Training Workshop could be held on 27–28–29 March 2000.

The second working meeting could be held in September 2000. (UNEP/ MAP/Blue Plan, 2000, p7)

As an aside, this first phase is self-evidently exploratory but does show signs of top-down determination of indicator numbers; why is 15 to 20 seen as a good range? As mentioned in Chapter 2, there is a sort of unreasoned assumption commonly expressed in a range of sources that the desirable number of such indicators be approximately 20. Note also the predetermination of dates and schedules prior to any work being undertaken and any results being forthcoming.

These are not meant to be negative or critical points, but they do show the form of reality that project environments impose on teams and indicate areas where such environments might militate against participatory design, particularly when one is dealing with such a diverse and contested area as SD.

Phase 2: Identification and representation of the level of sustainability: Connecting

The SSA team will need to identify an acceptable and feasible band of equilibrium for each key indicator. This will allow the team to have a schematic representation of the level of sustainability for the system as a whole. This representation can be undertaken for the past and present situation and undertaken in such a manner as to underline trends, pressures on the environment and crucial points.

Phase 2 will be ongoing over a three to four month period, September to December 2000. A large meeting (two days) could be held in January 2001 . . .

Phase 3: Future of key indicators: Modelling and experiencing

Trends and projections over 10, 15, 20 or 25 years will identify for each key indicator possible future situations and the resulting problems and opportunities for sustainable development. Images of future trends will be drawn at this stage.

From this trend information, desirable future outcomes will be defined and key indicators' objectives identified as well as the actions necessary to achieve these objectives.

Phase 3 will be ongoing over a four to five month period. A large meeting is expected to take place in June 2001.

Phase 4: Elaboration of a monitoring programme for the system within the CAMP project: Experiencing and reflecting again

This ultimate phase will constitute the output of the activity and will be also very important for the CAMP project as a whole. The objective is to propose a process which will follow progress or downturns towards sustainable development according to the key indicators.

This will be achieved by assessing the level of sustainability for key indicators according to a selected time span and by a periodical re-examination of key indicators' objectives and necessary actions, depending on achieved results.

Phase 4 will be ongoing over a six-month period. Final report could be presented in December 2001. (UNEP/MAP/Blue Plan, 2000, p8)

Again the language of the report, appropriate for such documents ('phase **will** constitute', 'This **will** be achieved') indicates a potential dislocation between the ethos of SSA (and indeed SD) and conventional project design.

The three Blue Plan phases integrated with the four stages of the Kolb learning cycle when applied to SSA provided a practical schedule for the work of the various teams.

Author's diary

It seems to me that the process is well set up at this stage. With agreement with Blue Plan on what we mean by terms . . . and a learning cycle roll-out of the SSA, the process seems clear. My worry is the capacity and willingness of the team in-country to do SSA given their existing workloads – we shall see.

The concern expressed above relating to the meaning of the word 'systemic' remains a constant cause of concern. Generally, 'systemic' means holistic and widely embracing of the relationships that make up situations that are appreciated as complex. 'Systematic' tends to mean that which is procedural: a cook book (step 1 is followed by step 2, which in turn is followed by step 3, etc). Of course the two can work together and it is often possible for systemic approaches to be applied in a systematic manner. However, to mistake one for the other would be to reduce the inclusive and systemic approach of SSA, an approach which can learn from its own activity, to a deterministic cook book approach of joining the dots. The potential for confusion on this point was constantly monitored by the authors.

In many ways the planning for CAMP Malta was a refreshing experience. Blue Plan showed imagination and courage in supporting the SSA approach and provided a positive environment for the collaboration that marked the three years of the project experience.

With the SSA firmly defined and agreed between Blue Plan and the authors as the procedure to be undertaken, a learning process to be engaged with and a timetable to be complied with, the first workshop for the core Maltese SSA team was seen as being a highly important event. The purpose of this event was to introduce a team to the use and application of the SSA. This also included what might not have been an insignificant task, that of convincing local professionals that this approach was worth investing their time and effort in! After all, the SSA approach remained at this time an untried and largely theoretical structure without local approval or acceptance. At this time it was not known what trade-off activity or negotiation would be necessary to gain wider approval.

The additional pressure on the authors at that time was not inconsiderable, mainly because the use of SSA as defined for the Blue Plan project in Malta was at the time completely untested in the field. Elements of it had been applied in various parts of the world (notably Pakistan and Nigeria), and many of the tools and techniques to be described here had been tested to destruction in other contexts, but at the time of the first workshop for the core SSA team in February 2000 the entire approach had never been used before. Furthermore, it had been envisaged (originally by the authors in 1996) that SSA might provide the basis for sustainability indicator software. The concept behind this was to provide a user-friendly front end (something like Microsoft's Excel) for data input, which could then create visual images including the holistic AMOEBA presentation of a range of indicators.

The workshop had a number of objectives. For example, to clearly define answers to the following questions:

• Who are we?
• What do we want to do?
• How can we do the project which we want to do?
• Select and agree on approach?
• What procedures will we apply to do project?

Note that the 'we' in the above list refers to everyone present at the workshop and was not meant to be a set of lectures informing those present what had to be done!

The workshop made use of soft systems methodology (SSM) to make the most of the event and to arrive at answers to the questions cited. SSM was used throughout the project and constituted the main workshop approach. We made use of it as a means to develop a shared vision of what we as a team intended to do.

Author's diary

Yet again I find myself making use of SSM and yet again I use it as feels best rather than running back to the texts for precise guidance. I am not sure I would want to read it all again now. I know that SSM works for me best 'organically' in context. I am not sure I could do an orthodox, cook book version of SSM now.

As mentioned in Chapter 1, SSM and its users have their critics. However, the authors were more concerned to make use of an approach which they had confidence in rather than advocating a single approach as definitively 'correct'.

In an overall sense the elements of SSM at this stage worked in practice as follows. An initial roundtable discussion provided the opportunity for participants to introduce themselves and their vision of the project context. Throughout it was seen as essential that the team 'own' its view on this. While members of the same team may have different perspectives, this was not a problem and the emphasis was on allowing the members to share their views.

From the discussion the team drew out tasks (things that needed to be done) and issues (things which can get in the way of the things needing to be done).

For example, the SSA team produced a series of issues of concern to them:

- *There is a need for an integrated, strategic management plan.*
- *There is agreed need for long-term, wide area, wide dissemination of the sustainability concept and practices.*
- *This must be both practical and pragmatic, providing usable tools and techniques.* (Bell and Coudert, 2000, p5)

Arising from the tasks and issues, the SSA team were encouraged to draw out some definite system of interest to them which would be the basis for the work which would follow. Again, multiple perspectives would have to be brought to the fore and the process is one of enrichment of ideas followed by an agreed focusing on core issues. This agreed 'core' was then refined into a vision statement or root definition of what would follow. The first step to achieving this is to produce an outline of:

- Who is to be the **client** or customer for the project?
- Who are to be the main **actors** or change agents?
- What is to be the main **transformation** to be achieved by the project?
- What is the key assumption or **worldview** behind the transformation?
- Who will be the eventual project **owner**?
- Under what **environmental** constraints will this all occur?

The team came up with the following definition:

> The **client** for the SSA: initially for the first two years, the clients for the SSA are the five projects, extending into a national level. Outreach would need to be considered after two years. An agreed learning process would need to be engaged in.
>
> The main **actors** in the SSA: initially the members of the core team and then developing into the wider five teams. This may be the basis of the March meeting. Possibly after this there will be further professionals included in each project team.
>
> The **transformation** we are seeking to bring about contains a five-fold set of activities. To provide the five project teams with **understanding** of and **competency** in the use of SSA, with a view to **co-developing** and **testing** a series of SIs for wider **application**.
>
> The main assumptions [**worldview**] behind the transformation. That the five main activities indicated in the transformation are **accepted, complied** with and **implemented**.
>
> The eventual **owner** of the SSA. This it was thought would be the Environmental Protection Department, the Economic Planning Division, the Central Office of Statistics and the Planning Authority. These are all co-owners of the process. Further, Blue Plan has some temporary ownership of resources and the project coordinator . . . . . has a leadership role.
>
> The (**environmental**) constraints on the SSA transformation we are trying to achieve. These were considered to be four-fold – access to sensitive information, lack of cooperation from data providers, data quality and timeliness and shifting priorities. (Bell and Coudert, 2000, p6)

The six features set out above and usually referred to in soft systems literature as CATWOE (client, actors, transformation, worldview, owner and environmental constraints) criteria were then developed into an overall statement or root definition for the project. In this case it is a restatement of the transformation:

> To provide the five project teams with **understanding** of and **competency** in the use of SSA, with a view to **co-developing** and **testing** a series of SIs for wider **application**.

This was the basis from which the use of SSA developed.

WHAT ARE SSA AND SPSA AND HOW ARE THEY DIFFERENT?

The origins, structure and processes of SSA are largely the topic of the earlier book produced by the authors in this series (Bell and Morse, 1999). SSA was a complete methodology, based on SSM, designed to develop sustainability indicators in a participatory manner. SSA was originally designed to deal with all stages of the learning cycle, reviewing past experience, planning and modelling for the present and looking to develop and change in the light of what is learned. In this sense SSA has reflection, futurity, systemism and modelling all included.

However, for the purposes of the Maltese project, there was from the outset a need to adapt SSA to reflect the values and concerns of Blue Plan and to include elements which had been used before in Blue Plan projects elsewhere. We have already noted the desire of Blue Plan to focus on using indicators to measure impacts of practice and policy, and Blue Plan was particularly keen on scenario planning as an approach within this. It had already developed a range of multiple scenarios that could emerge for different regions within the Mediterranean, for example Sfax in Tunisia. Combined with mapping and even GIS techniques to help visualization, such 'what if' planning can be a provocative and powerful tool (Chapter 1). This required a modification of the original SSA to reflect such an emphasis. The resulting approach is defined here as SPSA (systemic and prospective sustainability analysis, with 'prospective' stressing extrapolation in order to consider multiple scenarios). For the purposes of setting out a clear definition it is important to set out the main elements of SPSA here. Figure 3.4 provides an overall 'look' at the SPSA.

The figure is an adaptation of the original SSA model but clearly shows a 12-point process involving a major and minor cycle of activity. To provide greater clarity, the figure was redesigned as a simple cycle, and this is shown in Figure 3.5.

In Figure 3.5 the twin cycles are combined and the Kolb learning cycle can be seen more clearly. It is apparent that SPSA requires periods of reflecting on existing learning, connecting with the views of stakeholders, etc, modelling an AMOEBA or similar device for demonstrating the outcomes of indicator development and acting

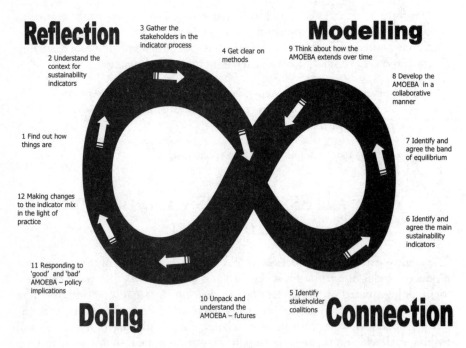

Figure 3.4 *SPSA in outline*

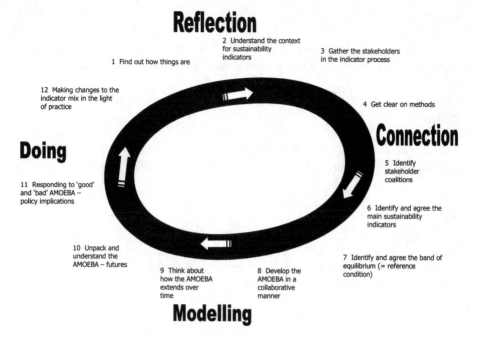

Figure 3.5 *The revised view of the SPSA*

in which populations are invited to make what they will from the 'story' of the indicators.

As SPSA was the flavour of SSA that was implemented in Malta, it will be referred to (rather than SSA) in Chapters 3 and 4. The 12 stages of SPSA as shown can be explained briefly as follows, and are set out in Table 3.1.

Stage 1

Find out how things are. This is the preliminary stage, where the analyst or facilitator of the SPSA process demonstrates openness to the context in seeking to find out as much as possible about the current situation in the context where SPSA is to be undertaken.

Stage 2

Understand the context for SIs. We have already described in this and in our previous book that SIs are not one thing and are not experienced by stakeholders as uncontestable. In this stage the value of such indicators in the current context is questioned.

Stage 3

Gather the stakeholders in the SI process. This usually refers to the internal stakeholders in the SPSA team. A preliminary review of context and potential problems.

Stage 4

Get clear on methods. In this stage the various elements of the SPSA are described and discussed. Any changes to the toolkit are best agreed at this stage.

Stage 5

Identify stakeholder coalitions. This means the identification of both internal (project related) and external (concerned and or interested) parties. This should be largely agreed by now for the internal stakeholders.

Stage 6

Identify and agree the main SIs. A large part of the following notes will be concerned with this activity. As a note of clarification it can be said here that the SIs developed within the SPSA approach arise from a participatory overview of the current situation by use of SSM.

Stage 7

Identify and agree the band of equilibrium. The band of equilibrium can be seen as both an agreed reference condition for sustainability and also as an aspiration. Items which arise around this include the management of expectation around the band. What is realistic and feasible as well as being desirable? At this point the wider stakeholder group agrees the reference conditions for the various indicators. The idea of the band of equilibrium is fully described in our previous book but for the purposes of a brief description, the thematic teams initially and later the wider stakeholder group are encouraged to consider how the indicators' outcomes could be considered. There are three possible outcomes for the value of an indicator relative to its band:

1 Outside the band and on the wrong side for sustainability. For example, an unsustainably high fishing catch or a level of water pollution that is too high. This is under-attainment.
2 Inside the band (equilibrium). This may be an agreed, sustainable fishing catch or an acceptable level of water pollution. This is usually a range and not a fixed figure, although it could, in theory at least, be a single figure.

3   Outside the band but on the right side for sustainability. For example, a lower fishing catch than what may be acceptable for sustainability, or perhaps a lower level of water pollution than what may be acceptable. In a sense this represents over-achievement, but may not necessarily be good news! For example, it could come at a cost if achieved at the expense of not dealing with another indicator that happens to be on the wrong side of the band.

The setting of the band of equilibrium is intended to be a participative process and is certainly not a scientific or objective undertaking. Hence terms such as 'acceptable' and 'agreed' that appear in the above points. Much depends, of course, on exactly who thinks it is acceptable. In practice one would likely see a mixture of such stakeholder reference conditions for indicators alongside those that are set by legislation (Malta is adopting the EU standards for many indicators, such as water quality).

However, there does obviously need to be care. After all, fishermen may wish to have a 'sustainable' catch (in their eyes) much higher than could be sustainable in a biological sense. They may be willing to see the resource destroyed in the medium/long term provided they get short-term gain. We are not saying that the band should only be set by fishermen. However, a key notion here is that the voices which influence the setting of the band should include all those with a reasonable stake in the undertaking. If this approach had been followed in the setting of the sustainable yield for the fishing in the North Sea then we argue that the task would have been undertaken by a mixed forum including fishermen and scientists. This would undoubtedly have made the negotiation process much more complex but it might have resulted in better management of expectations. At the very least it would have provided a forum where all could share their perspectives and allowed a better understanding of constraints and limits.

One should also note that the term 'equilibrium' does not imply stasis. We fully accept that an acceptable band can, and indeed should, change with time. As technology improves or as people's needs and ambitions change, then so should the reference condition.

Following the agreement on the band of equilibrium, all further analysis is engaged with finding out what SIs are and what this means in terms of sustainability.

Stage 8

Develop the AMOEBA in a collaborative manner. All development of sustainability indicators and the presentation of them in a visual format (about which there will be much more to say shortly) needs to be agreed. For the purpose of brief description the form of visual presentation selected in Malta was the AMOEBA (Chapter 2). The AMOEBA is a diagramming device intended to show all indicators and their bands of equilibrium in a single format (Figure 3.6). The 'circle and arm' style of indicator presentation has been commonly applied in the SD literature (Chapter 2).

In this diagram the band of equilibrium is set as the circle in the centre. The 16 indicators cover four general areas of concern: society, environment, technology and economy. Indicators for these four could be, respectively, levels of alienation, erosion, automobile pollution and poverty.

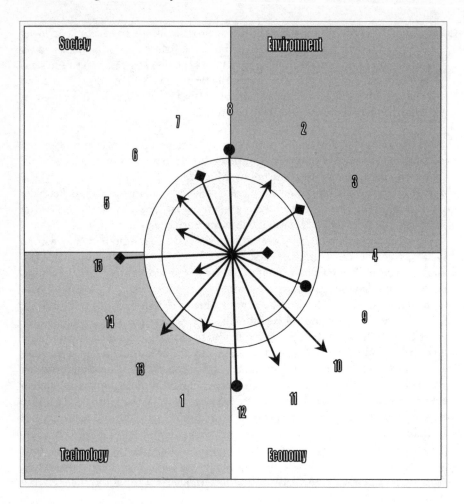

Figure 3.6 *AMOEBA and sustainability indicators*

Again, we do not wish to imply that our use of the AMOEBA somehow suggests that this is the only or indeed best such device. Indeed, current thinking in SD is tending to favour devices such as the sustainability dashboard. We rejected this particular device only because we wanted to keep each indicator clearly identifiable so as to allow an evolution of indicator choice during the project. Over-aggregation would tend to hide the indicators that had been selected and inhibit any further discussion over their selection. Our concern was to be able to clearly demonstrate how indicators combined together to give an overall 'vision' of the sustainability of a given context, but at the same time allow the users to disaggregate the vision with ease. This device needed to be both visually impressive and holistic in terms of its content. The AMOEBA seemed to offer this, and in addition could be easily generated with widely available software (the AMOEBA is a variant of the RADAR chart type available in Microsoft Excel). In the work described in the next chapter we show how our field work with the Blue

Plan in Malta led to the development of a simple macro programming device (from within Microsoft Excel) for teams to input the indicator data and produce AMOEBAs such as that shown above.

Stage 9

Think about how the AMOEBA extends over time. The real value of indicators is not so much related to any one snapshot of the current situation, even if powerfully presented against stakeholder views of an equilibrium state. Rather, the collection of a number of indicators extending over time provides insights into the fluctuation of sustainability, and this is the beginning of the search for trends.

Stage 10

Unpack and understand the AMOEBA: scenario-planning potential. At this point the value of the scenario-planning aspect of SPSA can reveal a range of options for the future. As already mentioned, Blue Plan was particularly interested in scenario planning and wanted to emphasize this within the original SSA methodology. Such planning may appear as guesswork, which it is to some extent, but nevertheless can provide SPSA teams with valuable means to engage local populations with the outcomes of SIs following policy and management decisions. In that sense it helps provide a direct association between 'doing something' and its outcomes.

This approach basically involves taking an historical set of indicator values and using them to conceptualize a range of possible future trends based on various policy/ managerial interventions. The result may be a set of future possible scenarios. For example, from a scenario-planning exercise (for which we use the appellation 'Prospective' here), three outcomes for a given indicator trend might be:

1   If car numbers show some decline (0.6 per cent/annum) following some active intervention by national government, then overall pollution will decline by 2 per cent and the effect on incidence of respiratory disease will be a reduction of a further 2.2 per cent/annum.
2   If car numbers show the present rate of increase (1.5 per cent/annum) following benign neglect by government, then overall pollution will increase by 1.7 per cent and the effect on incidence of respiratory disease will be an increase of a further 1.4 per cent/annum.
3   If car numbers show an accelerated rate of increase (3 per cent/annum) following active encouragement by government for a 'car owning democracy', then overall pollution will increase by 4 per cent and the effect on incidence of respiratory disease will be an increase of a further 3 per cent/annum.

Such scenarios provide local people with real choices for the sustainability of their future. This is rendered more powerful if the scenario arises from participatory and inclusive processes so people can make the links themselves between policy and outcome rather than expect others to do it. As described in Chapter 1, there may sometimes be a tendency for people to externalize the practical achievement of SD by expecting others to carry the cost or to do it. The result is that people may sometimes appear as nothing more than animated (or indeed passive) spectators of SD rather than the doers. Avoiding such a disentanglement is key to the SPSA approach.

It should be noted that a formal scenario-planning process is not the only way in which people can be kept engaged with practice and outcomes. One could, of course, take more of a reflective practice approach by asking people to dissect and analyse current practice and how this is impacting upon the indicators and sustainability. This is often the approach applied in community learning approaches in SD (Chapter 2). We will return to this later.

Stage 11

Responding to 'good' and 'bad' AMOEBA: policy implications. Options and choices mean implications for policy. The AMOEBA and scenario planning within SPSA can indicate hard choices for the future. At this stage these choices can be discussed in wider public fora. This stage is key to SPSA as it provides local communities with the legitimate power to devise how they will respond to indicators.

Stage 12

Making changes in the indicator mix in the light of practice. Sometimes an indicator does not work or completes its task and there is a need to move on and change the mix. This can be undertaken at this stage with the end of one cycle. Keeping indicators disaggregated within the AMOEBA device helps with this process of continual review. Highly aggregated devices, such as the dashboard, can (in the authors' view) inhibit this process of continual appraisal, and as a result indicators are more likely to become set in stone.

Table 3.1 demonstrates the evolving SPSA as an emergent property of the original SSA and prospective sustainability analysis approaches.

SPSA AND BLUE PLAN APPROACHES

As has already been stated, at the outset of the project Blue Plan made it clear that it already had a favoured approach to the development of and practical use of SIs. This approach has already been alluded to in the previous section as scenario planning or prospective sustainability analysis. As included here, it was taken from the original work of a French practitioner and academic, Michel Godet (Godet et al, 1999), although there are numerous sources for this type of approach. An overview of the Godet version is provided in Figure 3.7.

It is not the purpose of this book to set out the detail of the prospective sustainability analysis approach to scenario planning. However, some overall explanation is important if the process of SPSA given in the next chapter is to be clear. Prospective

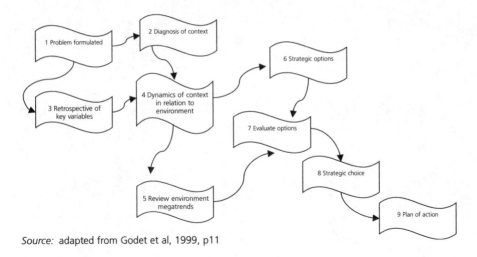

Source: adapted from Godet et al, 1999, p11

Figure 3.7 *Prospective sustainability analysis*

sustainability analysis encourages teams to explore potential futures as logical outcomes relating to the evidence which a SD project produces. Such outcomes or scenarios may be highly variable. For example, a worst case and best case alternative might arise. A scenario is made up of a number of separate features:

- An initial view of the system. This will include: knowledge of the system, including understanding of the evolution and current situation; trends; actors/stakeholders; processes; conflicts; challenges; stakes; and seeds of change.
- The choice of horizons of time.
- The choice of a set of hypotheses of evolution, with criteria of transparency, probability, consistency and relevance.
- Drawing up a pathway, a link between present and future.
- The description of final situation.

Godet's approach had been used in previous CAMPs and had been shown to produce useful outcomes. For example, in a Tunisian example three different scenarios relating to the level of urbanization of the coastal port of Sfax were designed, and GIS-based maps were produced to demonstrate outcomes. Such images can provide stakeholders with powerful visions for possible futures. However, at the same time we feel that it needs to be said that these visions can also be dangerous. After all, one must remember that these outcomes are based on opinion relating to observed trends and are not guaranteed to happen (even if no action were taken). Using GIS and other such technical devices can falsely suggest an objectivity which may simply not be present. The visions can be too powerful!

From this can arise a range of possible policy actions to make change. While this process is participatory and bottom-up, the result is typically policy change that may be outside the power of those involved in the SPSA process. The result may be akin to shooting an arrow into an empty void; you can't see where it went, how fast or what

Table 3.1 *SSA/Blue Plan (BP) training elements and comparison table: the origins of SPSA*

These actors . . .	in SSA stage . . .	use these methods . . .	and these SSM (and other) tools . . .	to achieve the Blue Plan item(s)
SSA and thematic teams	1 Find out how things are	SSM Blue Plan (BP) systemic and prospective approach: understand	Rich picture	Phenomenon studied, internal variables, context of external variables
SSA and thematic teams	2 Understand the context for SIs	SSM BP systemic and prospective approach: understand	Rich picture and root definition	Define the system
SSA and thematic teams and local stakeholders	3 Gather the stakeholders in the SI process	SSM BP systemic and prospective approach: understand	Rich picture, root definition, conceptual models, logical framework	Past and current analysis, relationships between elements of the system
SSA and thematic teams and local stakeholders	4 Get clear on methods	Reflect on the process so far	Reflect on the process so far	Reflect on the process so far
SSA and thematic teams and local stakeholders	5 Identify the stakeholder coalitions	SSM BP systemic and prospective approach: understand – explore	Rich picture Focus groups and informal meetings, role play	Choice of time horizons, choice of evolution assumptions concerning key variables, combination of the assumptions, choice of number and kind of scenarios
SSA and thematic teams and local stakeholders	6 Identify and agree the main SIs	BP indicator development	Pressure, state and response SIs: logical framework	Select a set of indicators, relevance, select prime indicators, calculate initially

SSA and thematic teams and local stakeholders	7 Identify and agree the band of equilibrium	Workshop BP systemic and prospective approach: understand, explore and suggest	Active listening	Elaboration of the scenarios Final images, presentation and discussion of possible strategies
SSA and thematic teams and local stakeholders	8 Develop the AMOEBA in a collaborative manner	Workshop BP systemic and prospective approach: understand, explore and suggest BP indicator development	Active listening, feasibility study, risk analysis	Elaboration of the scenarios Final images, presentation and discussion of possible strategies, recommendations
SSA and thematic teams, possibly local stakeholders	9 Think about how the AMOEBA extends over time	Workshop BP systemic and prospective approach: understand, explore and suggest BP indicator development	Active listening, feasibility study, risk analysis	Elaboration of the scenarios Final images, presentation and discussion of possible strategies, recommendations
SSA and thematic teams, invited stakeholders	10 Unpack and understand the AMOEBA – futures	BP systemic and prospective approach: suggest Monitoring and evaluation BP indicator development	Compare and contrast	Strategic planning
SSA team	11 Responding to 'good' and 'bad' AMOEBA – policy implications	BP systemic and prospective approach: suggest Monitoring and evaluation BP indicator development	Compare and contrast	Strategic planning
SSA and thematic teams and local stakeholders	12 Making changes in the SI mix in the light of practice	SSM BP systemic and prospective approach: suggest BP indicator development	Rich pictures, root definitions and conceptual models, active listening	Strategic planning

Notes: SSA = systemic sustainability analysis; SSM = soft systems method; SI = sustainability indicator it achieved. One could take this in another direction by asking people to reflect on what they currently do and consider how this contributes to sustainability (or unsustainability). This is more of an internal learning process that could also highlight issues that need discussion in a broader policy environment. The two are not mutually incompatible, as thinking of future scenarios could help with such reflection. Whatever the specifics, it is important in SD to keep people connected in terms of what they want, what needs to be done, how and by whom.

Author's diary

I find the Blue Plan approach quite interesting. Prospective sustainability analysis has less to do with the day-to-day operation of the SSA – with digging around for ideas and thoughts about sustainability. Rather, it focuses on the logical outcomes of the indicator process. I think SSA and prospective sustainability analysis could come together rather well. SSA will give us the indicators which local people think are important. Prospective sustainability analysis will allow us to set out a number of possible future scenarios which may follow from the work in hand.

In conversations with the Blue Plan it was decided that SPSA would form the basis for the production and development of sustainability indicators. The team would make use of prospective sustainability analysis as the means to develop scenarios and visions for the future, which can be drawn from the trends evident from the indicators. Again it was expected that SSM workshops would be the means whereby prospective sustainability analysis would be developed.

Table 3.1 is the logical outcome of this integration. The first column indicates who will undertake each stage. In column 2, the 12 stages of SSA are shown. In column 3, the main method used for each stage is set out, and the details of this in terms of tools and techniques is provided in column 4. Column 5 provides the wider Blue Plan goal and shows how the SSA or prospective sustainability analysis aspect fits into this.

Author's diary

This is a major achievement in my mind. Blue Plan have a firm idea of the process it wants and SSA has to work to this if we are to be successful. As it works out, SSA and the Blue Plan approaches seem to come together really well.

With the agreements on terms, integration of SSA and prospective sustainability analysis and the establishment of the core SPSA team in Malta, the process of doing SPSA could now begin. This would prove to be an interesting process, both in terms of making use of the approach now so rigorously agreed and set up, and in terms of adapting and changing in the light of need and following the request of stakeholders. The development of SPSA in Malta is the subject of the next chapter.

Chapter 4

Doing SPSA:
Some Reflective Experience

INTRODUCTION

In this chapter, we want to explore how the systemic and prospective sustainability analysis (SPSA) process played out in practice. To make the navigation of the stages fit with the original plan for the use of SPSA as already described in Chapter 3, and in light of the practicalities of the experience on the ground, we have set out each of the 12 stages in terms of where it fits within the original 12-point learning cycle set out in Figure 3.5, and also within the five substantive reports produced during the project's two-year process.

In this chapter, the stages of SPSA are described:

- as they were applied;
- as they were experienced from a craft point of view by ourselves; and
- as they were experienced by local stakeholders, both in the SPSA team and from within the local community.

Our contention has been that in the sustainability indicator (SI) literature, the craft concerns of consultants and researchers have been under-represented in the hothouse environment of conventional projects seeking 'impact' and 'deliverables' with limited resources and time. Also, and of more concern, the voices of those who aid with the development and roll-out of methodology on the ground have often not been heard at all.

However, the voice which is most significantly under-represented in the dialogue has been that of the local stakeholders, who have to take on board the implications that unpalatable things might be said or implied about the home which they take pride in. These stakeholders have to live with the costs of achieving sustainability or indeed not achieving it. Generally, the literature on SIs is woefully short on the real

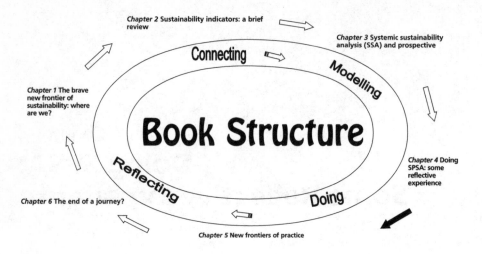

impacts of operations like SPSA. It is assumed that sustainable development (SD) and indicators to help gauge progress towards it are a good thing, and that local populations would be glad to get this important information. The implications for these stakeholders of achieving it or otherwise are rarely discussed.

Our experience in Malta has been that it is true that some elements of the local community share this view. It is also true that some feel that having indicators is rather like having a public health agency inspect your premises for evidence of rats or parasites. It implies ill-health, and this in turn might be a major turn-off to visitors.

Much SI work seems to be stunningly unaware of its own impact on the local community. This can best be explained by a myopia of self-reflection experienced by most practitioners of approaches which are assumed to be self-evidently 'good'. One supplementary point that can be made at this time is the plethora of approaches and acronyms which is evident in the SI literature. Models of best practice abound but often with little apparent critical comparative reflection on what approaches appear to 'work', what we mean by 'work', who says it does, and how it might work better.

This chapter will set out the stages of SPSA implemented in Malta. It should be remembered from Chapter 3 that what was done in Malta was governed by a number of factors, including the agenda of the coastal area management programme (CAMP) projects undertaken in the Mediterranean. The authors were asked to adapt the systemic sustainability analysis (SSA) methodology set out in Bell and Morse (1999) by including an emphasis on scenario planning (prospective sustainability analysis) towards the end of SSA (hence generating SPSA). While the chapter is descriptive in the sense that we wish to tell the reader what we did, it is also analytical in that we wish to analyse why things happened the way they did. Finally we will discuss the results of the SPSA process and what it told us about SD in Malta.[1]

STAGE 1: FIND OUT HOW THINGS ARE: REFLECTION

References: Bell and Coudert (2000); Ellul (2000)

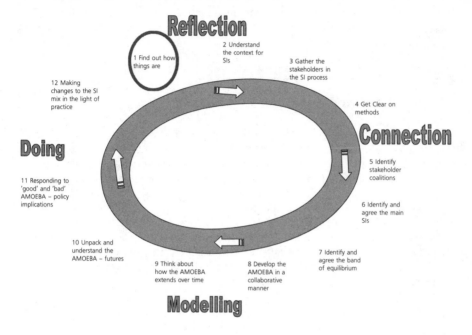

Aims of this stage of SPSA:

- To introduce main actors to each other.
- To scope the context.
- To gain insights.
- To open up the potential of SPSA to local people.
- To listen.

> There are a lot of extremes in Malta: we have environmental associations on one side and politicians and developers on the other side. There has never been an attempt to bring people together, and I very much believe that the way forward is to bring people together. (Comment from a stakeholder at a workshop in October, 2000)

The initial stage of SPSA is to find out about the minds and feelings of those who are working in the local context. To formalize this, one might refer to the stakeholder community but this is going too fast. At this stage the stakeholders within the project and outside the project are not known, and so to use this term would be to prejudge the community of interest. Rather, everyone and everything is considered in the frame of understanding and analysis at this stage. Voices come from many directions.

In Malta, the first stage comprised an inception meeting held in February in Sliema. Those attending the meeting included members of the SPSA team as well as members of all the other thematic teams. The experience of one of the authors is set out below.

Author's diary

The range of voices feeding into my thinking at present is very diverse. The inception meeting was formative in providing me with the formal project view and assumption of the context in mind. To some extent this view is surprising to me. SPSA demands that we think and do differently. Yet all project structures tend to demand a top-down and hierarchic structure which militates against hearing the voices of the real project community. There is a lot to learned here from the Chambers experience. I wonder if the format of the project as conceived is what the local population would consider to be valid?

This raises another issue: I wonder how 'participatory' this project is going to be? (The last note refers to the work of Robert Chambers, who has championed much of the modern focus on participatory approaches.[2])

This first part of the SPSA is a listening stage. It is a time for assessing ideas and speaking widely to as many interested parties as possible. Our experience led us to talk to several distinct groups:

- The Blue Plan team;
- delegates from the Priority Actions Programme Regional Activity Centre (PAP RAC);
- Maltese government officials;
- thematic team members; and
- local people.

The local take on the SPSA process is interesting in hindsight. Here are some views of one of the original Maltese SPSA team.

The first time I got involved in the SSA exercise, now called the SPSA, I could not imagine the involvement and commitment this would entail. The matter of SIs was familiar to me and from experience, [but] the identification of such indicators has always been an exercise carried out by experts. The SPSA has brought in a wider part-icipation in this exercise through the involvement of stakeholders and hence brings into the picture a wider understanding of the concept of SD and how this relates to the requirements and perception of the different stakeholders.

The need for SPSA to be participatory would continue to raise issues of time, effort and inclusion throughout the process. However, at this point no particular voices dominated but distinct themes did arise. We noted these as questions/themes not to be avoided or misplaced as the project develops:

- What is sustainability?
- Whose project is this?
- Does Malta want to be sustainable?
- What does unsustainable look and feel like?
- How much work will this involve?
- Do we get paid to do it, and if not who will do my existing work while I take on this extra responsibility?
- What is SPSA and how do we know it will work?

In the view of the authors these are all valid and powerful questions.

Another means to find out how team members in particular assess how things are is to make use of the first major tool within soft systems methodology (SSM): the 'rich picture'. In the early meetings and workshops, participants were introduced to methods for sharing their thoughts and expressing their concerns in such a manner that they could be discussed with and reviewed by colleagues. The rich picture is always a difficult tool to apply in the early stages. Adults tend to think that such diagram types are silly or childish. It is only when the picture is drawn and the outcomes shared with other teams that, amid the laughter, major themes of importance are raised and new foci for shared concern raised. An example of some of the work undertaken by the teams is set out in Figure 4.1.

It is worth noting at this point that many projects working in many contexts run on an assumption of the availability and interest of local staff. This is by no means restricted to SI projects. There is often an agreement between donors and local ministries that team members will be made available, but this is often (in our experience) without the consent, or even at times knowledge, of local staff. The problems that this apparently minor logistical issue can develop are legion. For example, secondment without release from other duties can result in tasks such as SPSA being seen as an add-on (at best) and expendable (at worst). This could affect targets and result in some teams being behind others in progress (with consequent effects on morale). Overall, project activities, in this case SPSA, could be relegated in the minds of the team to a secondary activity, and this could knock on to respective stakeholders.

It is not necessary here to go into the detail of the picture presented in Figure 4.1. However, it is useful to note the wealth of emotion and content which is described. In the picture are concerns for tourism, the wellbeing of local people, and the need to develop the island as a home for full-time residents as well as a playground for wealthy north Europeans. There is also the idea of a clock ticking away; there is an imperative that something needs to be done. The authors were most interested in the candour and passion which this early work evidenced. It did seem that the project was timely, offering the chance to review the current situation and review options in the light of a common understanding that 'something needs to be done'.

Stages 1 and 2 often ran together in the SPSA. The main differentiation between them is that Stage 1 is totally unstructured whereas Stage 2 involves working with the key teams of actors in the SI process and making more explicit use of SSM.

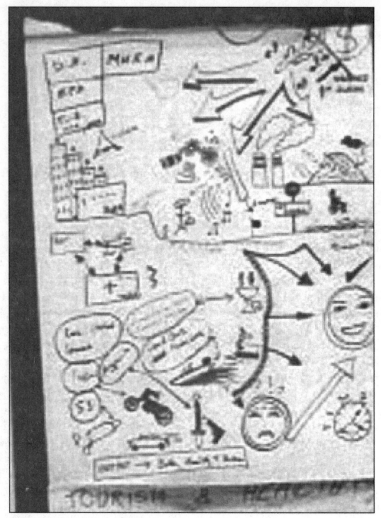

[low-resolution enlargement]

Figure 4.1 *An early rich picture*

Learning outcomes of this stage of SPSA:

- Understanding of local concerns.
- Insights into issues.
- Appreciation of the practicality of SPSA in this context.

SPSA craft points arising from Stage 1:

- Meet early and allow everyone and their view to be included and respected.
- Encourage participation.
- Use soft systems to map out the feelings about the context.

STAGE 2: UNDERSTAND THE CONTEXT FOR SUSTAINABILITY INDICATORS: REFLECTION/CONNECTION

References: Bell and Coudert (2000); Ellul (2000)

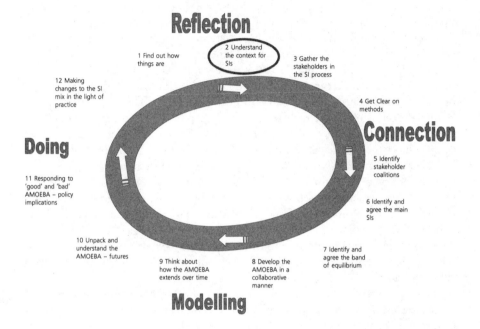

Aims of this stage of SPSA:

- To assess the context with others.
- To review multiple perspectives of the context.
- To assess local thinking about SPSA and SIs.
- To begin to scope the potential for the use of SPSA.

All processes of team working and collaborative learning require the integration of the SPSA team with the wider thematic teams and the still wider stakeholder community. From the outset this was problematic.

> The main failing, which otherwise would have led to a smoother process, was that the various (thematic) teams perceived this exercise as an added burden. In future, any such projects should include the SPSA as part of the thematic project and would therefore meet with more support and commitment. Stakeholders should also be involved in the drafting of the project proposal to ensure collaboration and post-project continuity. (Comment from one of the core SPSA team members)

This was to remain an issue for the rest of the project process. With hindsight it might have been wise to have formally included the widest stakeholder participation from the outset in the SPSA activity. Certainly there should have been some form of representation. At the time this was avoided because SPSA itself was so untested it was thought best to consolidate it in the mind of the main SPSA and thematic teams first to remove any possible points of confusion before they developed.

This in turn indicates the conventional project mentality that we, the authors, and the project team were experiencing. We were trying to get our approach to work and to be right. This is completely justifiable and appropriate for project approaches. However, in hindsight a more questioning and exploratory approach might have been more consistent with the espoused use of SPSA.

The purpose of the use of SSM at this stage was to allow thematic teams to work together with the SPSA team to define the key ideas behind sustainability and hence the indicators which they were likely to want to develop. This itself presupposes the understanding of the thematic teams. A large part of the workshop held in March of 2000 (Ellul, 2000) was to allow teams to share thinking and gain an overview of the demands which the SPSA process would put upon them. From the start it was to be understood that SPSA was not an activity to be undertaken only by the SPSA team, but rather it was an additional task for all those engaged in the CAMP. As can be seen from the team member above, this was not successfully communicated in all cases and there began a regular process of hounding thematic team members to attend the SPSA events. Concerns over who would or wouldn't attend meetings began to dominate discussions amongst the authors and SPSA team members. It should be noted that lack of attendance was not indicative of a lack of interest, but largely due to a clash with other duties.

The experience of the wider team and ourselves was that events went well and seemed to stimulate wide-ranging and insightful comments and understandings. Yet it must be remembered that the authors only visited the island for relatively short blocks of time – usually only a few days spaced out by some months. During those intensive periods of engagement by the authors things went well. The author's notes from this time do not yet allude to the emerging problem of attendance.

Author's diary

I am really pleased with the way in which the various teams are coming together. One un-looked-for bonus is the way in which SPSA is encouraging teams to share thinking and to talk together. Several of the thematic team members have said that the SPSA has allowed them to talk to colleagues for the first time. Serendipity could be a major aid to the task.

Possibly the main outcomes of this stage were the root definitions or visions for the way forward which were produced by the teams. Two of these, provided by the 'tourism impacts on health' and 'sustainable coastal management' thematic teams, are set out below.

> *Tourism impacts on health thematic team: The group started by identifying the mission statement for the project on tourism and health: An environmental health project designed and enacted by the WHO Collaborating Centre for the Tourism Ministry to understand the health impacts on tourists using the coastal zone, and to improve policy. Assuming willingness to make changes, under constraints imposed by stakeholders and existing knowledge to be owned by Mediterranean Action Plan (MAP), government agencies* (Ellul, 2000, p16)

> *The sustainable coastal management project is an 'umbrella' project in that it relates and coordinates the other projects to ensure integration. Therefore, it was agreed to prepare a project design to establish a participatory coastal planning and management system which achieves more policy integration among thematic activities. The root definition and the mission statement was defined as such: A sustainable coastal management project, owned by MAP/government, developed by CAMP teams with local stakeholders, for affected interest groups, to achieve balanced development and integrated policy-making, assuming public participation, support and political will under constraints of social inertia, economic growth pressures and sectoral thinking.* (Ellul, 2000, p18)

What is perhaps most striking about the reports from the teams is not the focus on indicators but that the definitions relate to the working of the teams as a whole. It became evident as the project progressed that many of the teams had never had an opportunity to really consider the tasks they had been asked to undertake, at least not in a systemic manner. Teams seemed keen to grasp the opportunity to think about their project from the widest angle. Most thematic teams seemed to experience a double life with regards to the CAMP project. On the one hand they had their thematic team duties. For many of them these were routine and consisted of applying their existing skills and capabilities to this specific project. On the other hand they were being asked to engage in an holistic and new experience called SPSA which encouraged them to think widely about their work and to coordinate with other teams.

Such sharing of old and new, familiar and unfamiliar was bound to develop tensions and new forms of thinking. One interesting insight was how, faced with having to consider the unfamiliar territory of SPSA, some individuals sought to refer to the familiar. We have already alluded to the dominance of the pressure–state–response (PSR) mindset in indicator development (Chapter 2), and indeed how Blue Plan highlighted this in their project documentation. The PSR framework does have advantages, notably its mechanical formality, and some team members began by dividing a sheet of paper into three columns with 'pressure', 'state' and 'response' as headings. The process then became one of filling in the columns with 'standard' indicators from memory! It took time to gradually wean them away from such textbook rigidity and to think more organically about their context and issues as a first step.

Certainly this process provided the team with a more focused view of the context for the indicators. Stage 3 now followed with the stakeholder thematic teams engaging in a deeper understanding of the tasks to be undertaken to develop such indicators.

Learning outcomes of this stage of SPSA:

- Clarity in the understanding of the internal SPSA teams.
- Craft skills in the use of SPSA.
- Co-understanding across the teams of their various needs and problems.

SPSA craft points arising from Stage 2:

- Allow teams to understand their core business better – don't just focus on SIs.
- Use soft systems to allow teams to define their purpose.
- Engage in preliminary conversations about the tasks needed to be undertaken in order to develop SPSA later.

STAGE 3: GATHER THE STAKEHOLDERS IN THE SUSTAINABILITY INDICATOR PROCESS: REFLECTION/CONNECTION

References: Bell and Coudert, 2000; Ellul, 2000.

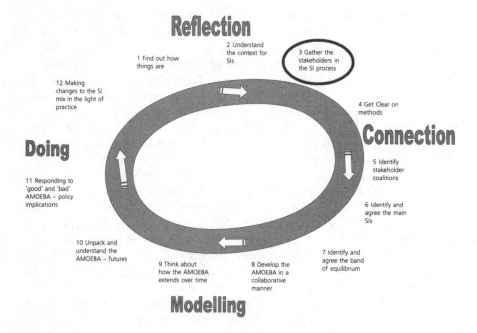

Aims of this stage of SPSA:

- To talk to stakeholders in the project teams.
- To assess views.
- To begin joint use of SPSA.

Initially the stakeholders engaged in the SPSA process comprised the internal, thematic teams. Later, the wider community was brought more inclusively into the process.

Author's diary

It would be great to have wider stakeholder involvement at this stage but in our view the process is not yet robust enough to gain the wider vision. There is room in SPSA for the external stakeholders to be engaged later on. From our angle it would be great to have them now but we are not prepared for the event.

A reflection on the reflection above is that, as noted earlier, SPSA is expected to work, and experimentation within a project context is not to be encouraged beyond a certain point.

At this point in the SPSA process the initial rich pictures and root definitions were developed further with conceptual models and, in some cases, Logical Frameworks for the development of the indicators. We will say more about Logical Frameworks shortly. Conceptual models are developed in soft systems thinking. The conceptual model is an activity model. All components or 'blobs' are verb-based, ideally begin with a verb, and set out the range of things that need to be done. The diagram is more than a task list however, as it demonstrates the activities which need to be set against the issues and tasks described in the original rich picture. Activities can be developed to deal with issues as well as addressing tasks. The thematic teams, as major stakeholders in the SPSA enterprise, were requested to develop their thinking and also to engage with the thinking of other thematic teams to compare their experience of the process to date. One example of the level of work that was undertaken by the sustainable coastal management thematic team is set out in Figure 4.2.

Author's diary

Seems to me that we are making really good progress; better than I could have hoped for given the number of teams we are having to work with. I have yet to see if the indicator work which we have begun can be seen through to completion and if the effort which we manage to elicit at workshops is maintained in the downtime between visits.

I must admit that the most interesting part of the whole CAMP activity was in fact the SPSA activity. Workshops were fun, highly interactive and, more than any other workshop, managed to keep us away from those occasional snoozes, so common during long presentations. The whole process through which the indicators were developed was innovative for me and my team, and definitely gave us all a sense of ownership and responsibility about what we were actually trying to do. The innovative way of tackling problems etc through diagrams made the issues so much easier to visualize and definitely brought out the best in us. Team work was at its best, something that is very lacking here in Malta due to our small size and a culture of 'protecting one's turf', and by the end of your first seminar, we all felt that we were rowing the same boat in the same direction. (Comment from a member of one of the thematic teams)

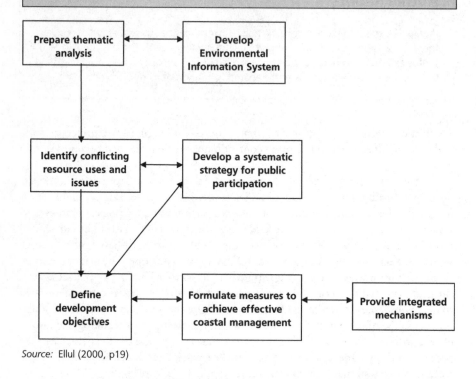

Source: Ellul (2000, p19)

Figure 4.2 *Thematic teams conceptual model*

A tool which had been planned to take on and develop the conceptual model was the Logical Framework, or Logframe. Logframes are described in great detail elsewhere.[3] For the purpose of this brief description, the framework is a four-by-four matrix (Table 4.1). The framework provides three views of a project. In the first column is the formal narrative, the story of what the project is expecting to engage with. In the fourth column are the risks and assumptions behind each of the formal aspects of the project. Some see this column as the counter-story or even anti-story of the project. For any formal activity, resulting output, achieved purpose or visioned goal, there must be some down-side or risk. The fourth column encourages the team to consider this down-side. If columns one and four tell the story of the project from formal and informal angles, then the middle columns provide the project with its accountability. Column two provides for indicators to map against activity, output, purpose and goal. Column three gives the means of verifying these indicators. An outcome of the development of the Logframe can be the encouragement of the teams to think in terms of indicators as means to understand how project processes and outputs can be assessed. They are not necessarily the same thing as SIs in the sense that they are driven more by a desire to appraise or evaluate project outcomes and processes, but they can be adapted into SIs.

Logical Frameworks have become increasingly popular within projects. They now dominate the thinking of a number of major donor agencies such as the Department for International Development (DFID) in the UK and the World Bank. They fit into the contemporary demand for defined outcomes at a defined cost in a defined place and over a defined time, which governs agendas of accountability and value for money. Logical Frameworks can be experienced as the written plan of blueprint-type projects.

In terms of the overall SPSA process, the framework can be made to arise from the soft systems review of SIs and can then provide for the development of a formal project. A concern of many agencies relating to the use of soft systems is that the work is not easily reportable or demonstrable to auditing authorities. Similarly, in the experience of the authors there is often a worry in teams that the work which they have undertaken in soft systems will be seen as being non-rigorous or unprofessional because of its use of diagrams and unfamiliar terms. The LogFrame can be used as a means to express the soft work in a more structured and formal manner, which may be more familiar to colleagues. It can be usefully seen as a bridge between highly formalized and less formalized project structures.

For example, the purpose of an SI project can be the root definition as developed in soft systems. The activities for a project set out in the Logical Framework can be derived from the actions developed in the conceptual model of soft systems. Most importantly, many of the issues and problems which were drawn out in the rich picture can be presented in the assumptions column.

In overview, the main strengths of using Logical Frameworks in SPSA are:

• They allow an indicator process to be mapped as a do-able project.
• They are widely used and understood in project work.
• They focus on real impact, not just project spend.
• They make explicit use of indicators.

The teams were encouraged to make use of the framework throughout the SPSA, but were also encouraged to develop it in ways which they were most comfortable with. As a result, there are few 'orthodox' LogFrames in the project documentation.

One example of the sustainable coastal management team making use of the LogFrame to make a more conventional presentation of their conceptual model is set out in Table 4.2. For each activity, outputs were established and indicators to assess the achievement of such outputs were identified.

It can be stressed that this was very early in the project (inception was in February 2000 and this work was completed by late March of the same year), but the team had now identified the key transformation which it was seeking to produce, and had some initial conceptions concerning the development of indicators. The authors were impressed by the level of progress but most impressed by the speed with which the SPSA approach appeared to be handed over to local teams.

Table 4.1 *The basic structure of a Logical Framework*

Narrative summary	Objectively verifiable indicator (OVI)	Means of verification (MOV)	Assumptions
Goal			
Purpose			
Outputs			
Activities			

Table 4.2 *Thematic team's Logical Framework*

Activities	Outputs	Indicators
Thematic analysis	Understanding of resource uses and processes	Trends (eg level of use, beach erosion, amount of cultivated land)
Environmental information system	Mapped data and descriptives	Amount and quality of policy-oriented information: accuracy, availability, timeliness, metadata, coverage, validity
Coastal profiling	Integrated assessment (conflicts)	Tourism employment/revenue/profitability Level of open space users/area (natural and urban) No and type of species Frequency of beach closure (because of health hazards) % of natural coastline (not developed)
Public participation strategy	Improved awareness	Knowledge level of environmental issue Amount of material produced No of participants Level of self-organization Levels of behavioural changes (less litter, fertilizers, off-roading)
Management strategy	Consensus/Objectives/Policies	Number of unresolved/resolved issues Trends in specific standpoints/positions % of land protected/scheduled % of non-buildable land (rural)
Integrating policies	Identified appropriate integrating mechanisms	Level of satisfaction of members Number of decisions implemented

Source: Ellul (2000, p19)

Learning outcomes of this stage of SPSA:

- Activity plans.
- Purposeful view of SPSA for the teams.
- Formal project definitions for the various teams.

SPSA craft points arising from Stage 3:

- Use soft systems conceptual models to develop activity plans for the teams engaging in the development of SIs.
- Use Logical Frameworks to plan out the activities and provide a formal present-ation of the insights gained making use of soft systems.
- Encourage team ownership of the SI process.
- Try to encourage team members to think realistically about the amount of time and effort which will be needed to complete the tasks.

STAGE 4: GET CLEAR ON METHODS: CONNECTION

References: Bell and Ellul, 2000a; Ellul, 2000.

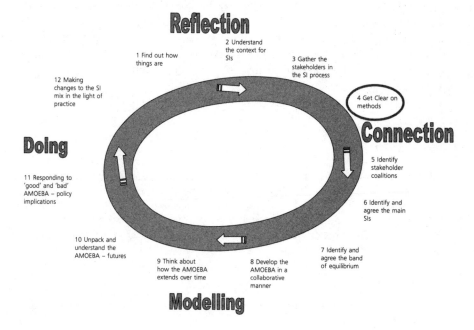

Aims of this stage of SPSA:

- To review progress.
- To make necessary changes to SPSA if required.
- To assess viability of the process so far.

If there is time for a collective intake of breath in any process, then this is it for SPSA. It was envisaged by the authors that the development and adoption of a new way to collect SIs would stretch the resources of many agencies. From years of professional work as consultants and researchers the authors were aware that many projects and project staff make quite major assumptions about the capacity and willingness of local teams to take on major new work commitments and develop new forms of investigation. This additional load is most noticeably felt in projects which work on the basis of short visits by 'experts', followed by long periods where the local team is expected to deliver on some key initiatives. We refer to this approach as 'hothousing'. To some extent it is the assumption of the project management that the development of indicators with local participation can be hothoused or forced. However, in any accelerated process there is always the risk that important factors are overlooked or that justified concerns and worries do not receive adequate attention. The authors were concerned that there would be a need to make sure that the SPSA approach was understood and that teams had resources to undertake the necessary work. It became clear in March of 2000 that the teams had very different demands being placed upon them by the wider project and by agencies outside the project. Some teams had a high degree of enthusiasm for the SPSA process, whereas others frankly saw it as an additional burden.

Early on some time was set aside for the core SPSA team in particular to question the process and to gain clarification on the way in which the various elements of SPSA came together. Given the conventional project form operating at the time and the commitments of team members to existing work, such questioning was limited but nevertheless important. This was also a good process for the authors as it provided an opportunity to find out where the main problems were and to review aspects which were not working so well.

Author's diary

My main view at this time is that the first few stages of SPSA all run together and it is plainly not useful to artificially segregate them. There clearly are distinct phases to the establishment of SPSA but the first five or six stages are all very closely related. I am particularly concerned to ensure that times of reflection do not get lost in the process. The teams need time to think and consider issues which could become problems even if they are not such as yet.

The outcomes of the stage are possibly set out most clearly in the report arising from the second workshop:

> *The main outcome of this training workshop is that each thematic group feels confident in redefining and establishing the key SIs related to the individual project and setting the Band of Equilibrium for each of the indicators selected.*

> *Teams also presented the progress achieved so far, since the March work-shop, on their particular projects.*
>
> *The teams were also provided with guidance relating to the use of additional tools from the SSA toolkit – the SWOC (Strengths, Weaknesses, Opportunities and Constraints) and Feasibility Analysis.*
>
> *Participants were also briefed on the use of the AMOEBA visual present-ation device for reviewing and monitoring of SIs.* (Bell and Ellul, 2000a, p1)

The outcomes as listed here may seem to be indicative that the SPSA process is running ahead of itself. According to the sequence set out in the 12 stages in Table 3.1, the time for review of indicators, setting the band of equilibrium and discussing the AMOEBA arises in Stages 6, 7 and 8. This is also true. However, as noted earlier, the SPSA as it was rolling out in Malta was initially focused on the requirements and needs of the SPSA team, the thematic teams and the internal stakeholders more generally. Stages 6, 7 and 8 refer to the consultation process which was subsequently undertaken with the wider stakeholder community.

At this stage two additional heuristic aids were presented to the teams. Firstly, it was suggested that the teams could assess indicators and how they are to be gathered as they are developed, by means of a feasibility analysis. The main elements of this simple questioning approach are set out below:

- We know **who** undertakes the activities.
- We know **what** activities are to be undertaken.
- We know **how** the activities will be undertaken.
- We know **when** the activities are to be undertaken.
- We understand the nature of the **impact** which the indicator is showing.
- We understand the implication on **workload** (high, satisfactory or low).
- We can state our **confidence** in the indicator (high, satisfactory or low).

The teams were also encouraged to question the nature of the work which they had undertaken so far. The tool employed for this was the SWOC analysis. This is described in more detail in Box 4.1.

The teams ended up applying SWOC to many areas of their combined work, above and beyond that which was expected for the SI work alone. Some examples of the outcomes are set out below.

The use of SWOC encouraged questioning of process and cross-thematic team comparison of progress and sharing of ideas for common solutions. More than this, it raised major concerns which might, without a process of thoughtful planning, become killer assumptions, threatening the integrity of the project as a whole. For example, the weaknesses identified above relating to dependencies between teams and lack of communication outside the formal workshops developed with the core SPSA team indicates that the cohesion of the project as a whole could be improved. Another concern raised here relates to the need for a big launch for the project as a whole. This relates back to the manner in which the work of the SPSA exercise is made known to

Box 4.1 *A word on testing indicators for SWOC*

The user can test the indicator's strength and thus get a view on its value. Usefulness can be gauged by expressing the indicator:

this indicator provides me with . . . . *(state nature of benefit) measure of sustainability.*

If the nature of the benefit of indicator monitoring is questionable or weak, then the SWOC should be completed accordingly. Similarly, if the benefit provides a powerful view of improvement in impact, again this should be indicated in the SWOC.

SWOC DETAILS

It should be noted that in this case the SWOC should show the following:

Strengths of the indicator	Its veracity as an indication of the sustainability of the area in question.
Weaknesses/problems with the indicator	Difficulties in collection, limitations of its scope (eg qualitative review may lack necessary figures to indicate progression).
Opportunities	The decisions which might arise from the effective use of the indicator. The insights it might supply.
Constraints	Limitations to decision-making in making use of the indicator.

wider Maltese society, and this in turn possibly reflects the ambivalence felt concerning the outcomes of SI work. Do we really want to tell everyone what could be rather bad news? This has wider implications. It relates to the value of the exercise and the commitment of individuals and agencies to the work in hand.

An anecdotal observation arising from years of project work undertaken on management information systems (MISs) is that such projects are welcomed if MIS is seen as equalling the provision of computers. However a very different reaction prevails if MIS is seen to result in transparency and accountability. SI projects are more obviously focused on accountability than are those dealing with MIS, but it may well be that commitment is dependent upon the nature of the indicators that arise. How do we manage the expectations of local communities and politicians? How does the news of what such indicators are telling us get into the public domain? This takes the conversation forward into areas relating to marketing and publicizing indicators. Maybe it also indicates a deeper questioning concerning how indicators are developed and for whom. These issues identifying how SIs are first conceived and developed are returned to later in the book. The issue of marketing and popularizing indicators is returned to later in this chapter.

Table 4.3 *Strengths and weaknesses across thematic groups*

Strengths	Weaknesses
Team A	
Well-defined objective	Work constraints, plus three months of half
Teamwork	time
Commitment	Human resources lacking
Training	Financial constraints which have emerged
Working in mixed groups	during the programmes
Co-learning and iteration between teams	Unavoidable delays
Sharing data	Availability and data format
	Weather constraints
	Lack of commitment from certain stakeholders
	Lack of contact with other teams
	Communication difficulties with MAP side:
	would be good if they were more available,
	especially email contact with consultants
Team B	
Complementary skills and knowledge:	Not enough communication between teams
diversity helps	Material produced not circulated well
Common stakeholders between teams	Time is a problem
Learning from other teams who are	Conflicting stakeholders
further ahead	Raising expectations can lead to scepticism
Positive response from most	Logistics and timing of input from consultants
stakeholders contacted	What strategy to adopt with stakeholders
Stakeholders see the project as a means	Teams may come out with recommendations
to obtain a gain: they see benefits from	which conflict with other teams
the project	Bosses not adequately informed about this
Raising expectations	project: what does the minister know?
Real benefits accrue	
Team C	
Other work: this means that other	Other work
projects can be aided by CAMP	Lack of incentives for field work: lack of a PR
activity	strategy and a big launch
Parallel projects can be used	Not all ministries are aware about CAMP
Existing data can be used	Need for a big launch
High level of ownership by stakeholders	Thematic teams have problems because
Data management activity is a strength	stakeholders don't know about the project
and in cross-communication	Lack of communication outside workshops
Own enthusiasm	Working in isolation
	Timeframes: too short to do all the things
	which need to be done
	Dependency on other activities. Some teams
	need the data from other teams. This
	compounds timeframe problems
	Fuzzy horizons: some team members did not
	know what the project involved and some
	do not know where it is leading
	Do not know what the policy role of this
	project is

Source: Bell et al, 2000a, pp12–13

Learning outcomes of this stage of SPSA:

- Understanding of the strengths, weaknesses, opportunities and constraints which the various teams are operating under.
- Engagement with the feasibility of the project.
- Appreciation of who needs to do what when.

SPSA craft points arising from Stage 4:

- Assume that SPSA needs to be questioned and confronted by local teams. Encourage this and encourage the development of the method.
- Use feasibility and SWOC to question the work done so far.
- Encourage reflective practice. Encourage the teams to think about what they are doing and what it means.

Stage 5: Identify the Stakeholder Coalitions: Connection

References: Bell and Ellul, 2000a and 2000b; Ellul, 2000.

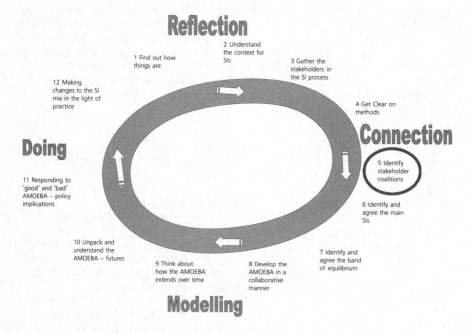

Aims of this stage of SPSA:

- To engage with the wider stakeholder community.
- To tell others what is going on.
- To listen to what they think.
- To make changes if necessary.

The requirement to develop a wider collaboration with stakeholders required new skills from the SPSA team. A skill which might appear routine or even human nature is the capacity of individuals to really listen to what is being said. Our experience is that hearing is common but listening is rare. What does this mean? Stakeholders often feel the context in which they are living with great passion. In our view this is often not appreciated in the literature on sustainability and indicators. This tends to present a semi-objective vision of sustainability, and indicators become the mechanical tools for handling progress. Yet people really do care about sustainability: their children, their lives, their jobs, their pleasure. They might not use quantitative indicators every day, but they use indicators all the time. A child's smile is something we all understand and appreciate.

When requesting information from stakeholders it is common to hear – that is, to nod assent or to record points; but to listen – that is, to take conscious understanding of the meaning of the conversation – is rare. One specific approach which was presented to the teams and was encouraged as a means to use with stakeholder workshops was 'active listening'. This is more fully described in Box 4.2.

Box 4.2 *Active listening*

If there is one skill that you need more than any other as a systems practitioner, it is how to really listen to other people. You have to be able to listen to them with sufficient care and understanding so that you can get their perspective on the situation – and it will usually be very different from your own. The most common mistake that people make when listening is that they assume that they know what the other person has said. This assumption comes from their own internal model of the other person and will be most active when they have very strong feelings and ideas about the other person, eg when they are critical of the other. Active listening is a technique for correcting this propensity to misinterpret other people.

The technique of active listening is very simple. In a conversation with someone you listen to what they say, and before you give your own response you say back to them, in your own words, what you have understood them to say – and invite them to confirm or correct your understanding. Here's how Gordon describes it more fully:

> *In active listening, the receiver tries to understand what it is that the sender is feeling or what his message means. Then he puts his understanding in his own words and feeds it back for the sender's verification. The receiver does **not** send a message of his own – such as evaluation, opinion, advice, logic, analysis or question. He feeds back only what he understands and feels the sender's message meant, nothing more, nothing less.* (Gordon, 1970, p53)

It is important that you use your own words to say what you have understood; mimicking the words the original speaker used is much less reassuring since the words may be taken with different meaning. By using your own words you clarify the meaning you took from the original speaker. Also, in your own rephrasing any misunderstandings are more likely to become apparent.

> *It is important to have your understanding checked and if necessary corrected. I am always amazed at how an apparently small oversight in what the responder*

> *failed to understand turns out to be critical in resolving a misunderstanding or a difference in perception of an issue.*
>
> *To the degree that you are able to make use of active listening the people with whom you converse will feel 'heard' by you. As a result they will be more open to hearing what you yourself have to say and also to disclosing to you more about what they think and feel.* (Bell et al, 1999, block 2, pp45–46)
>
> Source: by Professor Jake Chapman of The Open University

Active listening was seen as being a useful means to assist with the development of the stakeholder meetings which were to follow. The meetings certainly did raise a wide range of views concerning the SPSA approach and the indicators which the thematic teams had developed so far.

> This was one of the interesting aspects of the Malta project, particularly when stakeholders would discuss their understanding of the concept of SD, even though this understanding varied between stakeholders. This diversity in the level of understanding was also one of the disadvantages, since certain stakeholders (eg NGOs – non-governmental organizations) were very responsive to the exercise whilst other entities would just follow with little reaction. Thus it was a learning process for all. (Comment from one of the SPSA core team members)

The core SPSA team was largely responsible for organizing the workshop process, which was to invite a range of stakeholders to an exploratory event where the SPSA process and the indicators so far developed would be discussed. Stakeholders included representatives of key industries like tourism, agriculture and fisheries, concern groups like the Gaia foundation, and official bodies such as local councils. The selection of stakeholder groups was left entirely to the discretion of the Maltese SPSA team, with no involvement of either the consultants or Blue Plan. In all circumstances such selection is problematic. How representative is the sample? How many constituencies of interest are represented? Have some constituencies been excluded or overlooked? Such questions are valid, hard to check and a cause for concern in all participation-based projects.

The overall structure of the event was organized around some of the general themes of the focus group. The overall rules by which this method are usually applied are set out in Box 4.3.

The intention of the SPSA team was to provide an environment where stakeholders could be informed of the progress made so far in the work of the project and be encouraged to provide critical but constructive feedback. Often the natural instincts of teams in the context of stakeholder groups is to be defensive and even protective of the work undertaken and to deflect criticism as being either poorly conceived or maliciously devised. The understanding of the principles of active listening and the adoption of focus group methods were the means adopted to attempt to avoid these negatives. A note from the author's diary at the time indicates that this was not always the outcome.

Box 4.3 *Focus group interview*

- A recent addition to semi-formal techniques.
- Historically based in market research to gauge reaction of customers to new products.
- Focuses on reactions to potential changes.
- Participants discuss among themselves.

Some features of focus groups are set out below:

When applied	When a difficult issue needs to be reviewed When fresh insight is needed When inclusion is the primary requirement When ideas are muddled When people are in conflict and need to bring ideas together
Details of application	8 to 10 participants A specific topic is set out to a pre-ordered group All involved should participate
Participants are asked for	Ideas, issues, insights and experiences Discussion leader needs to focus and structure the range of the debate A number of such sessions will occur with different groups of participants
Benefits	The range of stakeholders is increased Views are interchanged Hidden problems can be revealed Local knowledge can lead policy
Potential problems to be aware of	Dominant members can lead the discussion to support their own views Careful discussion leadership is essential This can mean that control of the discussion leader is needed Can be prejudice forming not brainstorming Can alienate

Author's diary

I enjoy stakeholder events but must say that the forum developed for this occasion seemed rather formal and unimaginative. I am not sure if it is appropriate to try to make the event more chatty and informal or if this would be welcomed by those present. I feel that I need to let the SPSA team organize its own event. They know best what works well here. We certainly got some rich comments. I think I was not the only person present who did not feel comfortable with the format!

Learning outcomes of this stage of SPSA:

- Recognition of the concerns of major stakeholders.
- Adaptation to indicators if necessary.
- Understanding of how SPSA is perceived in the wider community.
- Acceptance from the local community that the process can continue.

SPSA craft points arising from Stage 5:

- Give the teams ways of developing stakeholder participation. Active listening and focus groups are good – there may be better ways which local teams know.
- Keep open to innovations.

STAGE 6: IDENTIFY AND AGREE THE MAIN SIs: CONNECTION/MODELLING

STAGE 7: IDENTIFY AND AGREE THE BAND OF EQUILIBRIUM: MODELLING

STAGE 8: DEVELOP THE AMOEBA IN A COLLABORATIVE MANNER: MODELLING/DOING

References: Bell and Ellul, 2000a and 2000b.

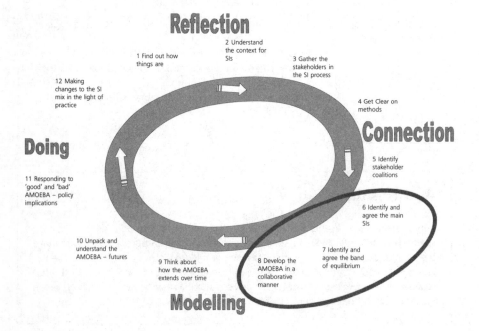

Aims of these stages of SPSA:

- To get to grips with SIs.
- To establish the bands of equilibrium.
- To make the AMOEBA.
- To get a picture of the sustainability of the context.

The main purpose of the stakeholder meetings was to discuss the work of the teams so far achieved, explain the nature of the SPSA process, seek ideas and questions from the wider stakeholder group, and specify indicators and bands of equilibrium. At the meeting in October 2000 each of the thematic teams presented their indicators and explained why and how they had been selected. An example of the indicator presentation is given in Figure 4.3. These were later to be tidied up and presented as shown in Figure 4.4.

The overall impact of the presentations was to provoke a wide-ranging conversation concerning the future of Malta and the need for sustainability planning. Some of the key points arising from the stakeholders included:

- *need to bring in the children;*
- *publicize;*
- *keep everything integrated – everyone is interested in the whole picture;*
- *use the WWW;*
- *there is a capacity to educate the tourists who come to Malta.*
  (Bell and Ellul, 2000b, p8)

Many of the points made at this point are reiterations of those identified in the SWOC analysis undertaken in Stage 4.

Figure 4.3 and the tidy version in Figure 4.4 show that the teams have identified indicators, and the band of equilibrium for each. It was very important to be able to go into the stakeholder meeting with this level of information. The stakeholders would probably not want to engage with an academic debate concerning the sustainability of the north. Rather, the teams had agreed that they would want to see real outcomes and real measures. For example, the health and tourism AMOEBAs relate to real and contentious issues such as the incidence of gastro-enteritis among tourists, changes in the results of pest control such as that relating to rats, and the effectiveness of garbage collection. These types of indicator engaged stakeholders, especially those representing the tourist industry.

Author's diary

There is a point worth noting here. I did ask the tourism group about the lack of standard indicators one often sees for other resorts. They replied that such statistics are kept by other agencies and they did not want to duplicate them. I don't know how common this was amongst the other teams – did they purposely select indicators on the basis that they knew others were collecting similar information? It may be argued, for example, that some teams could have taken a less imaginative stance and used indicators for which they already had lots of data (EU regulations). This helps describe the context within which SPSA took place. Governments do collect lots of data on a routine basis, and unfortunately there could be a tendency to see SPSA as yet another part of this effort – perhaps to be done by the same people in the same ministry.

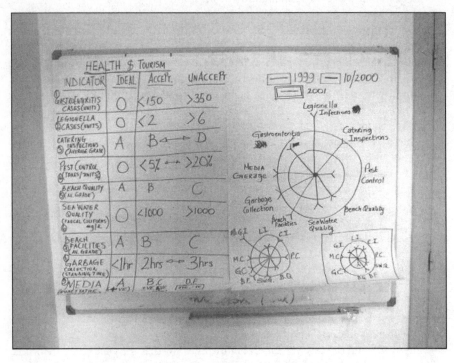

Figure 4.3 *Presentation for the stakeholder workshop*

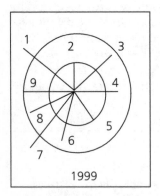
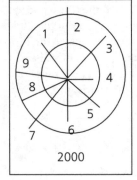
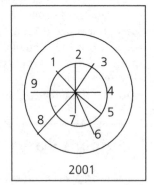

Source: Bell and Ellul, 2000b, pp12–13

Note: The numbers (1 to 9) refer to separate indicators, with the space between the two circles representing the band of equilibrium (the reference condition for sustainability).

Figure 4.4 *Health and tourism AMOEBA for three years: 2000, 1999 and 2001*

The authors saw the level of engagement of the stakeholders as a proxy measure of the effectiveness of the SPSA process as a whole.

At this time the wider stakeholder group did not want to make changes to the SPSA process or to the specific indicators so far described – the authors remain unsure why this was so. It might be that the stakeholders were happy with the process. Then again it might be that they did not have time or lacked trust in the process. However, they did feel the need for the process and sought to be informed about the developments of the project. Motives are unclear for this. This was useful information for the SPSA team, which had collectively been questioning if the indicators would be of value and if the sustainability question would be seen as being important to wider Maltese society.

The internal SPSA stakeholder team was provoked by the wider community stakeholder meeting at the level of its own working. It would be true that anecdotally there had appeared to be some sense of drift and dilemma between the workshop events. Teams had worried about their capacity to deliver on the SPSA and some concern had been expressed over the momentum needed to keep progress going. The concern over this process aspect of the project as a whole is well summed up below.

> The pity is that the seminars were spread too far apart, understandably so, since it would have been more costly and would have presented certain difficulties otherwise. However, your seminars usually left us full of enthusiasm and eagerness that would keep us going at a good momentum for some time, only to die down over the following months of silence, then panic: hurried meetings again because we were due to meet again and there were jobs that we still had to see to that we had forgotten all about. This sense of discontinuity would probably be less of a problem in your own country, but had we to repeat the process I would advise a few additional meetings or at least meetings held closer together. (Comment from a thematic team member)

This problem was recognized by the authors and Blue Plan representatives and some action was planned and undertaken. In particular the thematic teams met to discuss common problem areas and some potential solutions. The problems encountered included:

- What happens between events?
- Need to disseminate reports.
- Feedback lacking.
- Public launch of the project necessary.
- Funding required for public participation.
- More collaboration is required.
- Lack of technical support between visits and workshops.
- Engaging with participation.
- Formal integration is needed.
- Adapting the AMOEBA.
- Isolation.
- Project structurally defective.
- Learning more from other CAMP projects.

This range of identified problems in the SPSA process as encountered by the teams indicates an issue that we want to return to in the final section of this chapter; the issue of the institutional sustainability of SPSA. Put briefly here, how can conventional projects, working to limited deadlines with staff who already have full commitments in other areas, hope to be successful in developing sustainability in the continuous roll-out of SIs? Surely the project format as conceived leads to a short-term approach which must mean that there is an epistemological gap between the format of the project approach and the aims of the specific sustainability project. Put simply, how can we make indicator projects more sustainable?

From the series of issues identified above the team provided some ideas concerning solutions:

- Learn, plan and do not forget.
- Public launch.
- Passing the project to the public.
- CAMP is good for us.
- Keep talking and keep sharing (real integration).
- Come out of your box.
- Take control over design.

It might be argued that such processes might remain quite superficial. For example, the public launch might be high profile and politically useful, but how much real participation can it help deliver? After all, as it was conceived by the CAMP Malta it amounted to little more than publicity ('let's tell people what we are doing') rather than genuine public participation ('let's involve people in what we do'). This remained a concern as the project continued.

These were agreed to by the SPSA and thematic teams but an underlying problem for the process was twofold:

1   High-level political support for the SPSA process. Although SPSA was implicitly supported throughout the process of the project, this support was too often experienced as benign neglect and an absence of meddling rather than active support and freeing staff from existing work in order to be able to better undertake SPSA work.
2   Pace. The SPSA was taking too long to implement. With the gaps between training events being several months, the strengths of workshops were eroded over time and hard-won skills were lost.

Both of these issues are returned to in Chapters 5 and 6. The very process of the SPSA workshops in identifying the ranges of problems set out above was seen by some of the team members as being a success. Perhaps this is best put by a member of the SPSA core team.

The workshop sessions and the direct hands-on experience in understanding the various stages of the process has been the success of this project, particularly since groups would involve themselves in systemic discussions analysing the issues from different perspectives to come up with a collectively acceptable approach. All teams were unanimous on this. (Comments from a member of the SPSA core team)

Our own comments at this time read as follows:

Author's diary

I am surprised again by the integrative nature of some of the stages of SPSA in practice. As planned, Stages 6, 7 and 8 were all expected to absorb different time and space. As it has worked out they are simultaneous operations all being addressed by the same workshop format. A key output seems to be the legitimizing effect it has had on the thematic teams. It is as if they have been told that what they are doing is valid and OK. This could be a major empowerment for the project as a whole.

Again I can't help but feel that part of the popularity of SPSA was its sense of liberation and learning. I could imagine that all of the teams spend day after day doing their routine jobs, as well as their CAMP duties, with little time to reflect on what goes on elsewhere or the broader aspects of what they are doing. SPSA comes along and provides them with time and space to do just that – albeit with no allowance made from their line managers about time. It's not hard to see, especially with the way in which the sessions were run (ie no lectures), that SPSA would be popular. Sustaining that effort between workshops, with all the other calls on their time, would almost be expected to be the problem.

An interesting item, which figured prominently at this point of SPSA, related to the AMOEBA software which was being developed by Blue Plan. The initial idea of SSA (rather than SPSA) as first conceived by the authors had not made much provision for software, but it was recognized early on that software can make the process of presenting indicators easier and more obviously uniform and often helps to sell an approach to client organizations. The software would also fit well within the Blue Plan emphasis on scenario exploration. Once produced, the participants need only enter different values for the indicators to see how the shapes of the AMOEBA project change over time.

A cursory glance at the AMOEBA already set out in this chapter (Figures 4.3 and 4.4) demonstrates the range of ways in which indicators can be presented. For some purposes it is very useful to have a low-tech and hand-drawn presentation. However, for professional agencies and international donors a more professional format is demanded. Presentation and ease of scenario generation are only two of the drives to produce AMOEBA software. More importantly, it was considered necessary to provide the thematic teams with a means to rapidly store their indicators and for these stored indicators to be available across the thematic teams in the same format.

The main questions for the consultants in considering the AMOEBA software were how it was to be developed, using what program, and requiring what skills from the teams to make effective use of it.

It was agreed early on that the software should be developed using a standard and well-understood package like Microsoft Excel. This would widen out the community able to make use of it and make it more widely available.

It was at this point that the authors (initially) developed the AMOEBA (using the RADAR facility) as a macro in Excel. Blue Plan subsequently applied their resources in collaboration with the authors and began to develop Visual Basic for Applications (VBA) code for generating the AMOEBA. It was thought that the use of VBA code would provide far more flexibility in terms of how the AMOEBAs were to be presented than the use of simple macros.

An example of the type of AMOEBA which were produced (using the VBA program) for the project at the time of the fourth workshop is shown in Figure 4.5.

The main problem for the teams from the authors' point of view was the slow delivery of the software and the problems which all experienced in getting changes made to make the software more user-friendly. The literature detailing the problems of software development is vast.[4] The main problem in this case was the inability of the chosen delivery software to meet the basic needs of the client users, the thematic teams.

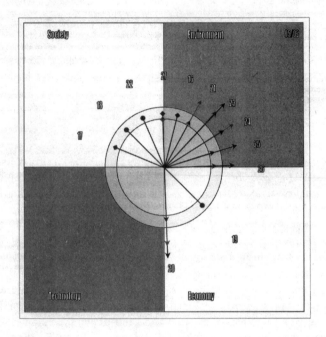

No	Indicator	Quadrant	Polarity	Measure	Max	Min	1996	1997	2000
16	Quality of water	1	<	% users	95	50	60	70	85
17	Use index	4	<	% of users	100	85	87	90	95
18	Water affordability	4	x	in cents per cu m	110	12	12	12	12
19	Water consumption per day	2	x	in litres per capita per day	150	90	110	120	120
20	Leaked water	2	>	% of total production	40	20	60	50	40
21	Abstracted ground water	1	>	in million cu m per year	8	2	10	10	6
22	Legionella cases	4	x	no of cases	6	2	3	4	4
23	Pest control	1	>	% of takes	20	5	30	25	25
24	No of breaches in rubble walls	1	>	no per Km	5	2	7	7	6
25	Rills and gullies	1	>	density per average sized field	4	1	5	3	3
26	Frequency of beach closures	1	>	no of beach days	5	2	6	3	2
27	Coast in public ownership	4	<	% of total coastal length	95	85	80	80	85

Source: Bell et al, 2001a, p18
Note: This diagram, called the AMOEBA, gives a visual representation of the indicators and the manner in which these have changed over three particular years. The indicators are categorized into four quadrants.

Figure 4.5 *Agreed AMOEBA*

Although the software did eventually provide output of the type set out in Figure 4.5, its development occupied a great deal of time and distracted some of the overall project effort away from the main issue of concern, the development of the indicators themselves.

At another level, the AMOEBA experience could be said to have been unsatisfactory because of a range of factors:

- The software was not adequately planned for within the project.
- There was a lack of clarity over the technical development of the specific elements of the AMOEBA as a software tool (polarity, band of equilibrium).
- The relevance of this technology for the various teams was questionable.

At this time the teams were encouraged to consider the risks involved in the development of any specific indicators. One means for assessing the risks was developed by Hughes and Cotterell (1999). The information given to the teams as part of a toolkit of such techniques is set out in Box 4.4.

Box 4.4 *Risk analysis*

Risks are identified in the soft systems process and then subsequently developed in relation to the indicators in the Logical Framework. For each indicator it is useful (subject to the costs of undertaking the exercise) to assess the risks in such a way as to identify if they are potentially fatal for the sustainability analysis as a whole. There are three elements to consider.

1 ASSESSING RISK VALUE

One risk analysis which is of general value is that set out by Bob Hughes and Mike Cotterell in their book *Software Project Management* (Hughes and Cotterell, 1999). What follows is taken from this book with some additional elements.

Some risks will be relatively unimportant whereas others will be of major concern. Some are likely to occur and some are unlikely. The probability of a risk occurring is the risk likelihood. If it happens it is known as the risk impact. The importance of the risk is known as the risk value or risk exposure. Risk value can be calculated as follows:

risk value = risk likelihood x risk impact

Likelihood is usually developed as a subjective valuation between 1 and 10, where 1 is considered to be completely unlikely and 10 is just about certain.

The estimation of the cost and probability of risk is a problematic issue and I will not deal with these here. Generally they are time consuming to generate and unreliable measures. However, there is still great value in developing some form of quantitative measure of the risks evident in any specific indicator development process.

Impact measures are assessed in a similar manner and take into account the total risk to the project, including such potential costs as:

- The cost of delays in gaining information.
- Cost overrun on sustainability indicator development.
- Compromises on quality set against schedule.

2 PRIORITIZING THE RISKS

Two strategies arise from risk value assessment:

1   Reducing the risk exposure by reducing likelihood or impact.
2   Drawing up contingency plans to deal with risk should it occur.

It is important that the major risks are given more attention to ensure that costs for contingency (for example) do not multiply on low-risk items.

Risk value is a starting point only. In practice, other factors need to be taken into account when prioritizing risks. All risks which have been valued should be prioritized by consideration of these factors.

Confidence of the risk value assessment	Some assessments will be poor and will need further investigation prior to action planning
Compound risks	Some risks are dependent upon others – in this case they need to be treated together as a single risk
The number of risks	In prioritization some risks might need to be temporarily ignored
Cost of action	Low-cost risk avoidance can be engaged in immediately without need for deep consideration, but some expensive risks will need to be compared in terms of costs of taking action set against the benefits of reducing the risk

3 STRATEGIES FOR REDUCING HIGH PRIORITY RISKS

For the risks which you assess to be of high priority, there are five generally agreed strategies for risk reduction. You will need to make your own assessment of the best strategy for your own cases.

Risk prevention	By early scheduling and prior planning in risks which relate to staff availability for example
Likelihood reduction	Again prior planning can reduce the likelihood of risk
Risk avoidance	By increasing budget, time or personnel for key sustainability indicator activities
Risk transfer	Contracting some risky activities out can reduce risk for the project itself
Contingency planning	Unpreventable risks need to be reduced in severity by contingency planning

By this point in the SPSA process the teams had been provided with a toolkit of methods and approaches for dealing with issues at the various stages. Although the risk analysis was seen as being a useful addition to the main tools applied, it was not widely used due to time constraints. An observation made in the author's diary at the time is pertinent.

Author's diary

I think the teams are suffering from technique and tool fatigue! The capacity of any team is limited and the demands on the time and resource of these teams might be too much. I am not expecting all the ideas we have provided them with to be applied. The core is the basic steps of SPSA itself and the AMOEBA. If we are to get to scenario planning we may well need to ease back on insisting that all tools are used to full capacity.

Learning outcomes of these stages of SPSA:

- Agreement on major SIs.
- Development of the initial AMOEBA.
- Understanding of some of the major sustainability issues arising.
- Visions for how things might change and develop as a consequence of the outcomes of the project.

SPSA craft points arising from Stages 6, 7 and 8:

- Try to keep the momentum going – workshops need to be closely spaced at this time.
- Don't overload the teams with tools and techniques – provide the toolkit but don't necessarily think that they will have time to do it all.
- Be a good listener at this point. The teams do now know what they are trying to do and they need you to be able to hear their problems and clear up remaining issues.

STAGE 9: THINK ABOUT HOW THE AMOEBA EXTENDS OVER TIME: MODELLING/DOING

STAGE 10: UNPACK AND UNDERSTAND THE AMOEBA – FUTURES: MODELLING/DOING

References: Bell et al, 2001a; Bell and Ellul, 2001b.

Aims of these stages of SPSA:

- To extend the AMOEBA over time.
- To begin to think into the future.
- To build scenarios for future policy.

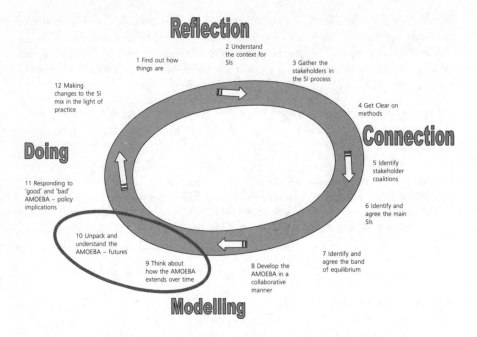

Previous stages had run together and so it proved at this point in SPSA. The two stages of linking together indicator observations to provide a record of change over time and then the development of this historical record into projections for potential futures ran together as one process. On reflection it was to be expected that they would. The historic trends of indicators would probably spontaneously indicate alternatives for how the indicators might develop in future.

At this time the wider stakeholder views were again assessed. During the stakeholder consultation there was some concern expressed that the indicator process could lead to an undue focus on virtuous but unprofitable change, and that the outcome of the SPSA process might be to indicate change of a painful or costly nature. The comment of a stakeholder at the time is instructive:

> By going from the negative into the positive, it could actually kill the business life of Malta. (Comment from a stakeholder at a workshop)

This risk of sustainability being seen as a negative had been predicted from the outset of the SPSA process but it was at this stage that the prediction took on flesh. The teams would need to manage the potential down-sides, costs and implications of SIs.

The scenarios for the future state of indicators arose from a soft systems review of the existing historical indicators so far gathered. Figure 4.6 provides one example, in this case from the soil erosion and desertification thematic team. The rich picture was the product of a brainstorming session arising from the review of the indicators developed so far. The scenarios relate to how one indicator, the claims for compensation for stormwater damage (a proxy indicator relating to the removal of soil-retaining features such as dry stone walls) might develop in the future.

As can be seen from Figure 4.6, the historical indicator values as gathered do not provide any consistent picture of a year-on-year tendency. In this case the teams were asked to use their imaginations as to where the trend might go. The resulting three scenarios indicate a wide spread of possible futures. What is possibly most interesting about the three scenarios is that they all indicate a rise in claims from the present situation. The second point of note is that the key to change is indicated to be global warming, a phenomenon which Malta as a whole can do little or nothing to affect. However, it is the level of the reaction to global forces and local economic tendencies (in this case, the tendency for farmers to sell their dry stone walls to builders for the cladding of fashionable dwellings in Valetta and Sliema) which indicates the change of the indicator values in different scenarios.

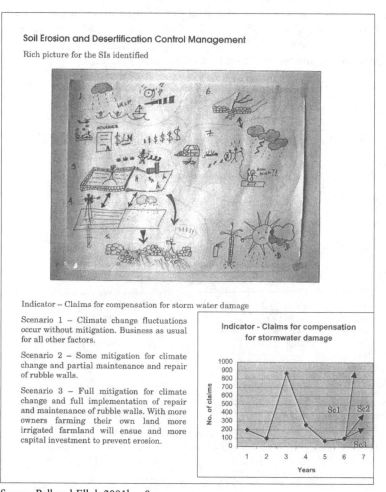

Source: Bell and Ellul, 2001b, p8

Figure 4.6 *Outcomes of extending AMOEBA over time and forecasting likely change*

The team was then asked to consider, by use of the conceptual modelling element of soft systems, what actions would need to be undertaken to achieve the three scenarios. These are set out in the next section.

Learning outcomes of these stages of SPSA:

- Clarification of how the AMOEBA extends over time.
- Appreciation of the variety of actions which any SI can lead to.
- Understanding of the policy implication of SPSA.

SPSA craft points arising from Stages 9 and 10:

- Be wary of software 'fixes'. The software can get in the way of developing good indicators and resulting AMOEBA.
- Realize that prospective sustainability analysis or other future thinking and scenario-planning approaches, if applied from within SPSA, need adequate time for learning about.
- Remember technique fatigue – take it easy on the teams.

STAGE 11: RESPONDING TO 'GOOD' AND 'BAD' AMOEBA – POLICY IMPLICATIONS: DOING

References: Bell et al, 2001a; Bell and Ellul, 2001b.

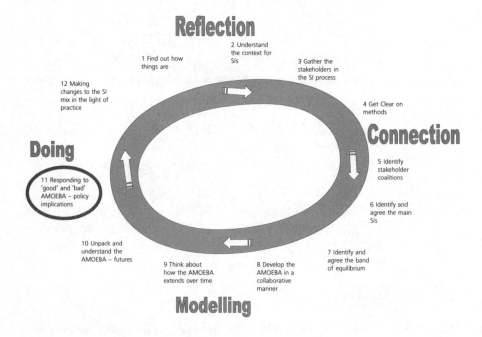

Aims of this stage of SPSA:

- To develop an agenda for action arising from AMOEBA and prospective sustainability analysis.
- To inform others.
- To market the outcomes of SPSA.

Following the development of scenarios, there is a review of the policy implications for undertaking them. This can be a worrying time for the teams and yet, paradoxically, this can be a time of insight and reward from the process. At this time it becomes apparent that some activities are not good for the sustainability of the context and that the statement of such may well have political fall-out. It is important to re-emphasize that the SPSA process presents options, and not 'the truth' or 'facts' as such. Working with options means that teams and local decision-makers have choices, rather than feeling that they are being bullied into courses of action that they do not like.

Author's diary

Ultimately, change and action means costs. It was noticeable how all the teams (it was all if memory serves me right!) began to translate their original indicators into monetary value. They saw this as essential in order to be able to illustrate the cost of **not** doing something or allowing it to get worse. This was a strong feeling at the time – I remember a number of people making the point. This gave rise to the idea of 'shadow' indicators – monetary-based reflections of the original indicators designed to raise public awareness (and that of politicians of course).

This apparent need for monetization of SIs to make them noticeable is perhaps a reflection of the world in which we live today. It has echoes of the weak sustainability approach (Chapter 2), and potentially suffers from the same sort of problems; how do you provide a monetary value for a 'good' environment? In microcosm, we saw in Malta the same arguments being played out. Maybe weak sustainability does resonate with our lives today, and although we can create indicators that capture an essence of sustainability, these may need to be shadowed by indicators that engage with the more immediate realities of economics.

Of course, there may be nothing to worry about on this score. As an aside at this point: Maltese stakeholders showed themselves to be keenly aware of the range of drivers to change. One interesting example is set out below. Maybe it shows two main points:

1 The willingness to make change.
2 The willingness to develop Malta in ways which may not be commensurate with its historic nature.

(Concerning customer satisfaction:) We have been hounding this to death. We need to have more water features . . . more open spaces, more drinking spaces, the more a country lies to the south and has a warmer climate, the more you need to emphasize what is not naturally there, especially for the northern mind . . . they are accustomed to certain standards. (Comments from a stakeholder at a workshop)

The actions which would lead to the three scenarios under Stage 10 were set out by the team as the activities of conceptual models and then presented as lists of likely tasks (Table 4.4). The activities set out in this way demonstrate clear choices for planners and stakeholders in Malta. They also highlight issues that Malta either has no or little influence to change, eg carbon dioxide.

Of course, it needs to be restated that the SPSA process is not attempting to develop a definitive or absolute model of the future for the island. By a process of active engagement with local stakeholders and international authorities, it attempts to provide a vision for how the sustainability of the island is measured at present, how this has changed over time and how it might develop in future. It is entirely up to the local community to ascertain what this means in terms of policy.

Table 4.4 *Three scenarios that could arise in Malta*

Scenario	
1	CO_2 levels continue to rise and international community fails to agree on control mechanisms
	Land tenure system as usual with owner prohibiting tenant farmer from turning dry land farm/units into irrigated fields
	Monetary compensation for storm damage remains ineffective
	Road and suburban development fails to take surface water runoff into account
	Farmer training programmes fail to take soil erosion prevention measures into curriculum
2	CO_2 levels taper off
	Some land ownership programmes get under way to promote farmer ownership of land
	Sewage treatment plants develop for northwest and yield second-class water for irrigation
	Local plans become more sensitive to problem of soil erosion
	Increasing mitigating measures with partial implementation of CAMP policies
3	Implementation of carbon tax system and CO_2 levels decrease
	Mitigation for climate change at local levels
	Repair and maintenance programmes in full swing
	Full sewage treatment and recovery of second-class water for irrigation
	Full compliance with CAMP recommendations on soil erosion
	Full set of incentives in place to achieve capital expenditure and repair/maintenance of soil erosion prevention measures

Source: from Bell and Ellul, 2001b, p9

At this stage in the SPSA process the results of the teams' work were shown and discussed at a public launch which was organized by the SPSA team without any input from the authors or Blue Plan. This was rather later than some would have liked but in the event it seemed to work well. The teams were confident by this time with the approach which they had been applying, understood the work which they had done and were able to make a coherent and engaging presentation.

As a final stage to the SPSA the teams were asked to think about how they might engage the public more actively in the use of indicators and respond to their import. In the literature there is a dearth of material relating to how indicators and sustainability more generally can be marketed (Chapter 2). At this point the thematic teams made use of the CATWOE (client, actors, transformation, worldview, owner and environmental factors) element of soft systems again to consider a marketing strategy (Table 4.5). One example of the outcome from this stage is shown in the rich picture of Figure 4.7.

Table 4.5 *CATWOE and action plan for the Marine Conservation Area thematic team*

Factor	Information
Clients	General public including bathers, yachters, divers, developers, tour operators, politicians, local councils
Actors	Environmental Protection Department, Malta Maritime Authority, Planning Authority, Malta Tourism Authority, NGOs, local council
Transformation	To secure public support for the marine conservation areas
Worldview (assumptions)	Mechanism and commitment to encourage cooperation between actors. Legal framework to establish an MCA
Owners	Extended MCA project team (CAMP)
Environmental constraints	Priorities, cooperation between agencies, development pressures
Marketing plan to achieve transformation (support for the MCA)	Marketing research to identify needs of clients/markets through surveys, eg focus groups, questionnaires Define promotional approach/es to the diverse client segments Choose mechanisms/media to send message to the client segments, eg seminars, TV, newspapers, meetings, web pages, information leaflets, etc Focus on sustainability indicators and their trends as part of promotional campaign Awareness exercise on MCAs in general and promotional campaign on the benefits of creating the MCA
Specific actions	Take key clients to visit success stories overseas Focus group meetings with key stakeholders/clients TV promotional campaign to the general public (strong visual message) Onsite stand to reach present users Indirect tourist support through the web page Monitoring/evaluation of promotional campaign – feedback, follow-up survey, observation

Source: after Bell and Ellul, 2001b, pp13–14

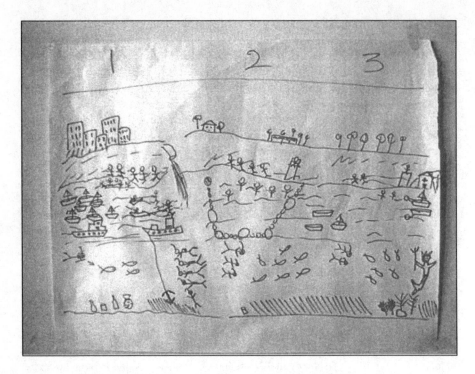

Figure 4.7 *Marine conservation areas: rich picture for marketing*

The rich picture in Figure 4.7 shows three visions of the marine environment as described by the scenario planning based upon the current indicators. To the left is the worst scenario – too much boating, tourism and pollution. To the right is Neptune in his element in an empty sea. The middle diagram shows restraint and responsibility. The team found the use of rich pictures particularly useful as ways of capturing new ways of thinking about the SPSA context.

Author's diary

It seems amazing to me how a simple diagramming technique like the rich picture can constantly lead to new insights in teams. Throughout this project the teams have been gaining in proficiency with the elements of SPSA. Soft systems seem to be a particularly engaging aspect.

As an aside, the authors wondered about two aspects of the SPSA. At one level the participants have achieved significant insights into how they can make use of indicators. On the other they have got to this point through a form of hothousing. By this we mean that they have undergone an accelerated form of training to arrive at SIs which they are now applying to make 'What If?' scenarios. From these scenarios they are considering how to market the outcomes to the wider population. A point we will develop in later chapters is the likely outcomes which such a hothousing approach may be expected to achieve and if other approaches to developing indicators might be applied which might result in different, maybe more insightful outcomes.

Learning outcomes of this stage of SPSA:

- Appreciation of the choices which SPSA provides.
- Understanding of the actions necessary to lead to the realization of the choices.
- Engagement with the policy problems and opportunities which the SPSA raises.

SPSA craft points arising from Stage 11:

- Stress that SPSA provides options and choices for the future. It is not expected to present a definitive 'truth'.
- Early public launch of indicators can leave the teams floundering.
- Marketing the indicators needs to be thought out. Soft systems can again be usefully applied to develop a strategy.

STAGE 12: MAKING CHANGES TO THE SI MIX IN THE LIGHT OF PRACTICE: DOING/REFLECTING

References: Bell et al, 2001a, Bell and Ellul, 2001b.

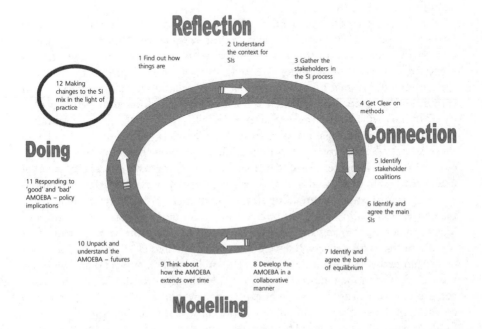

Reflection

1 Find out how things are

2 Understand the context for SIs

3 Gather the stakeholders in the SI process

4 Get Clear on methods

Connection

5 Identify stakeholder coalitions

6 Identify and agree the main SIs

7 Identify and agree the band of equilibrium

8 Develop the AMOEBA in a collaborative manner

9 Think about how the AMOEBA extends over time

Modelling

10 Unpack and understand the AMOEBA – futures

11 Responding to 'good' and 'bad' AMOEBA – policy implications

Doing

12 Making changes to the SI mix in the light of practice

Aims of this stage of SPSA:

- To adapt and change in the light of practice.
- To plan the ongoing use of SPSA.
- To establish resources for the continuing roll-out of SPSA.

No process, no matter how well intended, is perfect and the attempt of the SPSA to take forward the manner in which indicators are developed and presented naturally has not produced an uncontested success.

> I did feel a little lost when it came to the final stages. For me (once again I say that it may have been only my impression!), it seemed as if suddenly when we got close to the finishing line, the momentum slowed down and that we never actually finalized the end product to perfection. At the last seminar we were informed what to do and how to do it, but never actually worked our way right up to the polished end product . . . a bit of a frustrating experience after all the interest that your activity had built up. I feel that one other meeting at the end to help us as individual teams actually see our own AMOEBA set out would have worked wonders. In fact I have a meeting with XXXX next week to make sure that somehow I get across that finishing line. (Comment from a member of one of the thematic teams)

Maybe the notion of a finishing line is not consistent with the nature of SPSA, which was originally devised as a continuous learning cycle. But it is at this stage that the team needs to re-engage with the process as first conceived, and question how it might be improved.

A point to make at this time is the institutional nature of the indicators produced by the SPSA process. The indicators do have clear ownership with the thematic teams, but together the process is owned by government and development agencies. As suggested in Stage 7, the very project-based nature of the SPSA process can lead to a gap between the aspirations of the sustainability goal and the delivery capability of conventional projects. In short, there is the potential for a disjuncture between what we are trying to do and the way in which we are trying to do it. With the conventional project structure and organizational format, the emphasis of teams tends to be on short-term, high intensity inputs for rapid impact (hothousing). However, the needs of sustainable development tend to be focused on the long-term and knotty issues of macro changes in hearts and minds as well as short-term economic transformation. There appear to be two contending strategies within SPSA activity: the strategy of the conventional project with its related short-term outcomes, and the strategy of long-term conceptualizing and wide goals related to sustainable development. If, at the end of the SPSA process, the victorious strategy is that of 'the project', then the ownership of the resulting indicators will tend to lie with the project organization. If the victory is with the long-term sustainable development of the environment and community, then ownership might be expected to be more firmly focused on the local community. This would be an outcome more consistent with the aims and ideals of SPSA as originally conceived. This focus of ownership may itself restrict or promote real insight and, more importantly, the desire to make change and develop the overall framework. This is an issue to which we will return as we consider where SPSA goes from here in Chapters 5 and 6.

The final stage of SPSA involves active and purposeful reflection on what has been achieved and what has been problematic. Following this, it can be of great value to consider the meaning of the indicators and the scenarios as produced. There may well be meta issues which arise in the consideration of the whole picture, which have been lost in the general business of the project so far.

What are the themes? What is the learning? What needs to change both in the project and in the context if the indicators are to be taken seriously? Where does the team go now? If the project is the winning strategy, then there may be a tendency to wrap up the process at this point: 'we have the indicator lists and these have been developed in a participative mode, so end of story'. The vast majority of indicator projects that we are aware of have ended with this, even if the rhetoric suggests that the story should continue. What evidence has there been that is has? Do the indicator lists remain set in stone? Do they truly evolve and are they used to make real changes happen? The SD literature is largely silent on this, and one hears little of SIs that help bring about change to peoples lives, or which continue to evolve organically in a bottom-up fashion as people's ambitions and needs change.

By way of contrast, SPSA as originally devised, and indeed SPSA as operationalized in Malta, is designed to be a continuous process. Initial training and capacity building could encourage the continuous investment of national and international agencies in the annual renewal of indicators and the continuous development of the conversation around what they mean. Without this process, SSA and SPSA are exercises in short-term futility.

At the time of going to press, the SPSA project has successfully generated the first set of indicator lists (Appendix 1). Values have been found for some of these, and they did feed into a scenario-planning process. There is now a Maltese Commission for Sustainable Development in line with similar such commissions worldwide, and this would be the natural home for continuing to evolve the indicators and SPSA. The authors' official involvement in the Maltese SPSA has ended with the delivery of the indicator lists in Appendix 1, although unofficially they still maintain an interest. Has this all been yet another blueprint project that ends with an impressive list of indicators sitting in a final project report?

Learning outcomes of this stage of SPSA:

- Appreciation of the strengths and weaknesses of the current SPSA as undertaken in the context.
- Valuing what seems to work well.
- Identifying what needs to change.
- Establishing the long-term viability of SPSA.
- Establishing a long-term dialogue on sustainability issues.
- Appreciation of the range of perspectives which lie behind and within the indicators as at present constructed.

SPSA craft points arising from Stage 12:

- It is vital to reflect openly and with all members of the SPSA team.
- As with all brainstorming, nothing should be counted out at this stage.
- There will be a need to adjust indicators over time. It is a good strategy to make the changing of indicators an understood factor. Teams can become protective of their SIs.
- The needs of SPSA are consistent with the aims of sustainable development. There may be a need to actively engage with the boundary issues relating to the short-term needs of the project.
- Set in place the funding of the SPSA process for the coming year(s).

Chapter 5

New Frontiers of Practice

INTRODUCTION

As the reader would have gleaned from Chapters 1 and 2, there is much written on sustainable development (SD) and the use of sustainability indicators (SIs) as a tool to help with the gauging of attainment. The literature is vast and expanding rapidly, and both the authors can readily confirm that one can quickly become lost within the detail. Perhaps we shouldn't be too surprised at this, after all:

> *Achieving sustainable development is possibly the largest change challenge in human history.* (Ballard, 2000)

Much of the literature is written in a highly technical language (Chapters 1 and 2 provide only a taste!), and in itself this can inhibit digestion by all but the most dedicated and technically adept. By way of contrast, at least to us, our experience in Malta was with real people, dealing with real issues and articulated in everyday language. It was an emotional and subjective interaction and experience, and certainly could not be called 'science'. There were no 'objects' that sat outside the researchers (us) in a positivist sense that could be reduced and studied. We were as much a part of the systemic and prospective sustainability analysis (SPSA) as anyone else. It reminded us, if anything, of the conundrum faced by those working in sub-atomic physics. At these scales the researcher cannot be separated from the researched. The very act of looking at something can alter what one sees, and uncertainty is an integral part of the system.

Given that all of us in Malta took the SPSA journey together, there was inevitably a host of multiple perspectives that arose time and time again. This has been known for long in SD, but it is interesting how handling these has tended to take two quite divergent (in our opinion) directions. On the one hand one can sometimes detect an element of frustration that people are a component of SD at all. What we would call the 'sustainability as a science' route seeks to place all of the debate within a more familiar and controllable context of treating SD as a science. While people may be

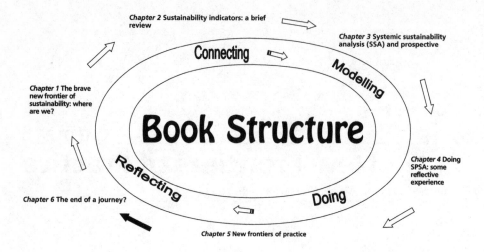

acknowledged (grudgingly) as components, the goal may be to find underlying scientific principles of SD, such as those of the Natural Step (Chapter 1), and call for them to be adopted. The following quotation sums it up for us:

> . . . *periodic attempts are made effectively to annex the theoretical found-ations of the concept of 'sustainability' as a proprietary sub-discipline of natural sciences such as physics and chemistry . . . At root, the implication of many such approaches is that 'sustainability', at least in its most important aspects, may be regarded as if it were an objectively determinate quantity.* (Stirling, 1999)

Seeing sustainability as science in this way has one advantage – the messy world of people can be ignored or at least passed to someone else to consider. However, while these principles may be based on good science, and promoted with the best of intentions to make the world a better place, they can be problematic in that they typically fail to take account of the imperfect human world in which they have to be applied; science and sustainability may not necessarily go hand in hand (Hutchcroft, 1996). We are constantly reminded that SD is about making things better for people; by definition and not as an inconvenient spin-off. As one SD practitioner puts it with regard to indicators of SD:

> *Since [SD] indicators are tools rather than answers, it is essential that their selection reflects people's values, concerns and dreams.* (Kline, 2000)

We would argue that this is hardly the language that suggests a sustainability science. This engenders a basis for compromise with all sorts of human activity, and can be an uncomfortable and frustrating reality:

> *The commonsense values underlying the nature-is-steward vision are not being communicated adequately to the public. We are losing the educational*

> *battle because the science underlying the nature-is-steward vision does not appear to be as convincing, let alone as dazzling, as is the science underlying the people-are-stewards vision of continuing growth and the conversion of wild habitat to manacled rivers and manicured forests.* (Harte, 1996)

> *Environmental sustainability (ES) is not pornography! Detractors claim that ES is like pornography: 'you'll know it when you see it'. Sustainability must not become a landfill dump for everyone's environmental and social wish lists.* (Goodland and Daly, 1996)

It is interesting to note the emotional divergence between the language of 'people's values, concerns and dreams' and the more disparaging vision of a 'social wish list'.

The second approach is to include people in the SD decision-making, and not just as passive recipients of someone else's directives. Agenda 21 was all about this encouragement of local action, and the word 'participation' is repeated time and time again in the conference reports. This immediately raises a problem though. Its all very well for a group of technicians to develop a set of Natural Step-type principles for SD, but what about the negative, as well as positive, impacts of these on people? If we really include people in the decision-making, and not just as token representatives, then we have to accept that they need to agree and be comfortable with any proposed changes. If the technical principles take precedence, then why bother to do 'participation'? Why not just tell people what they have to do and be done with it? No one wants, or even as far as we are aware, advocates this stance.

As we have seen in Chapter 1, there have been numerous attempts to widen public participation in SD. Various types of deliberative institution exist, and some workers are exploring how all of these pressures and divergent opinions can be combined into an integrated assessment. This is not easy. The 'public' is a highly diverse group, and trying to find a common denominator as to what they want and how to get it is like trying to hold water in a sieve. Even with such flagship SD projects as Sustainable Seattle, which is looked to by many as providing a guiding light (Besleme and Mullin, 1997), concerns have been raised:

> *The Sustainable Seattle approach suffers from a common notion that the measurement of 'sustainability' can be achieved through a public participation process.* (Brugmann, 1997a)

While Sustainable Seattle has been successful in terms of providing opportunities for debate and discussion amongst stakeholders, its limited impact in terms of influencing policy has been criticized (Guy and Kibert, 1998). This is a point we will return to later.

Inevitably there has to be compromise, and the result may well be a set of the 'wish lists' that Goodland and Daly (1996) are so concerned about, but some might not get all that they want. Will they feel disenfranchised by this? Will they feel the need to take to direct action to make others hear what they have to say? Quite possibly the answer is yes, but what are the alternatives? There are no perfect ways to get public participation for this very reason. All deliberative institutions make such compromises, and all can leave feelings of 'losing' and 'winning' in their trail. All are

applied by people, and can be highly variable as to public representation and participation (the two are different). In some situations perhaps it is only the most vocal
who are heard, while in others perhaps there is a tendency to only include 'opinion
leaders' and those with the most power and (it is assumed) influence. Perhaps one
could even say that those most likely to participate are those who are least mistrustful
of government (Pinfield, 1996). Given inevitable constraints on time and resources,
such short cuts can be highly tempting. We are highly sympathetic to these im-
perfections! Both of us have worked in developing countries where such participation
has been the byword of donors and projects for decades, and are only too aware of
the difficulties involved. Yet:

> *the application of different (but equally 'reasonable') value judgements and
> framing assumptions in analysis may lead to a situation where different
> studies yield radically different results.* (Stirling, 1999)

Ironically, if one takes these two responses to the extreme then the result can be dual
thinking (Brugmann, 1997a). Good science feeds into the turbulence of public
participation as rhythmic and structured waves strike an irregular and rocky shore.
The result could be a wearing down of both – the shoreline erodes and weakens, and
the waves lose their shape and rhythm. Technicians may become frustrated that their
message is not being listened to by policy-makers and politicians, and even more
frustrated with those fellow practitioners who adopt a social approach to sustainability
that appears to them to be weakening or detracting from the technical (Goodland and
Daly, 1996). We see increasing calls for better communication, the use of single
indices for SD to replace gross domestic product (GDP), calls for diagrams that
explain the state of SD in a clearer way (the dashboard and sustainability barometer),
or perhaps for more education. Yet we have had more than ten years of such efforts
and we still don't see the Policy Performance Index, sustainability dashboards or
similar devices appearing on our television screens or in our local newspapers on a
regular basis for us to respond to. There are exceptions, but in some cases early
attempts at such an engagement fell away. While the public can sometimes find these
in their local or national government Agenda 21 websites, they have to go and look
for them. Similarly, we have seen many projects that seek to encourage public
participation and we have yet to see any common denominators in perspective that
allow us to proclaim the discovery of a widely applicable set of answers (Stirling,
1999).

Perhaps a better approach is not to start with the technical, although this is not
to devalue the science that underpins these messages (Socolow, 1993), but with
people. Science feeds into this debate, but cannot be the sole concern (Fuentes, 1993;
Kellogg and Goss, 1997). Perhaps the answer may rest more with approaches in sustainability learning than with a more top-down technical driven process. This chapter
will explore some of the possibilities by drawing upon our experience in Malta and
combining it with the experience of others reported in the literature. We will begin
with an introductory discussion of dimensions in sustainability, before moving on to
develop a framework based on the Kolb learning cycle. We will end by making
linkages and suggestions that incorporate the dominant project approach to SD.

NEW WAYS OF THINKING ABOUT SUSTAINABILITY INDICATORS

It is often said that SD has many dimensions (Mitchell, 1996). This is perhaps most obvious in the sort of diagrams presented in Chapter 1, particularly the three inter-connected circles representing social, economic and environmental components. There are many other dimensions that one should consider. For example, let us take three basic questions relating to just one aspect of SD; namely the development and use of SIs as a tool:

Question 1: Who derived the indicator? The first dimension by which indicators may be characterized relates to their origin. They may be derived externally to the community (so-called 'expert' indicators) to which they are meant to be applied, or internally (so-called 'community' indicators). To date most attempts have been externally ('expert') led, but there is an increasing emphasis on internal ('participative') approaches. However, there is an ordinal graduation of participation, not all or nothing (Chapter 1 and Table 1.4).

Question 2: What is the indicator? It can be quantitative (numerical) or more qualitative (subjective). To date, most of them (and indicators in general) have been quantitative. Indeed, the typical definition of an indicator implies that it can be quantified (Chapter 2). This may seem a clear case of 'quantitative or not', without any sort of gradation. This may be so, but there may be some doubt, for example with the use of scores or ranks. It is true that these are numerical, but they are often used to make change something that is inherently qualitative (feelings, impressions) into a quantitative value.

Question 3: How is the indicator measured? It may be explicit (clearly articulated with standard methodologies for assessment and presentation) or implicit (not clearly articulated but assumed to apply). An explicit indicator would state the indicator clearly and provide the methodology and units that should be used to determine the value of the indicator. In addition there may be a stated target (reference condition) for the indicator, even if it is simply an expression of the direction of any desired change. To date, most indicators have been explicit, and again the definition of an indicator in many cases is something that has a clear, definable and replicable meth-odology. Chapter 2 provides a host of examples of explicit methodologies, including more exotic approaches such as fuzzy logic and weighted goal programming. How-ever, one could again imagine a gradation of implicit through to explicit, rather than only two extremes.

The result of all these questions is that one could imagine a series of three continuous axes within which to view SIs (see Figure 5.1).

The emphasis so far has been upon quantitative, explicit and external (QNEE) indicators, although there is an increasing emphasis upon quantitative, explicit and internal indicators (QNEI) derived by stakeholder participation. Both of these may be described generically as QNE* (see Figure 5.2).

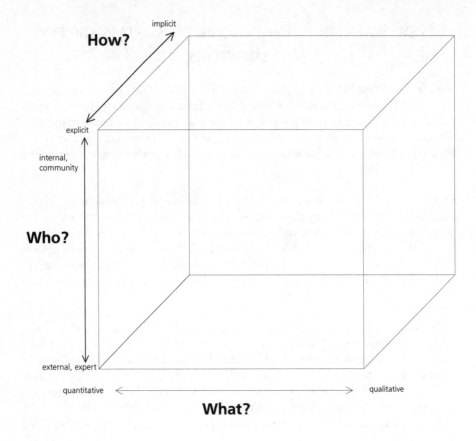

What is the indicator (on a scale of quantitative to qualitative in nature)?
Who developed the indicator (on a scale of external experts to internal community)?
How is the indicator to be gauged (on a scale of explicit methodology to an implied, 'gut feeling')?

Figure 5.1 *The how, who and what of sustainability indicators*

As already mentioned in Chapter 2, QNE* indicators are typically required to have the following characteristics:

- obviously must relate to some aspect regarded as important in sustainability;
- measurable in quantitative terms;
- definable and replicable methodology (explicit);
- sensitive to change; and
- data must be readily available/accessible.

Indeed, the QNE* group of indicators does have important advantages. Having an explicit set of defined indicators, with a replicable means of measurement, does have the advantage of allowing comparison across time and space. After all, one can prove

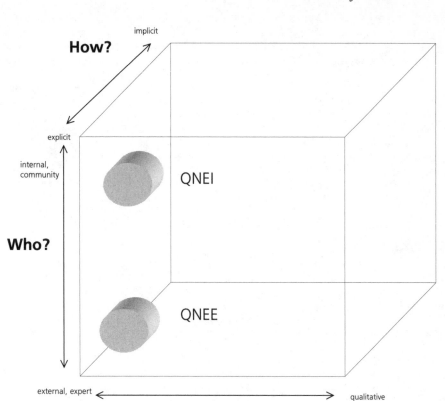

Figure 5.2 *The QNE* mindset of sustainability indicator development*
(quantitative and explicit). The form which dominates in most
sustainable development projects.

almost anything by perhaps only subtly changing the methodology: unsustainable becomes sustainable! The poor become rich! The polluter becomes the wise steward! By contrast, the qualitative and implicit ends of the three-dimensional spectrum have been almost completely unexplored (see Figure 5.3).

This may be highly ironic given that it is the qualitative and implicit (QLI*) types that are by far the most widely used in practice. Indeed, many would not realize that these are indicators, and that they use them. Individuals may not be in tune with QNE* indicators, even if presented as an attractive diagram, but all of us think that we know what constitutes sustainability, pollution or poverty. This is certainly so when we see ourself as the victim of the latter two, rather than being an unaffected observer! Linking such a 'you'll know it when you see it' stance in sustainability to 'pornography' (Goodland and Daly, 1996) is perhaps the most colourful (and dismissive?) way of expressing an awkward (for some) grain of truth.

Even terms such as: 'the density of cars on the roads is too high', 'we need to make more use of public transport' and 'there should be less pollution' may seem very

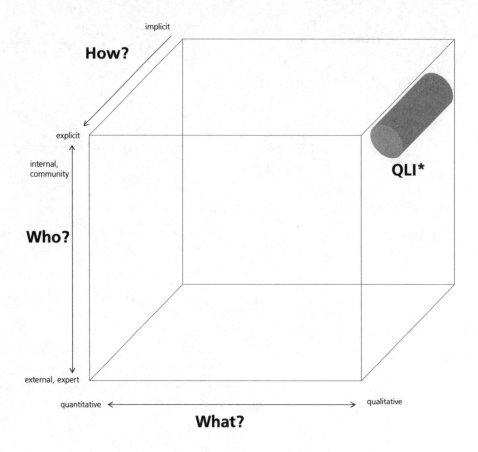

Figure 5.3 *The QLI* mindset of sustainability indicator development (qualitative and implicit). The form which dominates in our lives.*

subjective and emotional, but they are still indicators, and reference conditions (high, more, less) of a sort. Each statement implies a desired trend/level for sustainability and a notion of what the trend/level currently is. Therefore, while we may not typically quote QNE* indicators arising out of a scientific methodology, on an everyday basis we have gut feelings about what is good for sustainability. Terms such as 'more' and 'less' are not visualized in strict QNE* terms, but are inherently highly diffuse and nebulous. Nevertheless, does this make them of lesser value?

Even with these basic and simple dimensions one can begin to see some of the complexity involved, yet at the same time appreciate the contradictions of everyday usage of indicators as distinct from an assumption of relevance only to technocrats. In the next section we will take this analysis further by describing how almost every aspect of indicator development can be seen to encompass a host of potentialities, and how in practice we all make decisions at those points, often without consciously realizing it.

OTHER DIMENSIONS TO SUSTAINABILITY INDICATORS: A NEW SYNTHESIS (KOLB LEARNING CYCLE)

So far, this chapter has looked at the what, how and who at the level of modelling different types of indicator. This was intended as an introduction to alert the reader to the range of possibilities inherent within each axis of this three-dimensional space. However, there is a far richer story behind the indicators which are experienced. To find this richer story we need a heuristic device for developing an understanding and explaining a process for arriving at different visions of indicators. This will take us beyond the three dimensions displayed in Figures 5.1–5.3.

Of course, the case that we make in this book is tentative and exploratory. We intend to develop a model for understanding how and why different types of indicator arise in the work which we are undertaking at present in Mediterranean and in other European contexts. Our contention is that once we have such an analytical framework for appreciating decision-making in the formulation and application of indicators, this will help with the practice of such projects in the future.

The most fundamental emergent observation arising from our research is that indicators are not just a product of time and place, but in the conventional sense, as demonstrated in Chapters 1 and 2 of this book, they are also the outcomes of a host of epistemological assumptions made by the indicator developer. For example, we might expect scientists to seek indicators that are commensurate with their worldview, although they may or may not be aware of these assumptions and how they influence the decisions they make. However, in this case, and arising from our reading of the SI literature, the basis of most conventional indicators appears to arise as a function of a dominant mindset, which at best can be described as scientific and objective, and at worst appears almost pseudo-rationalist. Indicators that are presented to us in the most objective terms can hide a seething torment of cultural, epistemological, economic and professional influence. Even the most benign and neutral of indicators can hide this inner turmoil. For example, it is often said that car density on our roads is a key indicator in SD given the pollution cars generate and concerns over safety. Yet how is this measured? For example, when (day of the year and time of the day) and where (city, location in city)? Who funds this measurement, and will they continue to do so? Does the donor influence the way in which the measurement is done? For example, does the donor encourage cost-effective measurement and does this compromise more technically efficient alternatives? How does one determine the level of pollution engendered by car use? Is it necessary to prove to the donor that there is a problem with pollution in order to get funding, and do people's jobs and promotion prospects depend upon such funding? Is noise included as pollution? Even with such an apparently simple and uncontentious issue as car use, there are clearly thousands of such questions and dimensions that could be explored in thousands of different ways, and behind this may be the hidden and unhidden agendas of those paying for and carrying out the work, let alone the interest groups (drivers, pedestrians, environmental groups, etc) that may be involved and the post-war, liberal mindset which remains the foundation of much of the SD conventional wisdom.

In exploring this mindset, and the manner in which it infects the indicator conversation, we will make use of a formal thinking device or heuristic, the Kolb learning cycle (Kolb, 1984). Others have drawn a parallel between SD and the Kolb cycle (Hutchcroft, 1996) and the notion of SD as essentially a learning process (Meppem and Gill, 1998). We are applying Kolb for this purpose as the cycle represents a complete meta-methodology of the learning process, and as such can be applied in a number of different ways. The Kolb learning cycle is represented in Figure 5.4.

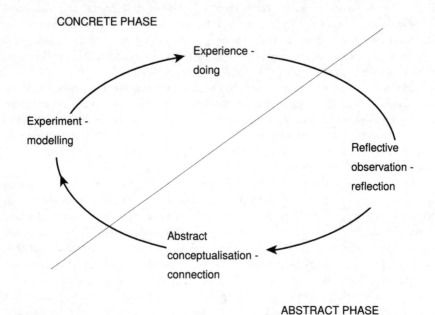

Source: after Kolb, 1984
Note: There are two phases and four elements of the cycle. The concrete phase represents the practice – the doing – while the abstract represents the 'thinking'.

Figure 5.4 *An Activity Sequence Diagram of Kolb's learning cycle*

As an example of how the cycle can be applied in different ways, Bell explored the cycle as being potentially representative of three different mindsets (Bell, 1999): the tyrannical, the scientific and the democratic (building from McGregor, 1960). Each model was true to its mindset and each could be reconciled to the four elements of the Kolb cycle in a manner that was commensurate with the needs of that mindset to learn and reflect according to its nature. The main elements of the three mindsets related to the relevant aspect of the Kolb cycle are set out in Table 5.1.

The Kolb cycle is applied here as the meta-methodology behind the three different types of intervention. The main point to be drawn from this is that the idea of a learning cycle can be applied in a manner that ranges from democratic participation through scientism to tyranny. The language can be the same but the experience of the intervention would be very different. Building on this, in the following section we

Table 5.1 *Theories W, X and Y and the Kolb learning cycle*

Elements of the Kolb learning cycle	Theory W Abuse	Theory X A systematic approach	Theory Y A systemic approach
Reflect	Interrogate those involved in the context	Label the thing you want to work with	Greet those in the intervention
Connect	Take over the context	Model the context in an objective fashion	Represent them in the system
Experiment	Instruct those in the context in the predetermined change	Intervene with the context	Invite them to engage in change
Experience	Measure the result	Appraise the result	Appreciate what is done

Note: The theories suggest how different people might respond when they apply the four elements of the cycle.

explore how the Kolb learning cycle can be applied in such a manner as to represent multiple mindsets in the visualization of SD and in the creation and application of SIs that match the vision. We will consider the nature of the surface of reality represented by these 12 mindsets by applying four different aspects of the learning cycle (with three dimensions at each of these).

It is important to note at the outset that we are not arguing that the four points of the cycle and the three dimensions in each that we have used are exclusive, definitive or definite. Rather we are using this approach to demonstrate that an indicator can arise from a range of different epistemological understandings and be used as a means to represent 'truth'. Indeed, it is a feature of this that all 'truths' are true to someone, somewhere and at some time, and the reader is encouraged to explore and create his/her own facets of the learning cycle and the possible dimensions that exist at each point. In fact, the epistemology may be highly idiosyncratic and quite unrepresentative of the needs of those who do not share the epistemological assumptions of the indicator author. In this case the indicators produced by an SD project may be experienced by those outside the project process as being inimical to their needs and divergent from their own understanding (as we experienced and described in the Malta context in Chapter 4).

Looking at Figure 5.1, it becomes evident that the three dimensions being applied in this simple analysis – engagement with stakeholders, approach to measurement and indicator type – are relevant to the Modelling aspect of the Kolb cycle. Our contention is that this is perhaps the aspect which would most appeal to those engaged in planning a new form of analysis and who were anxious to assess the value of different types of indicator. In a sense it perhaps represents the most obvious stage of the cycle to SD practitioners in that it focuses on methodology. However, in the Kolb cycle this is only one element of the four aspects underlying social action. In what follows we describe each of these four aspects and relate it to a similar three-dimensional continuum of conceptualization.

Figure 5.5 describes one view of the three-dimensional continuum of conceptualization relating to reflection. In our use of the term reflection an abstract process is engaged whereby the important aspects of learning are assimilated and either stored for subsequent action or dismissed as containing no relevant lessons. In order to provide reflection with a three-dimensional space we have considered it in terms of the three continua of:

1   Ideal to pragmatic type of focus; how we will 'do' the indicator?
2   Functional to dysfunctional approaches to change; who will 'do' the indicator?
3   Reductionist to systemic types of thinking; what form will the indicator take?

As we have already said, we do not consider these scales to be definitive or final but they do provide some interesting combinations of potential background to our reflection on indicators. For example, in our experience indicators are almost always considered by project teams and senior decision-makers as tending towards pragmatic measures with functional approaches to aspects of restricted and limited reductionist elements of wider reality. For example, the pragmatic is represented in choices of indicators which relate to small step improvements in the environment (eg an increase in the number of individuals of certain species such as salmon) rather than perhaps a more ideal but substantial change. The functional is seen in the focus on teams of applied 'experts' working to a project script which often seems written in advance of any understanding of specific contexts (eg the Malta CAMP project, see Chapter 3), and the reductionist is seen in the way in which indicators are often seen in relative isolation rather than considering the ways in which they interact and influence each other (beyond perhaps the cause–effect emphasis of the pressure–state–response (PSR) framework).[1] The third dimension may appear more provocative. By their very nature, of course, indicators can be seen as reductionist in that they are designed to reduce complexity to components and elements, but there are different degrees here. We would argue that tendencies towards reducing complexity to a single number or placement of the system in a category (eg the sustainability barometer) is one extreme, while allowing for a host of individual indicators covering elements of the economic, social and environmental dimensions of SD and allowing a range of interpretation represents the other.

Together, these characteristics place conventional indicator thinking in our experience in the element of the matrix which relates to the pragmatic, the functional and the tendency towards the reductionist (20 or fewer indicators, and the rise of highly integrative approaches). This is not a problem but might explain why systemic practitioners find so much of the indicator literature so frustratingly limited and the very basis of indicator projects to be at odds with the processes that they are intending to develop.

In the second aspect of the cycle we consider the continuum relating to connecting. 'Connecting' means linking personal and team reflection on experience to experiences from related and concerned areas and from others working in these fields. In this case we have selected the three scales of:

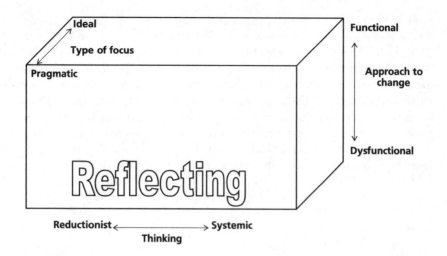

Figure 5.5 *A three-dimensional continuum of conceptualization in SD relating to the reflecting element of the Kolb learning cycle*

1 Anthropological to cosmological focus: how will we 'do' the indicator?
2 Pure to applied science: who will 'do' the indicator?
3 Control to partnership in social interaction: what form will the indicator take?

Again, these are not definitive or final. Rather they represent three continua that we personally find interesting and which we think might indicate some insights. Our own experience of the processes in the development of conventional indicators is that they tend to arise as a function of concern for mankind first and the environment second (ie weak sustainability). Please note that we are not saying that we agree with this, or that alternatives don't exist. We do of course acknowledge that a 'people first – environment second' interpretation within SD is highly contentious. We are not making a value judgement ourselves, only pointing out what we think is the centre of gravity in the SD literature at the turn of the century. For example, the focus on the needs of anthropos over cosmos is evident in the tendency to focus on over-production and income functions as shown in the harvesting of the seas and forests. Indeed, in our view the anthropocentric tendency in SD is focused more on issues of production and cost–benefit than quality of life or addressing poverty. Again this is a simplification but it might explain why those in the strong sustainability movement often complain that SIs are anthropocentric, with too little attention paid to the needs of the cosmos as a thing of value in and of itself.

Two other features of the use of indicators that we see as relevant at this connecting stage of the learning cycle are the tendency to see them as an outcome of applied science, and the endeavour to allow experts and others to 'control' social processes. The focus on applied scientific method is shown in the technological approach adopted in almost all indicators. There appears to be a definite tendency for indicators to be treated as quantities measuring processes 'in the world' or 'facts', as opposed to an approach which might include some questioning of the origin of the vision of SD being applied and the selection process of the indicators. Such questioning might be seen as a pure stance that takes time and effort away from the need to 'do something' (ie applied). The focus on the use of indicators to aid in the control of inherently social processes is evident in much of the indicator literature (Chapter 2). More recently, there has been a move towards the use of indicators as learning tools (the 'reactive' indicators of Moffatt, 1994), but for the most part they have been seen in a proactive sense as aids to policy development. In our view, the chain tends to be extractive-proactive in the sense that participation is seen as a means of getting relevant indicators to those in control who can then apply them. Whether this can be interpreted as a true partnership is open to question (see Figure 5.6).

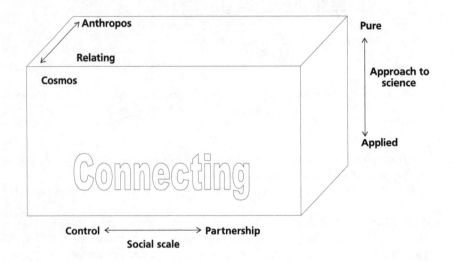

Figure 5.6 *A three-dimensional continuum of conceptualization in SD relating to the connecting element of the Kolb learning cycle*

The third, modelling aspect of the cycle is familiar from Figure 5.2 above. It relates to the:

1 Explicit or implicit indicator type: how will we 'do' the indicator?
2 Inclusivity or exclusivity of the engagement with stakeholders: who will do the indicator?
2 Qualitative or quantitative approach to measurement: what form will the indicator take?

Our observation, already described in this chapter, is that the conventional form of most SIs (with some notable exceptions given in Chapter 2) relates to a minimalist dialogue with stakeholders, seeking quantification at all costs and developing explicit indicators. Again this is a generalization, and is not intended to imply that all indicator projects have excluded stakeholders or taken a purely quantitative and explicit stance (see Figure 5.7).

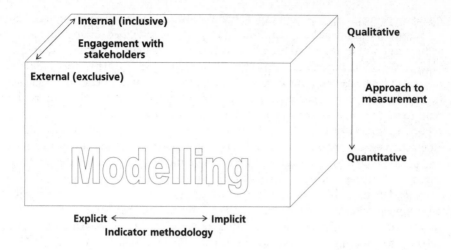

Figure 5.7 *A three-dimensional continuum of conceptualization in SD relating to the modelling element of the Kolb learning cycle*

Following on from the modelling of indicators comes their application in a wide variety of contexts and engaging a large number of different agencies. In considering the 'doing' of indicators we have applied the three scales of:

1 Singularity to diversity of outcome: how will we do the indicator?
2 Command to autonomy in approach to learning: who will do the indicator?
3 Purposive to purposeful projects: what form will the indicator take?

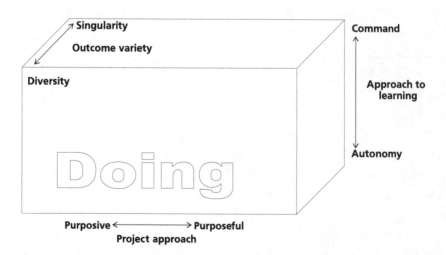

Figure 5.8 *A three-dimensional continuum of conceptualization in SD relating to the doing element of the Kolb learning cycle*

Again, working purely from our experience of working within SI related projects, the conventional wisdom indicates that most such projects are focused on single outcomes at any one point in space and time (for example, the northwest coast of Malta). The blueprint specifies outcomes to be achieved by the project and when they are to be reached. These have to be apparent in the sense that their attainment can be gauged (hence the objectively verifiable indicators of the logical framework). Projects also tend towards instruction and command as outcomes of learning (as seen in the reporting format of the United Nations development projects) as opposed to emergence and autonomy (as seen in many projects developed by non-governmental organizations), and in purposive projects where the project is an isolated and un-empowered cipher within the wider, determining scheme of programme or (for example) UN initiative. As already described (Chapter 3), the project approach is the dominant mindset in development, and key concerns are usually with achievement (have goals been reached?), accountability (has the money been well spent?) and getting the most impact from the resources allocated (value for money). Our contention is that, whether we like it or not, such features will continue to dominate. Taking the Kolb cycle as a whole, the dimensions combine as shown in Figure 5.9.

In Figure 5.9 we refer to 'prisons for thinking'. The prisons relate to traps for thinking. Our speculation is that certain types of reflection may well prejudice resulting connections, and this in effect will have an impact on modelling and doing.

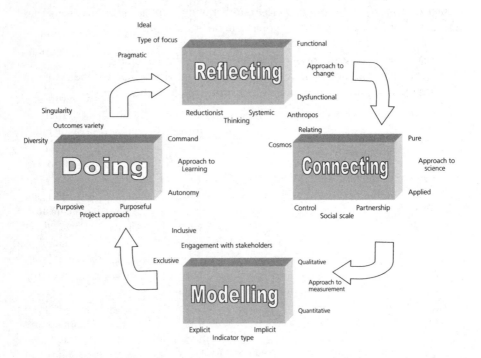

Figure 5.9 *Kolb and the four three-dimensional continua of conceptualization relating to reflection, connection, modelling and doing applied to an analysis of sustainable development and the use of indicators*

However, in considering the way in which the four elements of Kolb's learning cycle come together, we confronted a problem. We felt that the four aspects with their related three-dimensional matrix helped to inform us of mindsets and presumptions in the development of indicators. However, they did not as yet come together as a narrative, telling a story of the indicator process. A metaphor for this story arises from a consideration of physics and the use of space. Our interest was in the way in which ideas moved through conceptual space. Maybe we could find a metaphor if we looked at the way physical space behaves? Thinking about this, we noted that Euclidean concepts of space are distinguished by the simplicity of topological properties preserved through rubber-like stretching and compressing, but without any tearing. Similarly, in our model conceptual space is pulled around but there is no tearing, no disfigurement, of the Kolb cycle which provides the basis for various stages of thinking and action.

But, if space is a metaphor for conceptual space, what is the metaphor for the movement of practice and ideology through this space? Our attention moved from Euclid to the work of the US physicist John A Wheeler, the founder of geo-metro-dynamics. Wheeler pointed out the possibility of wormholes in space, analogous to the way in which the surface of a shape is modified if a worm bores through it. This is our metaphor. Figure 5.9 sets out a complex presentation of the integration of modes of action and the potential mindsets of SD and indicator practitioners. We refer to the Kolb learning cycle as our surface for human action and the potential path through the choices presented as the practitioner's wormhole. In effect, certain combinations of the coordinates at each node can be joined to form a wormhole through the cycle. Each point of the cycle has a multiplicity of combinations in the dimensions that exist there, and one could move effortlessly through a set of points in that space without even realizing that one is doing so. We would also contend that movement through one set of coordinates at one point in the cycle will tend to predetermine the exact coordinates for movement through other nodes. It is also possible that the wormhole changes shape by becoming broader at one point in the cycle (wide range of viewpoint) and narrowing at others (narrow set of viewpoint). Indeed, the sustainability wormhole could split into smaller wormholes and pass through a number of separate coordinates at one point in the cycle before merging to pass through one location at the next point. All sorts of possibilities exist. It could be postulated that each SD project constitutes a journey through the wormholes. Like Alice, SD project teams journey down into the burrow to discover what they will. Each choice results in further choices. Each assumption leads to its consequence. The journeys and choices are to be explored elsewhere in another publication. Alternatively each point could present a set of issues for discussion. Why a particular set of coordinates in that space is selected above all other possibilities could be analysed and reasoned rather than passing through a predetermined wormhole at speed and without questioning.

Now that we had a means to consider how the heuristic could be applied and developed, our task was to review how it performed under actual circumstances.

Taking our experience of conventional SI-related projects, the cycle appears as shown in Figure 5.10. We argue that this diagram not only describes the nexus for conventional indicator thinking and practice, it also explains the mental prison which allows and encourages this type of indicator experience: 'we must be here at this point because we were there at the previous point'.

Our initial concern had been to tinker with the modelling of indicators. It was only when we began to think about indicators as not just the atomized aspect of modelling but in terms of the wider elements of social action, both abstract and concrete, and then applied the Kolb cycle to develop this that we understood the nature of the glass ceiling which conventional indicator planning is up against.

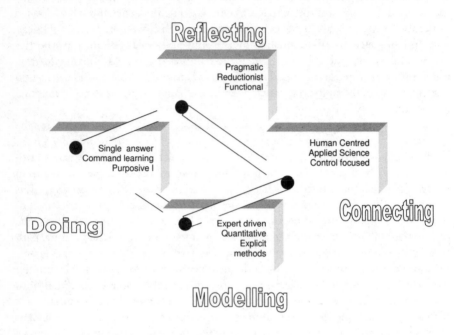

Figure 5.10 *Kolb and the four three-dimensional continua of conceptualization relating to reflection, connection, modelling and doing in conventional SD indicator experience within a typical project mindset*

Simply put, it is much more difficult to change the nature of the modelling of indicators if the team or project has not engaged first with the consciously or subconsciously held epistemic thinking which lies behind the modelling. What are the assumptions and worldviews behind the modelling process that has derived the indicators in the first place? Why do we find ourselves in this particular wormhole rather than another one? Why can't we pass through a different set of coordinates at a stage of the cycle rather than the one we seem destined to pass through? Why are we prisoners of the wormhole? Our heuristic encourages us to believe that the modelling used in the development of indicators is in main part a function of the epistemological mindset of social action as understood by the actors in the context. In the context in which we work with indicators the dominant mindset is described, as a simplified generalization, in Figure 5.10.

To make a fundamental change to the way in which indicators are modelled, we need to address the thinking and practice that go on at all stages of the cycle. This has fundamental implications for the project cycle approach to SD projects. It involves the consideration of project processes but also the power relations and mindsets which lie behind them. But the outcomes of an approach which sought to address all aspects of the cycle might be incalculable. To use a metaphor, for example, we do not know if a domino effect might be the outcome of a tendency to systemism at the Kolb stage of reflection. Purposeful projects (at the Kolb doing stage) might be the domino to systemic thinking in reflection. Valuing stakeholder views at the modelling stage might domino purposeful behaviour when engaged in doing. In terms of the cycle it could be argued that in order to develop autonomy-seeking connections the systemic reflection needs to be in place.

Making use of metaphors to appreciate the Kolb cycle makes the model sound rather deterministic and top-down. This would only be the case if the approach we advocate here were to be misconstrued as being 'true' or real. In fact, this is not the case. As we have stressed, the approach is an heuristic device, developed in order to assist the understanding of the social action of others, in this case others who develop indicators.

What it does imply is that it is not possible to change indicators (or any other outcome of social action) by piecemeal meddling at any of the four aspects of reflecting, connecting, modelling and doing. Rather, an holistic approach needs to be adopted whereby:

- The dominant power relations, mindset and assumptions (PM&A mix) of the stakeholders in the context are surfaced and respected.
- The likely outcomes of the PM&A mix are discussed.
- These outcomes are reflected upon and interpreted in terms of the desired outcomes.
- Changes to PM&A mix are agreed if appropriate.

In moving towards an understanding of the need to understand mindsets, outcomes and potential changes in mindset and assumptions, and making use of the Kolb learning cycle developed above, we have developed a 12-point questionnaire and from this a series of metaphors to describe the types of indicator which might be expected to arise from teams displaying different tendencies.

Depending on the outcomes of the questions, various patterns arise which, for the sake of defining PM&A, we have clustered into four distinct types. These types are:

1 the holistic;
2 the technocentric;
3 the organizational; and
4 the environmental.

These four types are not definitive or scientifically derived but they do represent certain tendencies which are interesting to speculate about in the formation of an SD project that intends to use indicators as a device. We argue that each of these has different strengths and weaknesses in such projects and also pose different opportunities and threats for their future (SWOC: strengths, weaknesses, opportunities and constraints). Table 5.3 shows the patterns of response to the 12 questions which might indicate a proclivity to each type.

Table 5.2 *Questionnaire for teams about to engage in SD indicator development*

	Question	Response Yes/No
1	When I reflect on my experience I am interested in lessons that provide me with wide-ranging and general guidance	
2	I am only interested in change which arises from an obvious need	
3	My SD indicators need to reflect the whole and not just parts of the context	
4	My focus is determined by the needs of mankind first	
5	I like to consider ideas from a wide and abstract spectrum when I consider SD and indicator contexts	
6	We need to bring people together to consider how we will do SD and develop indicators	
7	I like to have a wide and diverse team to work with for all aspects of project work	
8	Often SD indicators are unquantifiable	
9	Indicators can often arise from people's experiences rather than scientific observations	
10	Projects are at their best when they focus narrowly on limited outcomes	
11	Indicators teach us what we need to do	
12	A project works best when its goals are set by the project team itself	

The 12 questions could be asked of the project team members before the project begins. The definition of types could then be informative in terms of indicating the manner in which the project might develop. This information in turn might indicate the wormhole for the project and thus overall project strengths and weaknesses. Alternatively, the questions (or variants) could be applied during the life of the project, with stakeholders included throughout and reflective learning and practice a key outcome of the project and not just an emergent surprise. Whatever the mode, the cycle would allow a more reflective and questioning attitude towards the SD project so those involved know why they are moving through the particular sustainability wormhole that they have chosen.

Table 5.4 sets out the SWOC of each of the four types. Our intention is not to produce a tyrannical method for selecting the 'right' team for an indicator project. Rather, the intention is to develop a model for gaining better early understanding of the mindset of an indicator project team and so providing a scenario device for plotting the likely path which a project might follow – and so understand some of the problems which it might encounter.

Table 5.3 *Four tendencies and types in SD indicator development*

No	Question	Holisticic	Technocentric	Organizational	Environmental
			Tendency and type		
1	When I reflect on my experience I am interested in lessons that provide me with wide-ranging and general guidance	Y	N	N	Y
2	I am only interested in change which arises from an obvious need	N	Y	Y	Y
3	My SD indicators need to reflect the whole and not just parts of the context	Y	N	Y	Y
4	My focus is determined by the needs of mankind first	N	Y	N	N
5	I like to consider ideas from a wide and abstract spectrum when I consider SD and indicator contexts	Y	N	N	N
6	We need to bring people together to consider how we will do SD and develop indicators	Y	N	Y	N
7	I like to have a wide and diverse team to work with for all aspects of project work	Y	N	Y	N
8	Often SD indicators are unquantifiable	Y	N	Y	N
9	Indicators can often arise from people's experiences rather than scientific observations	Y	N	N	N
10	Projects are at their best when they focus narrowly on limited outcomes	N	Y	Y	N
11	Indicators teach us what we need to do	N	Y	N	Y
12	A project works best when its goals are set by the project team itself	Y	N	Y	N

Table 5.4 *SWOC for the four tendencies and types of Table 5.3*

Holistic	Environmental
Holistic Strengths · Mindset is wide ranging · Interested in relationships · Concerned with connectivity	**Environmental strengths** · Mindset is focused on environmental issues · Interested in natural cycles · Concerned with natural continuity
Holistic Weaknesses · Tendency for complexity · Hard to focus · Too many targets	**Environmental Weaknesses** · Misses the human need (eg need to address poverty) · Idealistic · Outcomes can be hard to justify to stakeholders
Holistic Opportunities · Seeing round the corner to the next issue · Seeing links to other issues · Engaging in future problem solving	**Environmental Opportunities** · Engaging in planet-level problem solving and the local becomes lost · Establishing the environment as the main basis for SD indicator formulation · Relating economic and social indicators to the environment
Holistic Threats · Confusion · Project creep · Babel (too much talk)	**Environmental Threats** · Ignoring other issues, such as the economic (strong sustainability) · Losing support from stakeholders · Tunnel vision
Organizational	**Technocentric**
Organizational Strengths · Mindset is human-focused · Interest in operational issues · Concerned with operational efficiency · Concerned with clear and tangible outputs	**Technocentric Strengths** · Mindset is technical · Interest in detail · Concerned with the way that specific elements operate
Organizational Weaknesses · Targets what is known to be needed · Avoids complex issues · Dismissive of long-term issues	**Technocentric Weaknesses** · Narrow focus · Avoids human issues · Avoids non-quantifiable issues · Quantification of the non-quantifiable (weak sustainability)
Organizational Opportunities · Developing organization-wide visions of SD indicators · Establishing the organization as the basis for indicators · Extending the organization view into indicator development	**Technocentric Opportunities** · Rigour as the basis for indicators · Focus and clarity in indicator development · Establishing clear standards in indicator formulation, including replication of method
Organizational Threats · Ignoring other issues · Losing support from stakeholders · Tunnel vision	**Technocentric Threats** · Concentration · Narrow limits · Monotony

APPLYING THE LEARNING CYCLE IN SUSTAINABLE DEVELOPMENT

All of the foregoing presents a picture of multiple-dimensionality in indicator development, and given that indicators are but a practical tool that helps solidify ideas, in SD itself. Yet perhaps the most noticeable outcome of our work in Malta was the joy that the participants showed in learning about SD through indicators. Perspectives were widened, and even if not a single indicator gets 'used' in the sense of helping to guide policy intervention, all agreed that much insight was gained and there were benefits as a result. This is not a new insight in itself, and others have had a similar experience. Elizabeth Kline, for example, describes a similar set of conclusions that arose out of the Boston Indicators project in the US (Kline, 2000). As already described, the SPSA process in Malta shadowed the Kolb cycle and decisions were made at each point by all involved to move in a certain way. Blue Plan, as the funder, was a major element of this, and the focus towards the end of the cycle on scenario planning (hence the 'P' that was inserted in SSA) was but one example of its influence.

It was as though the journey through the cycle in itself provided useful outcomes, even if none of the resultant indicators are ever used. SPSA did not set out to present the Kolb cycle and explore all options at each point, although in practice some of this did take place, particularly in the early phases of the SPSA. The project mindset was focused far more on the lists of indicators and implications for policy as outcomes than on stakeholder learning for sustainability as a valid outcome in itself. Exploration of scenarios in a 'What If?' mode was meant to project some future policy options to make things better, rather than provide a reflective analysis of Malta and why it is where it is in terms of SD. This is not a new insight. Moffatt (1994) has also described these two roles as proactive (designed to feed into policy) and reactive (to aid reflective analysis) indicators. Visioning is not a bad thing per se, and can feed into both reactive and proactive indicator development (Ballard, 2000). A knowledge of why one is in the position one is in can help with a better appreciation of how to get to some future goal. After all:

> *Effective learning involves not only discovery and adaptation but also the need to understand the assumptions or mental models of the decision-makers.* (Meppem and Gill, 1998)

Yet maybe the framework we have proposed in the chapter provides an opportunity for all of these dimensions to be considered – a merging of the bottom-up community with the 'expert' visions in a systemic learning for sustainability. Outcomes will be multiple and occurring at many places in the cycle, rather than ending with the sort of tables in Appendix 1 as the only valid (measurable) project outcomes.

Systemic learning for sustainability analysis founded on the Kolb cycle would therefore have all these outcomes built in and encouraged rather than see stakeholder participation as a better way of getting indicators. This may seem unpalatable for a project donor. After all, it is the tables in Appendix 1 that they may want, albeit while accepting that stakeholder participation is necessary to get there (extractive-proactive). Spending time and resources in discussing all points of the learning cycle may not appear to be productive in that sense, and could perhaps even be seen as inimical in that it deflects attention from the end point and could perhaps call into question the project blueprint process.

How is what we propose different from other foci on learning for sustainability? Meppem and Gill (1998) provide a case that is very similar to our own, and we agree with much that they say. Box 5.1 sets out their main conclusions.

Box 5.1 *Some conclusions expressed by Meppam and Gill following their analysis of sustainability as a learning concept*

Sustainability describes a state that is in transition continually:

- The objective of sustainability is not to win or lose and the intention is not to arrive at a particular point.
- Planning for sustainability requires explicit accounting of perspective (worldview or mindset) and must be involving of broadly representative stakeholder participation (through dialogue).
- Success is determined retrospectively, so the emphasis in planning should be on process and collectively considered, context-related progress rather than on achieving remote targets. A key measure of progress is the maintenance of a creative learning framework for planning.
- Institutional arrangements should be free to evolve in line with community learning.
- The new role for policy-makers is to facilitate learning and seek leverage points with which to direct progress towards integrated economic, ecological and sociocultural approaches for all human activity.

This describes a move away from a culturally inappropriate, exclusive epistemology of positive and normative definitions to a process that facilitates reflective insight and the genuine sharing of ideas.

Source: Meppam and Gill, 1998

Where we differ from Meppam and Gill (1998) is perhaps in their rejection of goal-orientated decision-making:

> *There is a need to be cautious of prescriptive goal-orientated decision-making which makes assumptions about the ability of policy-makers and resource managers to control systems under their jurisdiction.* (Meppam and Gill, 1998)

Cautious yes, but we live in a world that demands ever-increasing accountability from those providing resources to those expected to use them, let alone those meant to benefit. We have already seen how blueprint projects, and all the paraphernalia such as planning documents and Logical Frameworks that surround them, are still very much in vogue. How do such outcome-focused institutions, perhaps with 'remote targets', adapt to take on board the issues in Box 5.1?

We suggest that part of the problem rests with the separation that occurs in the minds of some sustainability workers. For example, some have typically referred to community indicators as distinct from those generated by experts, and the result is the sort of dichotomy presented in Table 2.4. Here community sustainable development indicators (CSDIs), designed to help facilitate the sort of learning engagement described by Meppam and Gill (1998), are at the other end of the spectrum from so-called expert indicators (created with or without public participation) designed to feed into policy. Projects, such as SPSA in the Malta CAMP, are intended more for the latter than the former. We suggest that a practical way forward may be to use the Kolb framework to help unite them all. On one level indicators provide us with a way of discussing important and contested issues; they become common currencies of debate and exploration. On a further level they become an end product to be used in policy. In that sense we are in tune with Meter (1999), who suggests combining community and expert indicators (Table 2.5). The difference is that we propose the development of these (community and expert) within a learning cycle in which they all (including the expert) take part. Neither would we necessarily expect the community (or stakeholders) to use the indicators in the sense that the project would use the word. Instead, their usage would be more as a learning device within the cycle. Yet at the same time the framework concedes that the dominance of the standard project approach, at least when seen in terms of outcomes at defined places, in defined timescales and at defined costs, is unlikely to diminish. We would like to call this process systemic learning for sustainability analysis (SLSA). It differs from our earlier SSA in opening up the debate at each stage of the cycle and encouraging reflection at all stages, while still allowing a valid end point to be a set of indicators intended for policy. SSA tended to focus more on the end product (Appendix 1), with participation seen as a better way of getting there, and less on reflective learning as an outcome in itself. SPSA, as applied in Malta, was SSA with an emphasis on 'What If?' questioning at the end of the cycle.

There still remains the gap between the generation of the indicator frameworks and putting these into practice in order to influence policy. Some rightly point out that public participation can lead to frustration if the indicators go nowhere in terms of practical use. Neither can we say that education in itself necessarily leads to change (Brugmann, 1997a). On the one hand our suggested emphasis on multiple outcomes would help alleviate some of this sense of frustration. It was noticeable in the Malta project how no such frustration set in, even though the usage of the indicators in Appendix 1 is uncertain. At the time of going to print, the intention is that the indicators will feed into a Maltese Commission of Sustainable Development. On the other hand, if policy-makers can be included in the learning process, and they should be, then one can imagine that such issues of eventual usage would form an important element for discussion throughout the process. After all, no holds are barred and even concerns such as 'but no one wants these things; we are far more interested in economic indicators that matter in political terms on the electoral campaign trail' are matters for dissection and discussion. The main point is that our learning framework helps keep 'contesting actors together' and 'provides them with a platform for fruitful debate' (Kasemir et al, 1999).

We believe that SLSA, which treats the very process of going through a cycle as an outcome in itself, sits comfortably with the more traditional project focus on hard lists of indicators that can be fed through to policy and ultimately change. It may require some courage on the part of donors to see such multiple outcomes as important in themselves, given that they may be uncheckable or even invisible in terms of devices such as the Logical Framework. We are not suggesting that funders abandon a focus on eventual outcomes. It is important that indicators feed into policy, and these should include elements of an assessment of performance on the part of implementing agencies (Brugmann, 1997b; Guy and Kibert, 1998). By way of contrast, Meppam and Gill (1998) call for a retreat from this quantitative-obsessed scenario planning that one often sees in the SD literature[2] into a pure learning mode:

> *Effort is then focused on understanding the inter-relationships in develop-ment planning, which leads to improved understandings of the dynamics of change, rather than quantitatively measuring parts of the economy or environment at particular points in time and making predictions about future states.* (Meppam and Gill, 1998)

There is one remaining problem that we did see a lot of in Malta. The standard project approach typically relies on secondment of government and parastatal staff to the project. No allowance is typically made for these additional duties, and the result can be a balancing act with surges of enthusiasm and engagement during workshops. Again, it is hard to see this changing given the way such projects operate and expect-ations from donors of trying to achieve as much as possible for as little as possible. Seconding staff is an obvious response. In these circumstances SLSA as an approach may offer greater advantages over single-outcome projects, as people may see something in it for themselves – enjoyment and liberation. We can't pretend that everyone will be happy with or enjoy the experience, but that's life!

What we suggest is open to a host of potential criticisms that usually surround participative approaches in SD. Unequal power relations still exist (Kasemir et al, 1999), and ultimately much depends upon the skill of the facilitator and the specific tools he/she applies. For example, it has surprised us somewhat how reviewers of our first book have tended to focus more on analysing and comparing methods (eg questioning the use of soft systems as distinct from another favoured methodology) without a consideration of the importance of the individual. Participative methods are highly dependent upon the skill of facilitators, and in our view this can override the impact of one method or another. Also, different groups may well come up with different outcomes in the learning cycle. This is not a problem in a learning sense, but policy-makers may find such multiplicity of end indicators confusing and this could perhaps provide an excuse for inaction. Navigation through this requires skilled facilitation, but even here there are limits. The bottom line is that this is art not science. SLSA in itself does not address these criticisms. A bad facilitation will result in poor participation and weak outcomes – although an indicator list akin to Appendix 1 will still be achievable and look like a reasonable outcome. But this will happen whether one is using citizen juries, study circles or consensus conferences.

SUMMARY

This chapter has been all about reflection on one specific practice and thinking of ways out of some of the boxes the typical SD project approach has got itself into. SD remains the holy grail for enlightened world planners, and SIs remain a popular means to assess levels of sustainability in communities, regions and nations. However, the box is evident and pernicious. Indicators appeal to a mindset for measurement yet they do not appeal to the popular imagination and this must limit their appeal to real people – the global community that is the target for the sustainability project. It is evident that a new way is needed, a new path forward, a way out of the box of our own understanding.

In this chapter we have discussed the various mindsets that characterize the types of indicator which beset us. We have talked about the mental prisons which our pre-conceptions place us in. We have made use of the Kolb cycle, the mindsets heuristic and the wormhole metaphor as a road through this multi-dimensional space to enable us to describe the reason why so many SD projects end in apathy and no change. We have championed the learning cycle (manifested as SLSA) as our key meta-methodology, as our way forward and as the noble outcome which we can always expect, even in times of the most severe adversity. The result is a set of multiple outcomes – the indicator lists as given in Appendix 1 – but also the enjoyment and fulfilment of learning and reflection. Perhaps we can paraphrase this as 'mixing business with pleasure'. However, we have also alluded that even with a reflective systemic practitioner who is epistemologically aware and knows of both the prison and the box, there is still every opportunity for the old mindset to maintain its dominance.

We might refer to this mindset as the 'projectified world'. Not a nice title and poor use of English but it does rather sum up the project format and mindset which continues to dominate and which, through its worldview of predetermined outputs, accountability and fixation on value for money, makes sterile and unchallenging the way in which SD is undertaken and perceived and utterly fails to engage with issues of power and conflict.

In our final chapter we will attempt some kind of synthesis and indicate a way forward.

Chapter 6

The End of a Journey?

*We shall not cease from exploration, and the end of all our exploring will
be to arrive where we started and know the place for the first time.* (from
T S Eliot's *Little Gidding*)

The authors see this book as the outer manifestation of a considerable number of
journeys. We have explored a number of domains in the broad church of sustainable
development (SD), and specifically focused on sustainability indicators (SIs). We have
reviewed the progress made by a number of practitioners in these domains of
experience, and tried to extract some commonalities. We have explained our own use
of a methodology – systemic sustainability analysis (SSA) – in the context of Malta,
and particularly how this had to operate within a project mindset. The influence of
the donor was particularly apparent in this project, hence the transition from SSA to
systemic and prospective sustainability analysis (SPSA), but this was but one of many.
Most importantly, from our point of view, we have explored the mindsets and
attitudes behind the experiences we have had and have tried to understand why things
are the way they are in the projectified world.

Table 6.1 sets out this process. It comprises four columns that set out the main
content of the chapters in the book, the personal insights we gleaned from the material
in those chapters and some characteristics of those insights.

The table is designed so that it can be read as a narrative by itself. As such it should
not need explanation. However, it is useful to draw out the main theme.

There appears to be a dislocation and dysfunction in the experienced world of
SD and SIs as a tool to help attainment. In our opinion, this dislocation is in part the
result of a gap between the espoused theory of the projectified world and the
experienced theory of the SD ideal; the very soul of sustainability. On the one hand,
we need control, accountability and known outcomes. Resources are scarce and
understandably people want assurance that what they fund will work and they are able
to know it has worked. Yet SD is meaningless without local control, emergence and
inclusion. People have to be given control over their lives and not fitted into a project
plan. This gap is significant because almost all actions to manage it are an attempt to

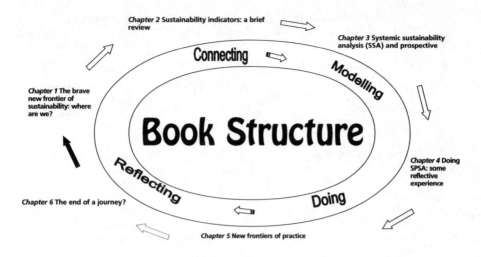

Table 6.1 *This book as an exploratory process of learning*

Chapter	Main content	Insights	Characterized by
1/2	In which we explore the sustainability indicator/sustainable development complex and experience it as vast, diverse and contested terrain. Typically project-orientated. At the same time, SD and indicators remain a popular approach.	The insight was the lack of insight. The terrain manifests as comprising the 'dialogue of the deaf'. Theory competes with theory and practice manifests very often as prejudicial use of favoured methods.	Everyone arguing their angle, turf war, tower of Babel.
2/3	In which we begin to work around the edges of the world order – the projectification of the world. This is time for a reality check. Is this just our experience or is it the 'real world?'. Our experience presents a desperate focus on accountability, tangible outcomes and value for money as key elements of the project. This is stylized in the predetermined outcomes evident in the Logical Framework approach, etc.	There appears to be widespread denial in the academic and practitioner community, but SD does occur in a projectified world. A world driven by a project mindset. It is both a prisoner and a victim of this mindset.	A community of bureaucrats seeking tangible and deliverable outcomes. There is a tendency to anxiously 'get busy', to show that we are 'doing something'. The project cycle neglects both learning and a cycle. Even if circularity is presented as desirable, there are rarely the resources and time to achieve it.

Table 6.1 *This book as an exploratory process of learning (continued)*

Chapter	Main content	Insights	Characterized by
3/4	In which we recognize the mismatch between the soul of SD on the one hand (inclusion, local decision-making, participation, emergent outcomes) and the drivers of the projectified world (top-down, donor agency agenda-driven). Therefore we discuss SPSA with the emphasis on systemic – maybe as a means to square the circle.	Managing the gap between the mindset of SD and the mindset of the project.	Paradox. We have what we do not want. We need what we cannot have.
5	In which we discuss self-knowing and epistemological shift – the systemic reflective practitioner. We suggest a prison is only a prison when you are constrained by it. Need to be aware of alternative roads before you can travel them.	The value of learning in itself. The 'eureka' moment in teams, when minds come together and insight is gained, can be captured, celebrated and applied in projects. So, is there a new variant of the methodology? SL(earning)SA?	Your chains are yours. I do not have to accept them as mine.
5/6	The constraints on the autonomy of SD communities are from a political/economic, conventional mindset. This mindset is a gross simplification of reality (see the insight). In terms of the experience of the projectified world, we know where we are right now and we know where we would like to be but to get there requires a shift in the conventional model. This would move us from an SLSA, where learning is benignly tolerated and is a valid outcome but is not sought or needed by the project mindset, to empowered SLSA, where the coalition of interests can set its own agenda and develop its own vision of the sustainable goal and develop indicators accordingly, as well as choosing what actions will occur to try to ensure sustainability.	There is too much simplification of apparent complexity. Projects, if they are to work, need requisite variety in order to manage complexity. Need to shift attention away from the doing of projects and the accounting of projects to the systemic and inclusive consideration of projects. Only complexity can know complexity.	Celebrating complexity. To consider outcomes and to take ownership of processes locally is not to lose control, but it does mean sharing control.

paper over the gap and not to fill it. The project mindset and its indicators of success are present and people are often slotted in as 'participants' with little (if any) real control over outcomes. At worst, they may be there to provide nothing more than a passive acceptance of project goals.

SPSA is one such attempt to paper over the gap. In SPSA we celebrate learning, but we remain victims of the 'projectified world order'; the indicator lists of Appendix 1 were the critical outcomes, not the learning of the people involved. We now believe we must go further, hence our new emphasis on learning and reflection in systemic learning for sustainability analysis (SLSA). The need is to hand over the means of assessing, planning and identifying sustainability to the people whom it affects.

We strongly believe that this cannot be achieved by conventional means.

Rather, for real SD to become a commonly understood value of civilized life in the 21st century, the reification of monetary value needs to be overthrown in a new vision of empowered stewardship. This isn't yet another attack on weak sustainability, although we do agree with much of the criticism espoused by others, but rather an acknowledgement of the way in which monetary issues dominate in our projectified worldview that encompasses SD by default. A more empowered stewardship would indicate not only the responsibility of a dominant species on a small planet, but also the willing service of a compassionate and humble humanity to the needs of a future utterly dependent upon it for its very existence.

Only by such a transition can the projectified world give sustainability a chance.

Systemic and Prospective Sustainability Analysis (SPSA) in Malta

The following tables present the indicator lists that arose out of one passage through the SPSA methodology in Malta. There were five thematic teams:

1 tourism and health;
2 soil erosion/desertification control management;
3 integrated water resources management;
4 marine conservation areas; and
5 sustainable coastal zone management.

Each team produced its own list of indicators, with help provided by the SPSA team.

For each table we have provided:

- the name of the indicators and the units in which they should be measured;
- bands of equilibria (ie reference conditions) for each of the indicators. These are the minimum and maximum values that equate to sustainability;
- historical values of the indicators (1990 onwards) if known; and
- some brief notes and explanations.

We don't intend here to discuss the pros and cons of each of the indicators, and neither do we intend to go into the debate that surrounded indicator selection and bands of equilibria. All we wish to do here is provide assurance that SPSA can generate indicator frameworks in a participative mode. At the funder's (Blue Plan) request, there was an emphasis on using these indicators to generate multiple (prospective) scenarios for sustainable development (SD) in Malta (hence the re-designation of systemic sustainability analysis, developed by Bell and Morse into SPSA for the Malta project).

The reader should also note that these indicator lists are the result of only one passage through the SPSA process. In SPSA they should form the starting point of a second round of the cycle.

We wish to thank Mr Tony Ellul of the Maltese Planning Authority for allowing us to reproduce the indicators tables here.

Table A.1 *Team 1: Tourism and health*

Indicator	Note	Band of equilibrium		Time series data (if available)						
		Max	Min	1990	1995	1996	1997	1998	1999	2000
Gastro-enteritis outbreaks in NW	No of total outbreaks in a year	3	1				2	1	6	5
Gastro-enteritis cases in NW	No of total cases in a year	9	5				8	6	5	7
Rodent control – bait placed	No of takes from baits placed	3	2							
Bathing water quality	% of samples meeting acceptable levels of faecal coliforms (<1000 milligrams per litre (mg/l))	95	85			98.5	98.7	98.6	97.4	98.3
Risk factor grading of hotels	% of inspections falling within grades A–C	90	70					76	72	68
Risk factor grading of catering establishments	% of inspections falling within grades A–C	90	70							57
Rodent control – residents' complaints	No of complaints from residents	5	1		9	6	9	7	14	1
Beach quality as compared to Blue Flag	In % points attained	210	71							
Beach quality as compared to health criteria	% of total beach sample observations falling within Grade A	100	80			75.4	80.6	81.6	65.7	71.7
Media interest in tourism health	% of positive/negative media coverage	90	50							

Table A.2 *Team 2: Soil erosion/desertification control management*

| Indicator | Note | Band of equilibrium | | Time series data (if available) | | | | | | |
		Max	Min	1990	1995	1996	1997	1998	1999	2000
Official flood warnings	No of warnings given	10	4							
No of claims for compensation	Annual number of claims	50	25		217		50	72		72
No of breaches in rubble walls	No of breaches	10	5							11
Length of breaches in rubble walls	Length in metres	100	50							69.8
Land tenure	% of agricultural land owned and farmed by owner	50	25							15

Notes: agriculture is not a major industry in Malta. Note the emphasis on rubble walls. Loss of the stone from these has become a major issue (used for decoration, building, etc). Results in a degradation of the Maltese scenery and also results in greater erosion.

Table A.3 *Team 3: Integrated water resources management*

Indicator	Note	Band of equilibrium		Time series data (if available)						
		Max	Min	1990	1995	1996	1997	1998	1999	2000
Quality of drinking water	Chloride level (mg/l)	800	200	457	771					517
Quality of drinking water	Nitrate level (mg/l)	50	15	75	54					56
Use index	% of total users	100	85	>99	>99					>99
Water consumption	Litres per capita per day	150	90	77.9	88.2					72.9
Pollution in groundwater	Nitrate levels (mg/l)	50	25	67.4	70.1					65.27
Water affordability	Maltese pounds (lm)/m³	1.1	0.12	0.105	0.327					0.516
Recycled water	% of water consumed	80	50	1.5	1.4					4.6
Quantity of produced water	Million m³/year	20	10	39.59	51.61					35.15
Piezometric levels	Metres	3.25	0.5	2.81	2.63					3.11
Leaked water	m³/hour	600	300	2421	2800					1200

Notes: Recycled water: this refers to the amount of recycled wastewater, and is measured as a percentage of water consumed. Many of the quality indicators are set by EU/national regulations. Note emphasis on abstraction, loss, recycling. Water is a big issue in Malta. Team did spend some time thinking about how it could get a handle on the illegal abstraction of water.

Table A.4 *Team 4: Marine conservation areas*

Indicator	Note	Band of equilibrium		Time series data (if available)						
		Max	Min	1990	1995	1996	1997	1998	1999	2000
Poly-hydrocarbons (PHCs) in effluent (bunkering)	mg/l	10	0							
Level of bunkering operations in Malta	% of total operations in Malta	20	5				20	17.5	25	19.3
Marine vessels in MCA	No of vessels	70	30							
Quality of bathing water	No of points obtained on faecal coliform readings	50	35		40	45	50	45	50	40
Complaints by visitors	% of visitors	10	5							

Notes: MCA = marine conservation area. Bunkering (flushing out cargo hold with sea water) is a major issue in Malta. Should be done out at sea and away from the coast. It leads to high concentrations of toxic hydrocarbons (PHCs) in the water. Also note the emphasis on bathing water and complaints. Reflects importance of tourism in Malta.

Table A.5 *Team 5: Sustainable coastal zone management*

Indicator	Note	Band of equilibrium		Time series data (if available)						
		Max	Min	1990	1995	1996	1997	1998	1999	2000
Applications granted – other	Granted as a % of m² submitted	70	30				1	63		
Applications granted – commercial	Ditto	75	40				23	64		
Applications granted – tourism/recreation	Ditto	60	35				34	2		
Applications granted – domestic	Ditto	90	80				49	54		
Scheduled/protected areas in NW	% of the total coastal area of the NW	80	65			7				66
Applications granted – agriculture	Ditto	95	75				0	24		
Applications granted – listed buildings	Ditto	90	70				0	0		
Abandoned agricultural land	% of total agricultural land	25	7			12	12	13	14	15
Fish farms in the NW	No of farms	5	2	3		4	4	4	4	5
Bunkering operations in NW	No of bunkering operations	NA	NA							
Hardstone quarries	Size of quarries by surface area (000 m²)	800	400							775
Production from hardstone quarries	% of national production	80	50			70				60
Cars travelling through the NW	Number of cars during peak	3000	1000	1630				4109		1000
Marine vessels in the NW	Number of marine craft during peak weekend	700	400			800				
Enforcement actions by planning authority (PA)	Annual number of cases	60	25			104	75	67	52	68
Reports to ALE	Annual number of ALE reports	60	25					34	67	109
Unemployed as a % of working population	% of working population in NW	3	1							1.8
Applications granted – industrial	Granted as a % of m² submitted	65	30				0	0		

Indicator	Note	Band of equilibrium		Time series data (if available)						
		Max	Min	1990	1995	1996	1997	1998	1999	2000
Applications granted – services	Granted as a % of m² submitted	95	80				100	77		44
Full-time farmers	% of total farmers	50	40							
Fish catch	% of total catch	30	15							
Fish farm production	Yearly production	NA	NA							
Tourist accommodation occupancy – winter	Occupancy % during winter	55	35					39	38	26
Tourist accommodation occupancy – shoulder	Occupancy % during shoulder	75	55					65	63	48
Tourist accommodation occupancy – summer	Occupancy % during summer	95	80					87	84	67
Employment in tourism	Full-time employees in NW (% of total)	35	30							14
Population growth in the NW	Annual rate of growth	5	2			19	1.6	1.3	1.3	1.4
Population density in NW	Population per km²	500	300			310	316	320	324	328
Full-time fishermen	% of total fishermen	15	5							
Beach closure	Number of days during summer	2	15			36	17	27	28	25
Tourist resident ratio – winter	Daily tourists as a % of residents	50	45				48	51	52	51
Tourist resident ratio – shoulder	Daily tourists as a % of residents	70	55				92	95	97	95
Tourist resident ratio – summer	Daily tourists as a % of residents	95	70				122	129	129	136
Marine conservation/protected areas	% of coastal length	20	10			0	0	0	0	0
Diving in the NW	No of dives	40000	15000							55000

Notes: NW = northwest. NA = not available. This was the largest team and acted as a sort of 'integrator' of issues. 'Shoulder' is the period of the tourist season between winter and summer in Malta. The PA (planning authority) is the body in Malta responsible for handling planning applications.
ALE: The Administrative Law Enforcement section of the Police Deaprtment.

Notes

Chapter 1: The brave new frontier of sustainability

1   See Crabtree and Bayfield (1998), de Kruijf and van Vuuren (1998) and Garcia and Staples (2000) for some examples and a discussion.

2   Some examples spanning a decade: Barbier (1989), Daly (1990), Wiggering and Rennings (1997).

3   For an interesting taste of this debate from the perspective of the ecology community (the 'subversive science', Sears, 1964) in the immediate afterglow of the Rio Earth Summit, see in the 1993 issue of *Ecological Applications* papers by Fuentes, Hilborn and Ludwig, Holling, Ludwig, Meyer and Helfman, Mooney and Salva, Salwasser, Slobodkin, Socolow.

4   See, for example, Langaas (1997) and Foxon et al (1999).

5   See, for example, discussions in Cohen (1995), Arrow et al (1995), Daily and Ehrlich (1996), Goodland and Daly (1996), Harte (1996), O'Neill et al (1996) and Schindler (1996).

6   A selection of websites on the ecological footprint, including summaries of ongoing projects in this rapidly expanding field, can be found at http://www.bestfootforward.com

7   For further elaboration of the ideas behind integrated assessment, see Rotmans and van Asselt (1996), van Asselt et al (1996), Rotmans (1998) and Kasemir et al (1999). A practical example of where IA has been attempted to help with bridging the gap between environmental science and policy can be found in the ULYSSES (urban lifestyles, sustainability and integrated environmental assessment) project. Details and documents describing the project, methodologies and results can be found at http://zit1.zit.tu-darmstadt.de/ulysses/index.htm An example of IA application within a modelling context can be found in van Asselt et al (1996) and Rotmans and van Asselt (1999).

8 For developed country examples see Webler et al (1995), Durant and Joss (1995), MacNaughton et al (1995) and Renn et al (1996). A summary of the issues and methods applied in deliberative institutions can be found at http://www.cpn.org/sections/tools/manuals/pew_delib_com.html (written by Michael Briand; accessed on the 22 February 2001). For PLA perspectives on participation see Chambers et al (1989) and Scoones and Thompson (1994).

CHAPTER 2: SUSTAINABILITY INDICATORS

1 For more detailed descriptions and examples of the PSR family of sustainability indicator frameworks, see Bell and Morse (1999), Guy and Kibert (1998), Crabtree and Bayfield (1998), Gallopin (1997), Mortensen (1997), Berger (1997), Rigby et al (2000) and Woodhouse et al (2000).

2 Examples of SD indicator frameworks can be found in the following publications: national and regional indicator sets: LGMB (1995), Hardi et al (1997), Moldan et al (1997), Rydin (2001); sustainable agriculture: Morse et al (2000), Woodhouse et al (2000); health and family planning: USAID (undated).

3 Explanations of the 'green accounting' methodology, and discussions of the value of the approach in sustainability, can be found in Hueting and Bosch (1991), Solow (1993), Mitchell (1996) and Bartelmus (1997).

4 Viewpoint attributed to Professor David Pearce from the Centre for Social and Economic Research on the Global Environment (CSERGE) (OECD, 1998).

5 Examples of the use of the AMOEBA approach to measuring sustainability include Wefering et al (2000) for a shellfish restoration project in North Carolina, Ten Brink et al (1991) for the North Sea, de Haes et al (1991) for lowland peat and Rotmans and van Asselt (1999) for future projections arising from a number of perspectives on SD (utopian and dystopian).

6 For some discussion of this point see Gallopin (1997), Stirling (1999) and Morse et al (2001).

7 For a discussion of this point based on the results of a six-year research programme focused on gauging agricultural sustainability in Nigeria, see Morse et al (2001). More detail regarding the village case study discussed in this paper can be found in Morse et al (2000).

8 See, amongst others, discussions in Mitchell et al (1995), Tschirley (1997) and Woodhouse et al (2000).

9 For discussions of the complexity and, often hidden, subjectivity involved in setting critical loads and levels in environmental studies, see Skeffington (1999), Reynolds and Skeffington (1999) and Cresser (2000).

10 For a technical description of the ESI and an interpretation, see World Economic Forum (2000 and 2001). For a sharp rejoinder, see *Ecologist* (2001).

11 For a flavour of the debates that can arise out of local governments attempting to meet these diverse, and sometimes conflicting, pressures, see reports such as Hyam (1999).

CHAPTER 3: SYSTEMIC SUSTAINABILITY ANALYSIS AND PROSPECTIVE

1   A word is necessary on 'teams'. The word is used a great deal in this text but in effect there were various teams. Clarity is needed to be sure who is being referred to at any one time.

- The SSA team were primarily the local Maltese engaged in SSA directly.
- The thematic teams were those working in the thematic sub-projects who also provided staff to work alongside the SSA team.
- The Blue Plan team included the Blue Plan staff and the authors.
- The stakeholders were of two types. 'Internal' stakeholders were the SSA and thematic teams as they engaged with the preliminary work on the project. 'Wider' stakeholders in the later stages refers to the local community in Malta as a whole.

2   Mediterranean Commission on Sustainable Development. In May 1999 a report was produced setting out a series of indicators for sustainable development (UNEP/MAP/Blue Plan, 1999).

CHAPTER 4: DOING SPSA: SOME REFLECTIVE EXPERIENCE

1   The Malta CAMP reports referred to in this chapter can be found at the Blue Plan website (http://www.planbleu.org/indexa.htm) in the section entitled 'Coastal Regions', where they are available for download in portable document format (pdf).
2   See Chambers, 1992, 1996, 1997.
3   See, for example, Bell, 1998 and 2000; Coleman, 1987; Cordingley, 1995; Gasper, 1997 and 1999; and PCI, 1979.
4   See Collins and Bicknell, 1997, for a summary.

CHAPTER 5: NEW FRONTIERS OF PRACTICE

1   See Chapter 2 for a discussion. De Kruijf and van Vuuren (1998) provide a good summary and set of critiques of the PSR framework, with which we largely concur.
2   For example, see the future projections developed by van Asselt et al (1996) and Rotmans and van Asselt (1999). These authors describe a range of scenarios set out by different groups in society: hierarchist, egalitarian and individualist. They include uncertainty ranges for each group. Such 'coordinated exploration of possible future trajectories of human and environmental systems' (Kasemir et al, 1999) is seen as a key element of integrated assessment. The Rotmans and van Asselt (1999) paper is particularly interesting to us because of their use of AMOEBA-type diagrams similar to those we used in the Malta CAMP.

References

Acton, C (2000) *Community Indicators for Sustainability: A European Overview,* Environ Trust, Leicester

Allenby, B, Yasui, I, Lehni, M, Züst, R and Hunkeler, D (1998) 'Ecometrics Stakeholder Subjectivity: Values, Issues and Effects' *Environmental Quality Management,* 8(1), pp1–18

Arrow, K, Bolin, B, Costanza, R, Dasgupta, P, Folke, C, Holling, C S, Jansson, B-O, Levin, S, Mäler, K-G, Perrings, C and Pimental, D (1995) 'Economic Growth, Carrying Capacity and the Environment' *Science,* 268, pp520–521

Ballard, D (2000) 'The Cultural Aspects of Change for Sustainable Development' *Eco-Management and Auditing,* 7, pp53–59

Barbier, E B (1989) *Economics, Natural-resource Scarcity and Development: Conventional and Alternative Views,* Earthscan, London

Bartelmus, P (1997) 'Greening the National Accounts', in Moldan, B, Billharz, S and Matravers, R (eds), *Sustainability Indicators: A Report on the Project on Indicators of Sustainable Development,* John Wiley and Sons, Chichester, pp198–205

Bartelmus, P (1999) *Sustainable Development: Paradigm or Paranoia?* Wuppertal Paper 93, Wuppertal Institute for Climate, Environment and Energy, Wuppertal

Bastianoni, S, Marchettini, N, Panzieri, M and Tiezzi, E (1998) 'Environmental Sustainability Indicators: Thermodynamic Aspects' *Annali di Chimica,* 88, pp755–760

Bauler, T and Hecq, W (2000) *Transitions Towards a Sustainable Europe: Ecology – Economy-Policy,* 3rd Biennial Conference of the European Society for Ecological Economics, Vienna, 3–6 May 2000

Bell, S (1996) *Learning with Information Systems: Learning Cycles in Information Systems Development,* London, Routledge

Bell, S (1998) 'Managing and Learning with Logical Frameworks: The Case of an MIS Project in China' *Human Systems Management,* 17(1), pp15–28

Bell, S (1999) 'Vulnerability and the Aware IS Practitioner: A Reflective Discourse on Unfinished Business', in Clarke, S (ed), *Human Centered Methods in Information Systems: Current Research and Practice,* Idea Group Publishing, Hershey, pp102–117

Bell, S (2000) 'Logical Frameworks, Aristotle and Soft Systems: A Note on the Origins, Values and Uses of Logical Frameworks' *Public Administration and Development,* 20(1), pp29–31

Bell, S and Coudert, E (2000) *Report on the Systemic Sustainability Analysis within CAMP Malta Workshop: 2 February,* UNEP/MAP/Blue Plan, Malta

Bell, S and Ellul, A (2000a) *Report on the Second Training Workshop on Systemic Sustainability Analysis (SSA) Within CAMP Malta: June*, UNEP/MAP/Blue Plan, Ministry for Economic Services/ Planning Authority, Malta

Bell, S and Ellul, A (2000b) *Report on the Third Training Workshop on Systemic Sustainability Analysis (SSA) within CAMP Malta: November*, UNEP/MAP/Blue Plan, Ministry for Economic Services, Malta

Bell, S and Ellul, A (2001b) *Report on the Fifth Training Workshop on Systemic Sustainability Analysis (SSA) within CAMP Malta: May*, UNEP/MAP/Blue Plan, Ministry for Economic Services, Malta

Bell, S and Morse, S (1999) *Sustainability Indicators: Measuring the Immeasurable*, London, Earthscan

Bell, S, Albani Wilson, C and Ellul, A (2001a) *Report on the Fourth Training Workshop on Systemic Sustainability Analysis (SSA) within CAMP Malta: March*, UNEP/MAP/Blue Plan, Ministry for Economic Services, Malta

Bell, S, Armson, R, Ison, R, Zimmer, R, Paton, G, Chapman, J and Blackmore, C (1999) *Managing Complexity: A Systems Approach*, Open University, Milton Keynes

Berger, A R (1997) 'Natural Environmental Change: A Challenge to the DSR Approach', in Moldan, B, Billharz, S and Matravers, R (eds), *Sustainability Indicators: A Report on the Project on Indicators of Sustainable Development*, John Wiley and Sons, Chichester, pp191–197

Besleme, K and Mullin, M (1997) 'Community Indicators and Healthy Communities' *National Civic Review*, 86(1), pp43–52

Bevan, P (2000) 'Who's a Goody? Demythologizing the PRA Agenda' *Journal of International Development*, 12, pp751–759

Bossel, H. (1997) 'Finding a Comprehensive Set of Indicators of Sustainable Development by Application of Orientation Theory', in Moldan, B, Billharz, S and Matravers, R (eds), *Sustainability Indicators: A Report on the Project on Indicators of Sustainable Development*, John Wiley and Sons, Chichester, pp101–109

Bossel, H (1999) *Indicators for Sustainable Development: Theory, Method, Applications*, International Institute for Sustainable Development, Winnipeg

Braat, L (1991) 'The Predictive Meaning of Sustainability Indicators', in Kuik, O and Verbruggen, H (eds), *In Search of Indicators of Sustainable Development*, Kluwer Academic Publishers, Dordrecht, pp57–70

Brown, L R, Renner, M and Halweil, B (2000) *Vital Signs 2000–2001*, Earthscan, London

Brugmann, J (1997a) 'Is there a Method in our Measurement? The Use of Indicators in Local Sustainable Development Planning' *Local Environment*, 2(1), pp59–72

Brugmann, J (1997b) 'Sustainability Indicators Revisited: Getting from Political Objectives to Performance Outcomes – A Response to Graham Pinfield' *Local Environment*, 2(3), pp299–302

Camilleri, M (1996) *Sustainability Indicators for Malta*, paper presented by Marguerite Camilleri for the International Conference on the Integration of Environmental and Economic Planning in Islands and Small States, Valletta, Malta, 14–16 March

Catton, W (1980) *Overshoot: The Ecological Basis of Revolutionary Change*, University of Illinois Press, Chicago

Chambers, R (1992) *Rural Appraisal: Rapid, Relaxed and Participatory*, Discussion Paper No 311, Institute of Development Studies, Brighton

Chambers, R (1996) 'ZOPP, PCM and PRA: Whose Reality, Needs and Priorities Count?', in Forster, R. (ed), *Zopp Marries PRA? Participatory Learning and Action – A Challenge For Our Services And Institutions*, Deutsche Gesellschaft fur Technische Zusammenarbeit, Eschborn

Chambers, R (1997) *Whose Reality Counts? Putting the First Last*, Intermediate Technology Publications, London

Chambers, R, Pacey, A and Thrupp, L A (1989) *Farmer First: Farmer Innovation and Agricultural Research*, Intermediate Technology, London

Chambers, N, Simmons, C and Wackernagel, M (2000) *Sharing Nature's Interest: Ecological Footprints as an Indicator of Sustainability*, Earthscan, London

Checkland, P B (1981) *Systems Thinking, Systems Practice*, Wiley, Chichester

Checkland, P (2001) 'The Emergent Properties of SSM in Use: A Symposium by Reflective Practitioners' *Systemic Practice and Action Research*, 13(6), pp799–823

Checkland, P and Jayastna, N (2000) *The Soft Systems Research Discussion Group: Taking Stock, Background, Current Position, Future Direction*, University of Salford, Salford

Checkland, P B and Scholes, J (1990) *Soft Systems Methodology in Action*, Wiley, Chichester

Cohen, J E (1995) 'Population Growth and Earth's Human Carrying Capacity' *Science*, 269, pp341–346

Coleman, G (1987) 'Logical Framework Approach to the Monitoring and Evaluation of Agricultural and Rural Development Projects' *Project Appraisal*, 2(4), pp251–259

Collins, T and Bicknell, D (1997) *Crash: Ten Easy Ways to Avoid a Computer Disaster*, Simon and Schuster, London

Cordingley, D (1995) 'Integrating the Logical Framework into the Management of Technical Co-operation Projects' *Project Appraisal*, 10(2), pp103–112

Cornelissen, A M G, van den Berg, J, Koops, W J and Udo, H M J (2001) 'Assessment of the Contribution of Sustainability Indicators to Sustainable Development: A Novel Approach using Fuzzy Set Theory' *Agriculture, Ecosystems and Environment*, 86(2), pp173–185

Corvalán, C, Kjellström, T and Briggs, D (1997) 'Health and Environmental Indicators in Relation to Sustainable Development', in Moldan, B, Billharz, S and Matravers, R (eds), *Sustainability Indicators: A Report on the Project on Indicators of Sustainable Development*, John Wiley and Sons, Chichester, pp274–282

Crabtree, B and Bayfield, N (1998) 'Developing Sustainability Indicators for Mountain Ecosystems: A Study of the Cairngorms, Scotland' *Journal of Environmental Management*, 52, pp1–14

Cresser, M S (2000) 'The Critical Loads Concept: Milestone or Millstone for the New Millennium?' *The Science of the Total Environment*, 249, pp51–62

Crilly, M, Mannis, A and Morrow, K (1999) 'Indicators for Change: Taking a Lead' *Local Environment*, 4(2), pp151–168

Curwell, S and Cooper, I (1998) 'The Implications of Urban Sustainability' *Building Research and Information*, 26(1), pp17–28

Cusworth, J and Franks, T (1993) *Managing Projects in Developing Countries*, Longman Scientific and Technical, Harlow

Dahl, A L (1997) 'The Big Picture: Comprehensive Approaches. Part One – Introduction', in Moldan, B, Billharz, S and Matravers, R (eds), *Sustainability Indicators: A Report on the Project on Indicators of Sustainable Development*, John Wiley and Sons, Chichester, pp69–83

Dahl, A L (2000) 'Using Indicators to Measure Sustainability: Recent Methodological and Conceptual Developments' *Marine and Freshwater Research*, 51(5), pp427–433

Daily, G C and Ehrlich, P R (1996) 'Socioeconomic Equity, Sustainability, and Earth's Carrying Capacity' *Ecological Applications*, 6(4), pp991–1001

Daly, H E (1990) 'Toward Some Operational Principles of Sustainable Development' *Ecological Economics*, 2, pp1–6

de Haes, H U, Nip, M and Klijn, F (1991) 'Towards Sustainability: Indicators of Environmental Quality', in Kuik, O and Verbruggen, H (eds), *In Search of Indicators of Sustainable Development*, Kluwer Academic Publishers, Dordrecht, pp89–105

de Kruijf, H A M and van Vuuren, D P (1998) 'Following Sustainable Development in Relation to the North–South Dialogue: Ecosystem Health and Sustainability Indicators' *Ecotoxicology and Environmental Safety*, 40, pp4–14

de Soyza, A G, Whitford, W G and Herrick, J E (1997) 'Sensitivity Testing of Indicators of Ecosystem Health' *Ecosystem Health*, 3, pp44–53

Deb, A (1998) 'Sustainable Cities in Developing Countries' *Building Research and Information*, 26(1), pp29–38

Ditz, D and Ranganathan, J (1998) 'Global Developments on Environmental Performance Indicators' *Corporate Environmental Strategy,* 5(3), pp47–52

Dumanski, J and Pieri, C (2000) 'Land Quality Indicators: Research Plan' *Agriculture, Ecosystems and Environment,* 81, pp93–102

Durant, J and Joss, S (eds) (1995) *Public Participation in Science: The Role of Consensus Conferences in Europe,* Science Museum, London

Ecologist (2001) 'Keeping Score' *Ecologist,* 31(3), pp44–47

Ekins, P and Simon, S (2001) 'Estimating Sustainability Gaps: Method and Preliminary Applications for the UK and The Netherlands' *Ecological Economics,* 37, pp5–22

Ellul, A (2000) *Report on the Training Workshop on Systemic Sustainability Analysis (SSA) within CAMP Malta: April,* UNEP/MAP/Blue Plan, Ministry for Economic Services of Malta, Malta

Envision Sustainability Tools (EST) (2000) *Overview of the QUEST Model,* Envision Sustainability Tools Inc, Vancouver, Canada

Foxon, T J, Leach, M, Butler, D, Dawes, J, Hutchinson, D, Pearson, P and Rose, D (1999) 'Useful Indicators of Urban Sustainability: Some Methodological Issues' *Local Environment,* 4(2), pp137–149

Fuentes, E R (1993) 'Scientific Research and Sustainable Development' *Ecological Applications,* 3(4), pp576–577

Gallopin, G C (1997) 'Indicators and their Use: Information for Decision-making', in Moldan, B, Billharz, S and Matravers, R (eds), *Sustainability Indicators: A Report on the Project on Indicators of Sustainable Development,* John Wiley and Sons, Chichester, pp13–27

Garcia, S M and Staples, D J (2000) 'Sustainability Reference Systems and Indicators for Responsible Marine Capture Fisheries: A Review of Concepts and Elements for a Set of Guidelines' *Marine and Freshwater Research,* 51(5), pp385–426

Garcia, S M, Staples, D J and Chesson, J (2000) 'The FAO Guidelines for the Development and Use of Indicators of Sustainable Development of Marine Capture Fisheries and an Australian Example of their Application' *Ocean and Costal Management,* 32, pp537–556

Gardner, J S, Sinclair, A J and Berkes, F (1995) *Comparative Analysis of Mountain Landuse Sustainability: Case Studies from India and Canada,* Natural Resources Institute, University of Manitoba

Gasper, D (1997) *Logical Frameworks: A Critical Look,* paper presented at a Development Studies Association conference held at the University of East Anglia, 1997

Gasper, D (1999) 'Evaluating the Logical Framework Approach: Towards Learning-Orientated Development Evaluation' *Public Administration and Development,* 20(1), pp17–28

Gatto, M (1995) 'Sustainability: Is it a Well-Defined Concept?' *Ecological Applications,* 5(4), pp1181–1183

Gilbert, A (1996) 'Criteria for Sustainability in the Development of Indicators for Sustainable Development' *Chemosphere,* 33(9), pp1739–1748

Global Reporting Initiative (GRI) (2000) *Sustainability Reporting Guidelines on Economic, Environmental and Social Performance,* Global Reporting Initiative, Boston

Godet, M, Monti, R, Meunier, F and Roubelat, F (1999) *Scenarios and Strategies: A Toolbox for Scenario Planning,* Report for the Laboratory for Investigation in Prospective and Strategy Toolbox, April, Conservatoire National des Arts et Métiers, Paris

Goodland, R and Daly, H (1996) 'Environmental Sustainability: Universal and Non-Negotiable' *Ecological Applications,* 6(4), pp1002–1017

Gordon, T (1970) *Parent Effectiveness Training,* Plume Books, New American Library Inc, New York

Grove-White, R (1993) 'Environmentalism: A New Moral Discourse For Technological Society?', in Milton, K (ed), *Environmentalism: The View from Anthropology,* Routledge, London, pp18–30

Guy, G B and Kibert, C J (1998) 'Developing Indicators of Sustainability: US Experience' *Building Research and Information,* 26(1), pp39–45

Haberl, H, Erb, K-H and Krausmann, F (2001) 'How to Calculate and Interpret Ecological Footprints for Long Periods of Time: The Case of Austria 1926–1995' *Ecological Economics*, 38, pp25–45

Hardi, P (2001) 'The Dashboard of Sustainability', paper presented at a conference entitled *Measure and Communicate Sustainable Development. A Science and Policy Dialogue*, Stockholm, 3–4 April

Hardi, P, Barg, S, Hodge, T and Pinter, L (1997) *Measuring Sustainable Development: Review of Current Practice*, Occasional Paper no 17, Industry Canada, Ottawa

Hart Environmental Data (1998) *Sustainable Community Indicators Trainers Workshop*, Hart Environmental Data, North Andover, Massachusetts

Harte, J (1996) 'Confronting Visions of a Sustainable Future' *Ecological Applications*, 6(1), pp27–29

Henderson, H (1991) *Life Beyond Economics: Paradigms in Progress*, Knowledge Systems Inc, Indianapolis

Herrick, J E (2000) 'Soil Quality: An Indicator of Sustainable Land Management?' *Applied Soil Ecology*, 15(1), pp75–83

Hilborn, R and Ludwig, D (1993) 'The Limits of Applied Ecological Research' *Ecological Applications*, 3(4), pp550–552

Hinterberger, F and Schmidt-Bleek, F (1999) 'Dematerialization, MIPS and Factor 10: Physical Sustainability Indicators as a Social Device' *Ecological Economics*, 29, pp53–56

Hodge, R A, Hardi, P and Bell, D V J (1999) 'Seeing Change Through the Lens of Sustainability', background paper for the workshop *'Beyond Delusion: Science and Policy Dialogue on Designing Effective Indicators of Sustainable Development'*, IISD, Costa Rica

Holling, C S (1993) 'Investing in Research for Sustainability' *Ecological Applications*, 3(4), pp552–555

Howlett, D, Bond, R, Woodhouse, P and Rigby, D (2000) *Sustainability Indicators for Natural Resource Management and Policy: Stakeholder Analysis and Local Identification of Indicators of the Success and Sustainability of Farming Based Livelihood Systems*, Working Paper 5, Institute for Development Policy and Management, University of Manchester, Manchester

Hueting, R and Bosch, P (1991) 'Note on the Correction of National Income for Environmental Losses', in Kuik, O and Verbruggen, H (eds), *In Search of Indicators of Sustainable Development*, Kluwer Academic Publishers, Dordrecht, pp29–38

Hughes, B and Cotterell, M (1999) *Software Project Management*, McGraw Hill, Maidenhead

Hutchcroft, I (1996) 'Local Authorities, Universities and Communities: Alliances for Sustainability' *Local Environment*, 1(2), pp219–224

Hyam, P (1999) *Sustainability Counts: Developing Local Sustainability Indicators for Cumbria*, report of the conference, 8 October, Projects in Partnership. Available at http://www.cumbria.gov.uk/environment/soer/html/confreport.pdf

Jesinghaus, J (1999) 'Indicators for Decision-Making', draft paper, 12 December, European Commission, Brussels

Jesinghaus, J (2000) 'The World Economic Forum's Environmental Sustainability Index: Strong and weak points', European Commission Joint Research Centre, Ispra, Italy. Review posted on the internet, April 9 2000

Jimenez-Beltran, D (2001) 'Measure and Communicate Sustainable Development: A Science and Policy Dialogue', paper presented at a meeting entitled *Measuring Sustainability in Sectors: The Development after Cardiff*, Stockholm, 4–5 April

Jodha, N S (1991) 'Sustainable Mountain Agriculture: Limited Options and Uncertain Prospects', *Appropriate Technology*, 17(4), pp9–11

Joly, C (2001) 'Is Enlightened Capitalism Possible?', available for downloading at the Storebrand website http://www.storebrand.com/ accessed in January 2002

Kasemir, B, van Asselt, M B A and Dürrenberger, G (1999) 'Integrated Assessment of Sustainable Development: Multiple Perspectives in Interaction' *International Journal of Environment and Pollution*, 11(4), pp407–425

Kates, R W, Clark, W C, Corell, R, Hall, J M, Jaeger, C C, Lowe, I, McCarthy, J J, Schellnhuber, H J, Bolin, B, Dickson, N M, Faucheux, S, Gallopin, G C, Gruebler, A, Huntley, B, Jäger, J, Jodha, N S, Kasperson, R E, Mabogunje, A, Matson, P, Mooney, H, Morre III, B, O'Riordan, T and Svedin, U (2000) *Sustainability Science*, Belfer Center for Science and International Affairs, Harvard University

Kellogg, R L and Goss, D W (1997) 'Development of Environmental Indicators for Use in Macro-economic Models' *Journal of Agricultural and Applied Economics*, 29(1), pp77–86

Kessler, W B, Salwasser, H, Cartwright Jr, C W and Caplan, J A (1992) 'New Perspectives for Sustainable Natural Resource Management' *Ecological Applications*, 2(3), pp221–225

Kline, E (2000) 'Planning and Creating Eco-cities: Indicators as a Tool for Shaping Developing and Measuring Progress' *Local Environment*, 5(3), pp343–350

Kolb, D (1984) *Experiential Learning: Experience as the Source of Learning and Development*, Prentice-Hall, London

Langaas, S (1997) 'The Spatial Dimension of Indicators of Sustainable Development: The role of Geographical Information Systems (GIS) and Cartography', in Moldan, B, Billharz, S and Matravers, R (eds), *Sustainability Indicators: A Report on the Project on Indicators of Sustainable Development*, John Wiley and Sons, Chichester, pp33–39

Lefroy, T and Hobbs, R (1992) 'Ecological Indicators for Sustainable Agriculture' *Australian Journal of Soil and Water Conservation*, 5(4), pp22–28

Lefroy, R D B, Bechstedt, H-D and Rais, M (2000) 'Indicators for Sustainable Land Management Based on Farmer Surveys in Vietnam, Indonesia and Thailand' *Agriculture, Ecosystems and Environment*, 81(2), pp137–146

Lindley, J J (2001) 'Virtual Tools for Complex Problems: An Overview of the *Atlas^{NW}* Regional Interactive Sustainability Atlas for Planning for Sustainable Development' *Impact Assessment and Project Appraisal*, 19(2), pp141–151

Liverman, D M, Hanson, M E, Brown, B J and Merideth, R W (1988) 'Global Sustainability: Toward Measurement' *Environmental Management*, 12(2), pp133–143

Local Government Management Board (LGMB) (1995) *Sustainability Indicators Research Project: Consultants' Report of the Pilot Phase*, LGMB, London

Ludwig, D (1993) 'Environmental Sustainability: Magic, Science and Religion in Natural Resource Management' *Ecological Applications*, 3(4), pp555–558

MacGillivray, A (ed) (1994) *Environmental Measures: Indicators for the UK Environment*, Environment Challenge Group, London.

MacGillivray, A (1997) 'Social Development Indicators', in Moldan, B, Billharz, S and Matravers, R (eds), *Sustainability Indicators: A Report on the Project on Indicators of Sustainable Development*, John Wiley and Sons, Chichester, pp256–263

MacGillivray, A and Zadek, S (1995) *Accounting for Change: The Role of Sustainable Development Indicators*, ESRC GEC Programme Briefings Number 4, February, New Economics Foundation, London

MacNaughten, P, Grove-White, R, Jacobs, M and Wynne, B, (1995) *Public Perceptions and Sustainability in Lancashire: Indicators, Institutions, Participation*, a report by the Centre for the Study of Environmental Change, Lancashire University, Lancashire Country Council, Lancashire

Mageau, M T, Costanza, R and Ulanowicz, R E (1995) 'The Development and Initial Testing of a Quantitative Assessment of Ecosystem Health' *Ecosystem Health*, 1(4), pp 201–213

Manyong, V M and Degand, J (1997) 'Measurement of the Sustainability of African Smallholder Farming Systems: Case Study of a Systems Approach' *IITA Research*, 14/15, pp1–6

Mayo, E, MacGillivray, A and McLaren, D (1997) 'The Index of Sustainable Economic Welfare for the United Kingdom', in Moldan, B, Billharz, S and Matravers, R (eds), *Sustainability Indicators: A Report on the Project on Indicators of Sustainable Development*, John Wiley and Sons, Chichester, pp293–298

McGregor, D (1960) *The Human Side of Enterprise*, McGraw-Hill, Boston

Meadows, D (1998) *Indicators and Information Systems for Sustainable Development*, Sustainability Institute, Hartland Four Corners, Vermont

Meppem, T and Gill, R (1998) 'Planning for Sustainability as a Learning Concept', *Ecological Economics*, 26, pp121–137

Meter, K (1999) *Neighbourhood Sustainability Indicators Guidebook*, Crossroads Resource Center, Minneapolis

Meyer, J L and Helfman, G S (1993) 'The Ecological Basis of Sustainability', *Ecological Applications*, 3(4), pp569–571

Mitchell, G (1996) 'Problems and Fundamentals of Sustainable Development Indicators' *Sustainable Development*, 4, pp1–11

Mitchell, G, May, A and McDonald, A (1995) 'PICABUE: A Methodological Framework for the Development of Indicators of Sustainable Development' *International Journal of Sustainable Development and World Ecology*, 2, pp104–123

Moffatt, I (1994) 'On Measuring Sustainable Development Indicators' *International Journal of Sustainable Development and World Ecology*, 1, pp97–109

Moldan, B, Billharz, S and Matravers, R (eds) (1997) *Sustainability Indicators: A Report on the Project on Indicators of Sustainable Development*, John Wiley and Sons, Chichester

Mooney, H A and Salva, O E (1993) 'Science and Sustainable Use' *Ecological Applications*, 3(4), pp564–566

Moran, V (1994) 'A Different Perspective on Sustainability' *Ecological Applications*, 4(3), pp405–406

Morse, S, McNamara, N, Acholo, M and Okwoli, B (2000) *Visions of Sustainability: Stakeholders, Change and Indicators*, Ashgate, Aldershot

Morse, S, McNamara, N, Acholo, M and Okwoli, B (2001) 'Sustainability Indicators: The Problem of Integration' *Sustainable Development*, 9, pp1–15

Mortensen, L F (1997) 'The Driving Force–State–Response Framework used by CSD', in Moldan, B, Billharz, S and Matravers, R (eds), *Sustainability Indicators: A Report on the Project on Indicators of Sustainable Development*, John Wiley and Sons, Chichester, pp47–53

Newman, P (1998) 'Can Sustainability be Measured?' accessed on line at http://www.renewableway.co.uk/sustain/measures.html on 31 May 2001

Novartis Foundation for Sustainable Development (2001) *Sustainable Development: A Common Challenge for North and South*, Novartis Foundation for Sustainable Development, Novartis, Basle http://www.foundation.novartis.com/sustainable_development.htm

Odum, H T (1988) 'Self-Organization, Transformity and Information' *Science*, 242(4882), pp1132–1139

OECD (1998) *Sustainable Development Indicators*, OECD Expert Workshop, 8–9 October, OECD, Paris

O'Neill, R V, Kahn, J R, Duncan, J R, Elliott, S, Efroymson, R, Cardwell, H and Jones, D W (1996) 'Economic Growth and Sustainability: A New Challenge' *Ecological Applications*, 6(1), pp23–24

Opschoor, H (1991) 'GNP and Sustainable Income Measures: Some Problems and a Way Out', in Kuik, O and Verbruggen, H (eds), *In Search of Indicators of Sustainable Development*, Kluwer Academic Publishers, Dordrecht, pp39–44

Owens, S (1994) 'Sustainability and Environmental Policy: Five Fundamental Questions', in Miliband, D (ed), *Reinventing the Left*, Polity Press, Cambridge, pp207–215

Pannell, D J and Glenn, N A (2000) 'A Framework for the Economic Evaluation and Selection of Sustainability Indicators in Agriculture' *Ecological Economics*, 33, pp135–149

Paton, G (2001) 'A Systemic Action Learning Cycle as the Key Element of an Ongoing Spiral of Analyses' *Systemic Practice and Action Research*, 14(1), pp95–112

Paulesich, R and Reiger, H (1997) 'Methods of Eco-auditing and Verifying Environmental Statements Derived from Qualitative Methods of Social Research' *Eco-management and Auditing*, 4, pp44–56

Pearce, D W and Atkinson, G D (1993) 'Capital Theory and the Measurement of Sustainable Development: An Indicator of "Weak" Sustainability' *Ecological Economics*, 8, pp103–108

Persson, G A (2001) 'The Chairman's Report', conference entitled *Measure and Communicate Sustainable Development: A Science and Policy Dialogue*, Stockholm, 3–4 April

PCI (1979) *The Logical Framework: A Manager's Guide to a Scientific Approach to Design Evaluation*, Practical Concepts Inc, New York

Pinfield, G (1996) 'Beyond Sustainability Indicators' *Local Environment*, 1(2), pp151–163

Prescott-Allen, R (1997) 'Barometer of Sustainability', in Moldan, B, Billharz, S and Matravers, R (eds), *Sustainability Indicators: A Report on the Project on Indicators of Sustainable Development*, John Wiley and Sons, Chichester, pp133–137

Pretty, J (1995) *Regenerating Agriculture: Policies and Practice for Sustainability and Self-reliance*, Earthscan, London

Pretty, J (1998) 'Participatory Learning for Integrated Farming', in Eng-Leong, F and Della Senta, T (eds), 'Proceedings of the Internet Conference On Integrated Bio-Systems', www.ias.unu.edu/proceedings/icibs/jules/paper.htm

Probert, S (1997) 'The Metaphysical Assumptions of the (Main) Soft Systems Methodology Advocates', in Winder, R L, Probert, S K and Beeson, I A (eds), *Philosophical Aspects of Information Systems*, Taylor and Francis, London, pp131–151

Probert, S (1998) 'A Critical Analysis of Soft Systems Methodology and its (Theoretical and Practical) Relationship with Phenomenaology' *Systemist*, 21, pp187–207

Quarrie, J (ed) (1992) *The Earth Summit '92: The United Nations Conference on Environment and Development*, Regency Press, London

Reid, D (1995) *Sustainable Development: An Introductory Guide*, Earthscan Publications, London

Renn, O, Webler, T and Wiedeman, P (eds) (1996) *Fairness and Competence in Citizen Participation*, Kluwer, Dordrecht

Rennings, K and Wiggering, H (1997) 'Steps Towards Indicators of Sustainable Development: Linking Economic and Ecological Concepts' *Ecological Economics*, 20, pp25–36

Reynolds, B and Skeffington, R A (1999) 'Critical Loads' *Progress in Environmental Science*, 1(4), pp371–381

Rigby, D, Howlett, D and Woodhouse, P (2000) *A Review of Indicators of Agricultural and Rural Livelihood Sustainability*, Institute for Development Policy and Management, Manchester University, Manchester

Rotmans, J (1998) 'Methods for IA: The Challenges and Opportunities Ahead' *Environmental Modeling and Assessment*, 3(3), pp155–179

Rotmans, J and van Asselt, M B A (1996) 'Integrated Assessment: A Growing Child on its Way to Maturity' *Climatic Change*, 34(3/4), pp327–336

Rotmans, J and van Asselt, M B A (1999) 'Perspectives on a Sustainable Future' *International Journal of Sustainable Development*, 2(2), pp201–230

Rubenstein, D I (1993) 'Science and the Pursuit of a Sustainable World' *Ecological Applications*, 3(4), pp585–587

Rydin, Y (2001) *Interim Report of the PASTILLE Project: Promoting Action for Sustainability through Indicators at the Local Level in Europe*, accessible on the project website: http://www.lse.ac.uk/depts/geography/pastille

Salwasser, H (1993) 'Sustainability Needs More than Better Science' *Ecological Applications*, 3(4), pp587–589

Schindler, D W (1996) 'The Environment, Carrying Capacity and Economic Growth', *Ecological Applications*, 6(1), pp17–19

Scoones, I and Thompson, J (1994) *Beyond Farmer First: Rural People's Knowledge, Agricultural Research and Extension Practice*, Intermediate Technology, London

Sears, P B (1964) 'Ecology: A Subversive Subject' *Bioscience*, 14, pp11–13

Skeffington, R A (1999) 'The Use of Critical Loads in Environmental Policy Making: A Critical Appraisal' *Environmental Science and Technology*, 33, pp245A–252A

Slobodkin, L B (1993) 'Scientific Goals Require Literal Empirical Assumptions' *Ecological Applications*, 3(4), pp571–573

Socolow, R H (1993) 'Achieving Sustainable Development that is Mindful of Human Imperfection' *Ecological Applications*, 3(4), pp581–583

Solow, R (1993) 'An Almost Practical Step Towards Sustainability' *Resources Policy*, 19, pp162–172

Spangenberg, J H and Bonniot, O (1998) *Sustainability Indicators: A Compass on the Road Towards Sustainability*, Wuppertal Paper no 81, Wuppertal Institute for Climate, Environment and Energy, Wuppertal

Stirling, A (1999) 'The Appraisal of Sustainability: Some Problems and Possible Responses' *Local Environment*, 4(2), pp111–135

Syers, J K, Hamblin, A and Pushparajah, E (1995) 'Indicators and Thresholds for the Evaluation of Sustainable Land Management' *Canadian Journal of Soil Science*, 75, pp423–428

Templet, P H (1995) 'Equity and Sustainability: An Empirical Analysis' *Society and Natural Resources*, 8, pp509–523

Ten Brink, B J E, Hosper, S H and Colijn, F (1991) 'A Quantitative Method for Description and Assessment of Ecosystems: The AMOEBA Approach' *Marine Pollution Bulletin*, 23, pp265–270

Tschirley, J B (1997) 'The Use of Indicators in Sustainable Agriculture and Rural Development: Considerations for Developing Countries', in Moldan, B, Billharz, S and Matravers, R (eds), *Sustainability Indicators: A Report on the Project on Indicators of Sustainable Development*, John Wiley and Sons, Chichester, pp221–229

Tyteca, D (1996) 'On the Measurement of the Environmental Performance of Firms: A Literature Review and a Productive Efficiency Perspective' *Journal of Environmental Management*, 46, pp281–308

UNEP/MAP/BluePlan (1999) *Indicators for Sustainable Development in the Mediterranean Region*, Blue Plan Regional Activity Centre, Sophia Antipolis, France

UNEP/MAP/BluePlan (2000) *Systemic Sustainability Analysis Within CAMP Malta: Technical Specification*, Blue Plan Regional Activity Centre, Sophia Antipolis, France

UNEP/PAP/MAP (2000) *MAP CAMP Malta Project Inception Report*, Priority Action Programme, Split

United Nations Development Program (UNDP) (1998) *United Nations Development Report*, UNDP, New York

USAID (undated) *Health and Family Planning Indicators: Measuring Sustainability*, Volume II, Office of Sustainable Development Bureau for Africa, US Agency for International Development

van Asselt, M B A and Rotmans, J (1996) 'Uncertainty in Perspective' *Global Environmental Change*, 6(2), pp121–157

van Asselt, M B A, Beusen, A H W and Hilderink, H B M (1996) 'Uncertainty in Integrated Assessment: A Social Scientific Perspective' *Environmental Modeling and Assessment*, 1, pp71–90

van der Hamsvoort, C and Latacz-Lohmann, U (1998) 'Sustainability: A Review of the Debate and an Extension' *International Journal of Sustainable Development and World Ecology*, 5, pp99–110

Victor, P A (1991) 'Indicators of Sustainable Development: Some Lessons from Capital Theory' *Ecological Economics*, 4, pp191–213

Webler, T, Kastenholz, H and Renn, O (1995) 'Public Participation in Impact Assessment: A Social Learning Perspective' *Environmental Impact Assessment Review*, 15, pp443–463

Wefering, F M, Danielson, L E and White, N M (2000) 'Using the AMOEBA Approach to Measure Progress Toward Ecosystem Sustainability Within a Shellfish Restoration Project in North Carolina' *Ecological Modelling*, 130, pp157–166

Wiggering, H and Rennings, K (1997) 'Sustainability Indicators: Geology meets Economy' *Environmental Geology*, 32(1), pp71–78

Winograd, M and Eade, J (1997) 'Environmental and Sustainability Indicators for Latin America and the Caribbean: The Use of Geographical Information Systems', in Moldan, B, Billharz, S and Matravers, R (eds), *Sustainability Indicators: A Report on the Project on Indicators of Sustainable Development*, John Wiley and Sons, Chichester, pp40–46

Woodhouse, P, Howlett, D and Rigby, D (2000) *A Framework for Research on Sustainability Indicators for Agricultural and Rural Livelihoods*, Institute for Development Policy and Management, Manchester University, Manchester

WCED (World Commission for Environment and Development) (1987) *Our Common Future*, Oxford University Press, Oxford

World Economic Forum (WEF) (2000) *Pilot Environmental Sustainabilty Index: Annual Meeting 2000, Davos, Switzerland*, WEF, Switzerland

World Economic Forum (WEF) (2001) *2001 Environmental Sustainability Index, Annual meeting 2001, Davos, Switzerland*, WEF, Switzerland. Available on line at http://www.ciesin.columbia.edu/indicators/ESI

Index

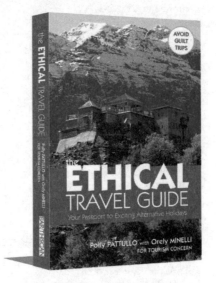

Join our
online community
and help us save paper and postage!

www.earthscan.co.uk

By joining the Earthscan website, our readers can benefit from a range of exciting new services and exclusive offers. You can also receive e-alerts and e-newsletters packed with information about our new books, forthcoming events, special offers, invitations to book launches, discussion forums and membership news. Help us to reduce our environmental impact by joining the Earthscan online community!

How? – Become a member in seconds!

>> Simply visit **www.earthscan.co.uk** and add your name and email address to the sign-up box in the top left of the screen – You're now a member!

>> With your new member's page, you can subscribe to our monthly **e-newsletter** and/or choose **e-alerts** in your chosen subjects of interest – you control the amount of mail you receive and can unsubscribe your-self

Why? – Membership benefits

✔ Membership is free!

✔ 10% discount on all books online

✔ Receive invitations to high-profile book launch events at the BT Tower, London Review of Books Bookshop, the Africa Centre and other exciting venues

✔ Receive e-newsletters and e-alerts delivered direct-ly to your inbox, keeping you informed but not costing the Earth – you can also forward to friends and colleagues

✔ Create your own discussion topics and get engaged in online debates taking place in our new online Forum

✔ Receive special offers on our books as well as on products and services from our partners such as *The Ecologist, The Civic Trust* and more

✔ Academics – request inspection copies

✔ Journalists – subscribe to advance information e-alerts on upcoming titles and reply to receive a press copy upon publication – write to info@earthscan.co.uk for more information about this service

✔ Authors – keep up to date with the latest publications in your field

✔ NGOs – open an NGO Account with us and qualify for special discounts

Join now?

Join Earthscan now!

name

surname

email address

Earthscan Member

[Your name]

Click to Change

My profile
My forum
My bookmarks
All my pages

www.earthscan.co.uk

The Natural Advantage of Nations
Business Opportunities, Innovation and Governance in the 21st Century

Edited by Karlson 'Charlie' Hargroves and Michael Harrison Smith

Forewords by Amory B. Lovins, L Hunter Lovins, William McDonough, Michael Fairbanks and Alan AtKisson

'I am particularly pleased with the new book, *The Natural Advantage of Nations,* which will, in effect, follow on from *Natural Capitalism,* and bring in newer evidence from around the world' AMORY B. LOVINS, Rocky Mountain Institute

'This is world-leading work, the team deserves the loudest acclamation possible' BARRY GREAR AO, World Federation of Engineering Organisations

'A seminal book, a truly world changing book... As part of the process of pulling together the people whose ideas they wanted in the book, [the editors] have pulled together a whole movement' L. HUNTER LOVINS, Natural Capitalism, Inc

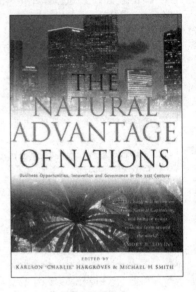

This collection of inspiring work, based on solid academic and practical rigour, is an overview of the 21st century business case for sustainable development. It incorporates innovative technical, structural and social advances, and explores the role governance can play in both leading and underpinning business and communities in the shift towards a sustainable future.

The team from The Natural Edge Project have studied and incorporated key works from over 30 of the world's leaders in sustainability. The book is also supported by an extensive companion website. This work takes the lessons of competitive advantage theory and practice and combines them with the sustainability paradigm, in light of important developments in economics, innovation, business and governance over the last 30–50 years.

Far from being in conflict with economics and business practices, this book demonstrates how we can improve the well-being of society and the environment while driving innovation in an increasingly competitive world.

Hardback 1-84407-121-9 Published January 2005

HOW TO ORDER:

ONLINE www.earthscan.co.uk
CUSTOMER HOTLINE +44 (0)1256 302699
EMAIL book.orders@earthscan.co.uk